D1542860

A QUESTION OF JUDGMENT

The Fortas Case and the Struggle for the Supreme Court

Robert Shogan

THE BOBBS-MERRILL COMPANY
Indianapolis   New York

The Bobbs-Merrill Company, Inc.
Indianapolis • New York
Copyright © 1972 by Robert Shogan
All rights reserved
Library of Congress Catalogue Card Number 74-173224
Designed by Jack Jaget
Manufactured in the United States of America

For Cynthia and Amelia

A
QUESTION
OF
JUDGMENT

CONTENTS

CONTENTS

JUSTICE FORTAS'S resignation from the Supreme Court in May of 1969 jarred and bewildered the country. The story came out in bits and pieces, amid a welter of rumor and innuendo, and some of it never came out at all. I have tried to pick up the pieces, some strewn over the past forty years, and put them together. Where it seemed appropriate, I have drawn conclusions. But my main purpose has been to provide a balanced and accurate account so that readers could make their own judgments.

Because of personal and official sensitivities, some questions remain unanswered. Fortas himself declined to be interviewed, as did Chief Justice Warren. But others, in and out of government, thought the issues raised by the Fortas affair significant enough to share their recollections with me. Among them were Attorney General John Mitchell, his immediate predecessor Ramsey Clark, members of Congress, White House aides and Fortas's former partners and law clerks. Most are cited by name in the source notes at the back of the book. Those who preferred to remain anonymous are listed as confidential sources.

This book owes a great deal to a great many people. *Newsweek's* Washington bureau chief, Mel Elfin, made the suggestion that prompted me to begin work, and his flexibility in arranging work schedules enabled me to finish. Holly Camp, Angus McEachran and Seth Goldschlager helped with interviewing and research. William Lambert of *Life* took considerable time to explain how he unearthed the story that led to Fortas's resignation. Samuel Shaffer, Henry Hubbard, John Lindsay, Tom DeFrank and Richard Stout, all of *Newsweek*, searched their files and their memories for relevant information, as did Ronald Ostrow and Robert Jackson of the *Los Angeles Times*, Fred Graham of the *New York Times* and Lyle Denniston of the *Washington Star*. I am grateful for having had access to the clipping files of the *New York Times* Washington bureau, the *Washington Post* and *Newsweek*, where Barbara Brandt, Ted Slate and Gerson Zelman were particularly helpful. Johnny Killian of the Congressional Research Service was an invaluable guide to the resources of the Library of Congress.

Professor Philip Kurland, of the University of Chicago Law School, and Tom Allen read portions of the manuscript, and the finished product has greatly benefited from their suggestions. Thelma McMahon typed and, very often, retyped the manuscript with unfailing accuracy and good humor.

My wife, Ellen, was encouraging and patient throughout, in the best tradition of authors' wives. More important, in the midst of my creative labors she gave birth to a daughter, our second. It is to our children that this book is dedicated, in the hope that they will come of age in a nation governed by the rule of law.

Chevy Chase, Maryland   *October 1971*

"The President, who exercises a limited power, may err without causing great mischief in the State. Congress may decide amiss without destroying the Union, because the electoral body in which Congress originates may cause it to retract its decision by changing its members. But if the Supreme Court is ever composed of imprudent men or bad citizens, the Union may be plunged into anarchy or civil war."

Democracy in America, ALEXIS DE TOCQUEVILLE

A
QUESTION
OF
JUDGMENT

THE PRESIDENT

IT WAS midafternoon when the Justice Department called from Washington. Minutes later a United States marshal was on his way from the Federal courthouse in lower Manhattan. He stopped first at the offices of *Life* magazine in Rockefeller Center, where, after his credentials had been duly scrutinized, he was entrusted with a manila envelope, double sealed with Scotch tape. Then he rushed off to catch the next plane to Washington.

On his arrival in the capital, the envelope was delivered into eager hands at the Justice Department and its contents hurriedly Xeroxed. By nightfall, one copy was in the hands of the attorney general. Another was at the White House, awaiting the attention of the President.

On this day, May 2, 1969, Washington as yet offered no outward hint that the newly installed Administration faced a test of will and nerve that would challenge the strictures of the Constitution. It was Friday, and the Federal agencies were slowing to their customary weekend lull. The city relaxed in the spring sunshine. Taking advantage of the balmy afternoon, the President had strolled down Pennsylvania Avenue to pay a call on his Treasury Secretary. The White House press corps tagged along, snapping photos and making notes as the

Chief Executive greeted passersby. It was a brief outing, but the newsmen could ill afford to let any opportunity pass. In 102 days in the White House, Richard Nixon had done conspicuously little to advertise himself or his presidency.

The First Hundred Days in office, which Franklin Roosevelt had established as a milestone of presidential accomplishment, had, in Nixon's case, been a study in modesty and caution. There were good reasons for this. On assuming his stewardship, the new President found the nation more sharply divided than at any time since the Civil War. He had been elected by less than a majority of the electorate, his victory margin so slim it could scarcely be considered a mandate. Another President might have projected his own personality into the breach. But Nixon, whose style was not suited to inspiring the citizenry, had so far devoted himself instead to the limited but essential task of restoring calm and order in the land.

His Administration lacked even a catchy cognomen like the Great Society or the New Frontier. The only slogan heard much in Washington under the new regime reflected its subdued aspirations: "Keep a low profile." Rather than charting a bold new course, Nixon had simply pledged to bring his fellow citizens together again. Instead of trying to rouse public opinion with dramatic rhetoric, he urged one and all to lower their voices, and proceeded himself to set a prime example.

By tempering his own abrasive tendencies, the new President had blunted the partisan edge of political debate. His efforts to disentangle American forces from Vietnam had helped muffle the thunder against the war. His promise to reform the welfare program was aimed at easing the grievances of the ghettos. Critics pointed to long-neglected national problems and charged that the President had not manifested nearly enough imagination or concern. Some complained simply that he had reduced the Federal government to a state of dreary dullness. Certainly he had not achieved national tranquillity. Nevertheless, after its long binge of violence, the country was showing hopeful signs of sobering up and calming down. And whether or not Nixon was really responsible for this improvement, the latest Gallup poll showed that sixty-one per cent of the nation approved of his early performance.

But the President knew as well as anyone else that one false move or one harsh speech could wreck the fragile consensus he had labored to achieve. To avoid discord, he had approached every major policy decision and pronouncement with utmost caution. Whenever possible, every action was weighed against the lessons of the past. Now, however, as this first weekend in May began, Nixon was confronted with a set of circumstances that were both unforeseen and unprecedented.

The envelope from *Life* magazine had been rushed to Washington Friday evening to give the President and his close advisers an advance look at a journalistic exposé that could have momentous consequences. The story, scheduled to appear on the nation's newsstands the following Monday, touched on the Supreme Court of the United States. Its central figure was Associate Justice Abe Fortas, friend and counselor to former President Lyndon Johnson and Johnson's unsuccessful candidate for Chief Justice of the United States. Information uncovered by William Lambert, author of the article, suggested that Fortas had committed what at the least appeared to be a serious indiscretion.

In 1966, soon after joining the High Court, Fortas had accepted a $20,000 fee from a charitable foundation established by Louis Wolfson, the free-wheeling financier. Ostensibly, Fortas had been given the money in return for his help in planning the foundation's activities. But at the time the arrangement was consummated Wolfson had been under investigation by the Securities and Exchange Commission. The SEC's probe ultimately led to criminal charges against Wolfson and some of his associates. Some months after these indictments were handed down, Fortas had returned the $20,000. Since then, Wolfson had been tried and convicted on two separate charges. Only the week before, on April 25, Federal prison doors had slammed shut behind him.

All this was fact. But the most damaging aspect of the story was based on hearsay. When the government investigation was at a crucial point, Lambert reported, Wolfson had sought to reassure his associates by implying that Fortas would help stave off trouble. *Life* conceded that it had uncovered no evidence that Fortas did anything of the kind. But the magazine pointedly quoted a section of the canons of judicial ethics that required a judge to be free not only from impropriety, but also from even the appearance of impropriety. The public was left to ponder whether Fortas had kept faith with that high standard.

The Nixon Administration had first learned of *Life's* impending disclosures in early April of 1969. Since then, for the past three weeks, the Justice Department had been conducting its own discreet but intensive investigation. Information gathered from the files of Federal agencies had confirmed *Life's* findings, and given rise to suspicions that Fortas's associations with Wolfson went beyond what the magazine had discovered. The evidence in hand was far from conclusive. But the Justice Department viewed the matter so seriously that the attorney general's staff had furnished him with a memorandum on the legal grounds for impeachment and prosecution of a Supreme Court Justice.

For tactical reasons, the Administration had decided to keep its information about Fortas and Wolfson to itself, at least until *Life* had published its story. This was no easy task in gossip-hungry Washington. The few officials who knew about the case were sworn to secrecy. But an awkward situation, created by Louis Wolfson himself, almost forced the government to tip its hand.

A man of wealth and influence, Wolfson was not the type to go quietly off to jail. He continued to proclaim his innocence, and when the Supreme Court refused to consider his appeal from his first conviction, he turned for help to Congress. In his last days of freedom Wolfson wrote to several friendly legislators, including Senator Spessard Holland of Florida, asking them to appeal personally to the President to delay his imprisonment until he could try one more plea to the courts. On April 22 Holland obligingly called the White

House, asking for an appointment for himself and Wolfson's other friends in Congress. Under ordinary circumstances the President probably would have agreed to see them, if only as a matter of courtesy. But the circumstances were hardly ordinary. The President took the matter up with his attorney general, John Mitchell, then had an aide phone Holland to tell him he had turned down the request on Mitchell's advice.

Later that day Mitchell himself called Holland to soothe the senator's feelings. The attorney general could not tell Holland specifically what the problem was. He said only that "something would occur" later on that would make it obvious why the President "should not be connected with the matter at this time."

Having avoided any involvement with Wolfson, the President on the very next night found himself face to face with Justice Fortas, and the other members of the Court, at the White House. The occasion was a presidential dinner in honor of the retiring Chief Justice Earl Warren. With Warren due to leave the Court in only two months, the guest list naturally stirred speculation about whom the President had in mind as a successor. Newsmen noted that all the men most prominently mentioned as possible candidates, including Thomas E. Dewey, former Attorney General Herbert Brownell, Jr., and the present attorney general, John Mitchell, were in attendance. No one, however, was astute enough to point out that the guest list included only one judge from the lower Federal courts. He was Warren Earl Burger of the U.S. Court of Appeals in Washington, an outspoken critic of the Warren Court's doctrines and the man who in June would become the next Chief Justice of the United States.

One jurist whose name, naturally enough, did not even enter into the speculation over the Chief Justiceship was Abe Fortas. His nomination for that position had failed to get Senate approval the year before. But Fortas seemed to have recovered from that setback. Self-assured as usual, he exchanged amenities with his host and the attorney general and once again made himself comfortable in the Executive Mansion where he had been such a frequent visitor. He had one fault to find with the new management. The air conditioning was turned on so high that he was forced to cover his wife's back with a handkerchief. "Next time, I'm going to bring a fur-lined handkerchief," he wisecracked to newsmen later. "The Republicans may have turned on the lights, but they turned off the heat."

The President, for his part, was striving to set party differences aside for the evening in the interests of harmony. To add a bipartisan flavor he had invited, along with the flock of Republican dignitaries, California's former Democratic governor and Nixon's former political rival, Pat Brown. The President now could afford to laugh off his defeat by Brown in 1962. If Brown had not beaten him, he told his guests, he might still be governor of California.

The President's warmest words appropriately enough were reserved for his guest of honor, the Chief Justice, with whom he had not always been on good terms. Hard feelings between the two men dated back to the time when Warren was governor of California and Nixon a young senator from the same state. In 1952 Governor Warren nurtured hopes of getting the Republican presidential nomination. His supporters suspected that Senator Nixon was scheming to pull California delegates at the Republican convention away from Warren to support Dwight Eisenhower in order to boost Nixon's own ambitions for the vice presidency. That had been long ago. But Warren's affection for Nixon had certainly not increased during the 1968 presidential campaign, when candidate Nixon had sharply attacked the decisions of the Warren Court. Under the East Room's crystal chandeliers, in the presence of the full Court and ten members of his cabinet, Nixon sought to make amends for any offense he had given over the years. He offered a gracious toast to Warren's family and recounted in glowing terms Warren's long career in public service. Earl Warren, the President declared, had served his country well. Warren's response made clear that he was willing to let bygones be bygones. He would leave the Court, he said, with "no malice in my heart."

It was one thing for the President to set aside his old differences with the Justices for an evening, in bidding farewell to their departing leader. But it would be quite another matter for him to deal judiciously with the grave new trouble brewing over the Court. Here, history offered Richard Nixon little in the way of guidance.

During the life of the Republic, while scandal had stained nearly every other branch of government at one time or another, the Supreme Court had remained by comparison a symbol of rectitude. Back in 1804 one of its members, Justice Samuel Chase, had been impeached. But the charges against him were clearly political in nature, and he was duly acquitted. In the ensuing years the personal conduct of members of the Court had been called into question only on rare occasions, none of which had produced serious consequences. Since Samuel Chase's trial before the Senate, no Justice of the Supreme Court had been impeached. Nor had any ever been forced to resign because of criticism of his behavior.

The allegations about Justice Fortas, then, might well raise unique ethical and constitutional questions. But that was only part of the problem. With Richard Nixon in the White House, anything bearing on the Supreme Court was bound to be charged with political significance.

The political ramifications were a product of both the Court's stormy record in recent years and Nixon's stance as a candidate and President. "We go with the cases that come to us," Earl Warren once said, truthfully enough, in response to criticism of the High Court's activist approach to jurisprudence. But it is also true that the Supreme Court has wide discretion in selecting which cases it will consider from the hundreds crowding its docket. In sixteen years under Warren's leadership, the Court had heard cases and handed down rulings that took it into areas where the judiciary had never before ventured. It struck down racial segregation, commanded the reapportionment of state legislatures, restricted the observance of religion in public schools, and vastly strengthened the rights of criminal defendants.

The reaction was inevitable. If it is to fulfill its role as a protector of minority interests, the High Court can never be a widely popular institution. The Warren Court, in its zeal to expand the rights of so many minorities, provoked the assault of a multitude of majorities. Demands for Warren's impeachment were heard throughout the land. Public indignation against him and his liberal colleagues was emblazoned on billboards and bumper strips and given sanction by congressmen, governors, and even the chiefs of the state judiciaries. The Warren Court was charged with, among other things, abetting violence and crime by its permissiveness. So in 1968, when Richard Nixon sought the presidency of the United States, with crime rates rising and riots erupting in ghettos and campuses, resentment against the Court was more intense than ever.

In the past, presidential candidates had generally steered clear of attacking judicial doctrines, considering it too sensitive an issue to raise in the midst of a campaign. Even Franklin Roosevelt, frustrated by the "nine old men" who had stymied his economic reforms, restrained himself from striking directly at the Court during the 1936 campaign. FDR preferred to wait until after his landslide victory to unveil his abortive "court-packing" scheme. But candidate Nixon, leery of discussing the war in Vietnam, found himself short of issues that would stir the electorate. The Court offered a tempting target. As he barnstormed around the land, all the while professing his lawyerly respect for the Court as "an institution," Nixon fired away.

In keeping with his main campaign theme of law and order, the Republican nominee concentrated his attack on the Court's criminal law opinions. Reeling off bloodcurdling examples of murder and rape, he charged that the Court had caused a "weakening of the peace forces as against the criminal forces in this country." Civil rights was another fertile field, although here the candidate was more subtle. Wary of alienating potential supporters in the North, he conveyed his views to the burgeoning Republican constituency in the South mainly through such spokesmen as Senator Strom Thurmond of South Carolina. They recalled Nixon's remarks on judicial efforts to end school desegregation made to a caucus of Southern delegates at the Republican National Convention earlier in the year. "I know there are a lot of smart judges," Nixon had said. "But I don't think there is any court in this country, including the Supreme Court of the United States, that is qualified to be a local school district and make the decision as your local school board."

In the course of the campaign, Nixon outlined what sort of Supreme Court he thought the nation should have. To no one's surprise his vision was very different from what the Warren Court had been. "I believe in a strict interpretation of the Supreme Court's functions," he said. "In a sense this means I believe we need a Court which looks upon its function as being that of interpretation, rather than of breaking through into new areas that are really the prerogative of the Congress of the United States."

Nixon's critique was not aimed at any one justice in particular, but Abe Fortas's judicial views as well as anyone's embodied all that Nixon deplored. From the time he joined the Court, in 1965, Fortas had aligned himself with the liberal bloc. And when in 1968, in the middle of the campaign, Earl Warren announced his intention to retire and Lyndon Johnson picked Fortas as his replacement, he seemed the logical inheritor of Warren's liberal legacy.

Nixon had immediately hit out at Johnson for making the nomination. Instead, Nixon argued, LBJ should have deferred to the President who would be elected in November, and who, Nixon certainly hoped, would be Richard Nixon. Nixon avoided public comment on Fortas's qualifications for the post. But he quietly encouraged the Republican senators who opposed the nomination and, combined with Southern Democrats, eventually forced the President to withdraw Fortas's name. That represented a significant victory for Nixon. Warren, having delayed his retirement after Fortas's setback in the Senate, had agreed to leave at the end of the current Court term in June, when Nixon would appoint his successor. But Fortas himself remained on the bench, where he would undoubtedly continue to be a forceful spokesman for the Warren Court's philosophy. With his vote the liberals on the Court would most probably remain in ascendancy for some time to come.

This was definitely not a sanguine prospect for the new President. The liberal justices would not retreat from the doctrines on criminal law that Nixon had inveighed against so often during the campaign, nor would they countenance any effort the President might make, on behalf of his Southern supporters, to soften the impact of desegregation rulings.

Now, however, the discovery of Fortas's relations with Louis Wolfson had introduced a new factor into the Administration's considerations about the Court's future. The accusation of impropriety, which would be threatening to any Justice, had extra sting in Fortas's case. His friendship with Lyndon Johnson and his earlier career as a high-powered Washington lawyer had already colored his reputation. And during the struggle in the Senate over his nomination as Chief Justice, it had been disclosed that Fortas had received a $15,000 fee, solicited from wealthy businessmen, for conducting a series of law school seminars. That revelation proved to be the death blow to his hopes to replace Earl Warren. All these factors made it seem likely that, barring some convincing explanation from Fortas, disclosure of the Wolfson episode would set off demands for the Justice's resignation and threats to impeach him.

Fortas's departure from the bench would make it possible, far sooner than anticipated, for the new President to shift the balance of power among the Justices in a direction much more in keeping with his tastes and political needs. This was a tantalizing prospect. But the advantage offered would be as apparent to everyone else as it was to Nixon himself. The President could be certain that his Administration's actions and motives in the Fortas affair would be closely scrutinized. By law, by precept and by hallowed tradition, the independence of the judiciary was held to be inviolable. If the President permitted himself or his agents to trespass the boundaries protecting the High Court, he would risk outraging the judiciary, the legal profession, and the Congress, and he might reap a political disaster. It behooved him, then, to act with great care.

Lacking any specific precedent to govern his actions, the President could draw on the personal experience of his own turbulent past. Early in his career, in the Alger Hiss case, Richard Nixon had learned that prestige and powerful friends do not make a man's reputation invulnerable. Hiss's service in the State Department had won him high esteem. At first few could believe the charges of Communist espionage leveled against him by Whittaker Chambers. But Congressman Nixon, with his own future at stake, pressed the attack. Hiss was convicted of perjury and ruined. Nixon, suddenly a bright new political star, won election to the Senate and his party's nomination for Vice President.

Then Nixon himself was nearly destroyed by scandal. During the 1952 campaign word got out that some wealthy Californians had raised an $18,000 "trust fund" to help defray Senator Nixon's political expenses. Amid demands from within his own party that he withdraw as vice presidential candidate, Nixon made an emotional appeal to the public on television in which he laid bare his personal financial history and assured the nation that the only political gift he had received was a cocker spaniel named Checkers. The Checkers speech kept Nixon on the ticket, probably saved the Republicans from defeat in November, and provided a memorable demonstration of the restorative powers of confession and sentimentality.

The ensuing years were filled with more personal challenges: President Eisenhower's heart attack in 1955, Nixon's cliff-hanger loss to John Kennedy in 1960, his defeat by Pat

Brown in California in 1962. That election seemed to finish him politically. Nixon moved to New York and became a prosperous Wall Street lawyer. Still, he yearned for public office. Endowed by his background of triumphs and debacles with remarkable resiliency, Nixon returned to national prominence, captured the presidential nomination again in 1968 and outlasted Hubert Humphrey to win the White House.

Richard Nixon came to the presidency unencumbered by ideology but equipped with a homemade philosophy for operating under conditions of stress. He was absorbed by techniques and tactics, and, as he had made strikingly clear in his self-revealing memoir, *Six Crises,* he tended to view public leadership in personal and psychic terms. "A leader is one who has the emotional, mental and physical strength to withstand the pressures and tensions created by necessary doubts and then, at the critical moment, to make a choice and to act decisively," Nixon wrote. "The men who fail are those who are so overcome by doubts that they either crack under the strain or flee to avoid meeting the problem at all."

Nixon's rules for leadership varied somewhat, of course, depending on circumstances. But his faith and experience in applied psychology would serve him well in the tense days ahead. "Confidence in crisis depends in great part on the adequacy of preparation," Nixon observed. The Administration had prepared as well as it could for the Fortas crisis. The *Life* story was in hand and the Justice Department's own investigation was off to a flying start. Now the President could relax in confidence and enjoy the weekend.

On Saturday morning, May 3, accompanied by an escort of congressmen from both parties, Nixon boarded Air Force One and headed for Louisville and the ninety-fifth running of the Kentucky Derby. The excursion offered him a chance to mix politics with pleasure. On the way down he chatted amiably with legislators from Kentucky and South Carolina. He stopped off in Columbia, South Carolina, to greet James F. Byrnes, a former Supreme Court Justice and one of the patriarchs of Southern politics, on his ninetieth birthday. Then on to Churchill Downs, which was warm in its welcome of the first President ever to witness the Run for the Roses. Nixon backed the Derby favorite, Majestic Prince. As the California colt crossed the finish line first by a neck, the exultant President shouted: "He won, he won." Newsmen wondered whether Nixon had more than a rooting interest in the race, but his staff refused to say whether he had placed a bet.

After the race the big jet returned to Washington, where that night the President was-guest of honor at the annual White House Correspondents' Dinner at the Washington Hilton. This is the largest of the social affairs that bring together the press and officials who maintain a symbiotic relationship in the capital. In attendance that night, besides almost every member of the Washington press corps, were six members of the President's cabinet, nearly two score senators and congressmen and even one Supreme Court Justice, Byron L. White. But the main diversion at such gatherings is always a combination of shop talk and gossip, and on this night the hottest topic of conversation was the forthcoming story about Justice Fortas.

Details were scarce. But bits and pieces of information had leaked out since the Federal marshal had visited *Life's* offices the day before. It was bruited about the Hilton that the story involved some sort of fee Fortas had accepted from Louis Wolfson's foundation. Meanwhile *Life* had arranged to make advance copies of its next issue, containing the complete story, available to the press on Sunday afternoon. Justice Fortas had let it be known that he would issue a statement on the story as soon as he had read it. Newsmen at the Hilton, scurrying around for more information, confronted Justice White and asked his reaction; the startled Justice said he knew nothing whatever about the matter.

Aloof from the hubbub, the President chatted amiably with his hosts at the head table. He appeared to enjoy the bantering tone of the after-dinner speeches and entertainment. In presenting a Gay-Nineties review, Nixon's hosts pointed out that the program, "following Republican tradition, looks backward, while moving forward." The President's cheerful mood was reflected in his own brief remarks to the gathering. "I know the job I have is supposed to be the most difficult in the world," he said. "But it has not yet become for me that great awesome burden that some have described." Then he made his way home down Connecticut Avenue toward the White House.

A few years before, looking back on what was already more than an average lifetime's share of stress, Nixon had written: "Going through the necessary soul searching of deciding whether to fight a battle or to run away from it, is far more difficult than the battle itself." Still more soul searching lay ahead on the Fortas affair, but the battle was about to begin.

THE ATTORNEY GENERAL

WHATEVER action the Nixon Administration took on the Fortas matter, the President, of course, would bear ultimate responsibility. But the nature of his office limited his personal participation. A host of other problems demanded the Chief Executive's time and attention. And in view of the political and constitutional ramifications, expediency dictated that some other official of the Administration take direct charge of the situation. The inevitable choice was the attorney general of the United States, John Newton Mitchell.

As the chief legal officer of the government, the attorney general customarily serves as liaison between the executive and judicial branches. He often plays an influential role in the selection of members of the Supreme Court, and he has a direct interest in the operation of the judiciary. Also, as a member of the Supreme Court bar and an officer of the Court, the attorney general has some concern with the dignity and prestige of that institution. But more significant than custom and statute in the present case was the special relationship between this President and this attorney general. In the early days of the Nixon Administration it had already become clear that of all his advisers, it was Mitchell in whom the President's greatest trust reposed.

Nixon had known Mitchell only five years, and Mitchell had never held public office until Nixon made him attorney general. Other men in the cabinet had worked with the President longer and had far more experience in public service. Among them were Robert Finch, Secretary of Health, Education and Welfare and former lieutenant governor of California, and Secretary of State William P. Rogers, himself an attorney general under Dwight Eisenhower. The reasons why Nixon seemed to rely more on Mitchell than on Finch, Rogers or others are best understood by those genuinely close to Nixon and Mitchell, a notably exclusive group. But Mitchell's background and bearing suggest that the President trusted his attorney general mainly because Mitchell never doubted himself.

Mitchell, who was fifty-five years old when he entered Nixon's cabinet, was born in Detroit and reared in the suburbs of Long Island. In the midst of the Depression he took his law degree from Fordham University, working days and going to class nights. He had five years with a small Wall Street law firm before joining the Navy during World War II. The Navy sent him to the South Pacific, where he commanded a torpedo boat squadron, one of whose junior officers and heroes was the captain of the celebrated PT 109, John F. Kennedy.

Back from the wars, Mitchell rejoined his old firm as a full partner and concentrated on municipal-bond law. This hitherto obscure field was taking on increasing importance with the postwar proliferation of publicly financed construction projects. Over the next two decades Mitchell quietly supervised the amending of state constitutions, the redrafting of municipal charters, and other legal engineering which permitted states and cities to borrow billions of dollars for housing, schools and hospitals. He was acknowledged to be one of the best in his business, a reputation that permitted him to earn more than $200,000 a year and to serve his own convenience. "He was so good, he had it made," an admiring young associate said. "He could pick his clients and set his hours and go home to Rye to play golf at four in the afternoon."

Though he was not a pretentious man, Mitchell's sense of assurance verged on arrogance. "He is a very hard-nosed guy," said one New York State official who often sought his advice on financial proposals. "And like all bond lawyers he is three steps above the archangels." His clients considered him a pillar of strength. "We were just a bunch of farmers from the Midwest," a Wisconsin legislator recalled of his first encounter with Mitchell. "But the overwhelming impression we all got was here was a guy you could rely on. He was in our corner."

Richard Nixon met him in the early 1960's when the former Vice President came to New York to practice law. Nixon was just beginning to make his way in private practice; Mitchell was already on top of the heap. Nixon came to share the general high opinion for Mitchell's expertise when Nixon's firm, like so many others, sought Mitchell's advice on fiscal matters. More than that, after the two firms merged in 1967, Nixon came to realize that Mitchell also had a better than fair grasp of politics. His wide bond practice had given him firsthand experience in political maneuvering and a host of contacts in state capitals and big cities around the country.

In early 1968, when Nixon's presidential drive began in earnest, the candidate asked Mitchell to lay the groundwork for campaign organizations in a number of states where he was well connected. Mitchell performed so successfully that, as he later put it, "I got sucked into running the whole campaign." "Nixon didn't need a political strategist," one Republican official explained. "That was *his* department. He just wanted somebody to manage things efficiently."

Managing, as Mitchell construed it, included responsibility for making judgments. On the eve of the Republican convention in Miami Beach, Mitchell, who was already on the scene, got a phone call from Nixon.

"Is there anything I need to know before I come down there?" the candidate asked.

"No," said the manager, and the subject was closed.

The two men got along well, in part because they were both

locked inside themselves, Nixon given to brooding introspection, Mitchell closemouthed and remote behind his habitual pipe. "They're a couple of loners," said one member of Nixon, Mudge, Rose, Guthrie, Alexander & Mitchell. "They're not at ease with most people. They'd rather learn something from a piece of paper than from a person."

No one was surprised when after his election Nixon prevailed upon Mitchell to surrender his lucrative practice and the comforts of Westchester County life to serve as attorney general. Mitchell, who had insisted beforehand that he would never come to Washington, later explained that he realized that the new President "had a helluva job to do. And if he felt I was going to make all that difference, I couldn't refuse him."

Mitchell made it part of his public style to take a sour view of life and work in Washington. Embassy receptions and other large social functions bored him, he said. Typically, he was not among the cabinet members in attendance at the White House correspondents' dinner. He complained that his job was tough, time-consuming and lacking in the satisfactions of private practice. He was not "overjoyed at being attorney general." To a group of young government interns who sought his views on the issues of the day, he put it even more bluntly. His first priority as attorney general, Mitchell said, "is to get the hell out of this town."

But Mitchell's associates at the Justice Department viewed his protestations with some skepticism. His grumbling served to keep those he dealt with off balance. Meanwhile Mitchell himself seemed to be managing the Nixon Administration much as he had managed the Nixon campaign. He sat, at the President's request, on high-level policy-making groups, including the National Security Council, whose concerns in international affairs were far removed from his immediate responsibilities. Indeed, Mitchell estimated that he spent fully one-third of his working hours on matters assigned to him by the President that had no connection with the Justice Department. He saw the President face to face on the average of three times a week and talked with him daily on the phone. In a city where contact with the Chief Executive is considered the hallmark of power and prestige, it was commonly agreed that no one in the government, outside the immediate White House staff, had readier access to the President than did his attorney general.

In his first months at the Justice Department Mitchell set a brisk and efficient tone. At his desk promptly every morning at quarter past eight, he stayed until seven at night, usually lugging home a briefcase bulging with legal papers. Members of his staff talked admiringly of his retentive powers and his capacity for analysis. And all were impressed by his close ties with the President. But some found his manner unsettling. "He just sits there and smokes his pipe and doesn't say anything," said one assistant attorney general. "He doesn't show you much," said another staff member. "He plays a tough brand of ball."

When he did respond, Mitchell was usually civil but often brusque. His features, under a fast-receding hairline, were normally fixed in a stern expression. He was no storyteller, but he occasionally indulged in caustic ribbing. When his second-in-command, Deputy Attorney General Richard Kleindienst, mentioned that he had decided not to attend a dinner sponsored by some lawyers' group, Mitchell gibed: "What's the matter, Dick, did you find out they have a cash bar?"

Richard Nixon's campaign criticism of Ramsey Clark, Lyndon Johnson's attorney general, had led the public to expect Clark's replacement would be a hard-boiled prosecutor, and Mitchell certainly looked and acted the part. No two men could have presented a sharper contrast in style and outlook. Warm and unassuming, Clark had won the affection of the Justice Department staff. On law enforcement he took a broad view, arguing that the crime problem could best be met not by harsher laws and crackdowns but by raising police salaries and reforming the prisons. He talked frequently of the social and economic roots of crime, and he defended the Supreme Court as a champion of the oppressed.

Mitchell believed that Clark had worried too much about the wrong things. "You don't solve the social problems of the country as attorney general," he said. "The Department of Justice is a law enforcement agency; that's its primary purpose. Other concepts shouldn't get in the way."

Early on, Mitchell's approach to crime fighting brought him into conflict with the doctrines of the Warren Court. The issue was wiretapping, which Clark, out of concern for civil liberties, had declined to use except in national security matters. Mitchell was determined to carry out his responsibilities "like another lawyer would set about doing a job for a client, using the best tools available." He considered wiretapping an excellent tool, and as soon as he took office he began authorizing phone taps in organized-crime investigations. Consequently he was much disturbed when in mid-March the Supreme Court ruled that under certain circumstances the government could be compelled to turn over the records of tapped conversations to defendants. Justice Fortas voted with the majority.

The Justice Department immediately petitioned for a rehearing on the case, which the Court subsequently turned down. While an appeal was being prepared, Mitchell publicly complained about the ruling before a Senate crime committee. The Court's decision, he said, "has been a great disappointment to the department," and he warned about its consequences. In some cases affected by the edict "national security is involved and in some other instances the very life and existence of witnesses are involved."

Disturbed by the tenor of these remarks, Michigan Senator Phil Hart, a vigilant civil libertarian, was prompted to remind the attorney general, "whether it is popular or not, that restraints and inhibitions on the police was the purpose of the Bill of Rights." The Supreme Court, Hart added, was "ultimately responsible for delivering on the guarantee." To complain that the Court's decision restricted the police "is in a sense a so-what argument, because that is precisely what the Bill of Rights is intended to do."

The attorney general's public criticism of the Court was considered unseemly by many liberals. The episode contributed to their growing concern that John Mitchell, in his zeal to combat crime, was prepared to undercut the Constitution and the Supreme Court. Mitchell scoffed at such talk as "a lot of rhetoric" left over from the campaign. "I don't think I'm tough," he said. Instead he considered himself as "businesslike and pragmatic, without too much concern about ideology, but with more concern about getting the job done."

It was in this businesslike manner that he approached the Fortas affair. While *Life* was putting the finishing touches on its story, Mitchell was overseeing the government investigation into Fortas's relations with Louis Wolfson. He had taken counsel with a few close advisers and of course with the President. But he was deeply troubled. In "gravity and magnitude," he acknowledged, this problem exceeded any he had encountered before. He was primarily concerned, he told his associates, about the prestige of the Court. But as Richard Nixon's former campaign manager, he needed no one to point out the political implications, which created, he said, "a not very pleasant situation." Accustomed to following well-established procedures, Mitchell now had no bench mark to rely on. For once, he realized, he was "operating on uncharted seas."

THE JUSTICE

JOHN MITCHELL had seen Abe Fortas perhaps half a dozen times since coming to Washington, at judicial functions and social affairs, most recently at the White House dinner for Chief Justice Warren. He considered him, more by reputation than on the basis of his own limited acquaintance, "a very able individual and a very able judge," an opinion, he added, which he shared with the President.

Everyone in Washington would agree with the attorney general's appraisal. Beyond that surface judgment, however, Fortas was a puzzlement, even to those close to him. Few public men are simple: the strain of presenting a certain image to the world invariably creates internal convolutions. But Fortas had more than his share of complications. "It wouldn't surprise me," one of his law clerks said, "if he was robbing banks on the side or writing novels under another name."

Visitors to the Court saw a short, small-framed figure with a seamed face and moody, narrow eyes. The gentle accents of his native Tennessee still flavored his deep voice. But his manner was crisp and peremptory, his words often edged with sarcasm as he leaned forward to set a trap for some hapless advocate. Off the bench, Fortas's life was rich in comfort and culture. He had a handsome wife who was a brilliant attorney in her own right, a lavish home in Georgetown complete with swimming pool, and a 1950 Rolls Royce restored to its original elegance. A first-rate amateur violinist, he gave chamber music recitals for his friends. He collected objets d'art and served on the boards of museums. Most of his fifty-eight years had been spent in Washington, where few men had provoked such vigorously opposing reactions. Many admired him, in Lyndon Johnson's words, as "a profound thinker," and "a man of humane and deeply compassionate feelings." Others mistrusted him as a relentless opportunist who, to put it delicately as the *New York Times* once did, was "insufficiently holy."

Fortas's career offered evidence to support either point of view. After making a brilliant record at Yale Law School he had come to Washington in the first flush of the New Deal and worked his way up through the new alphabet of reform from the AAA to the SEC. During World War II, as deputy to Interior Secretary Harold Ickes, he fought to permit the return of Japanese-Americans who had been uprooted from their West Coast homes. As a private attorney, when McCarthyism was at its height, Fortas and his partners, Thurman Arnold and Paul Porter, had defended scores of suspected security risks. His brilliant argument before the Supreme Court on behalf of a penniless convict led to a momentous decision guaranteeing the right of every accused criminal to free legal counsel. Since he himself had become a Justice of the High Court, his record had won him further professional acclaim.

The other side of the ledger was murky, a collection of suspicions and innuendos. "Mr. Fortas had something of a reputation as a fixer," said Michigan Senator Robert Griffin, who led the opposition to Fortas's nomination as Chief Justice. As with most such allegations, this was based more on intuition than on facts, and it stemmed in large measure from Fortas's background as a Washington lawyer.

Lawyers in the capital are widely believed to play a potent, mysterious and not always scrupulous role in the operations of the Federal government, a belief fostered by the large number of private attorneys who formerly worked for public agencies and by the extravagant fees they charge for nebulous tasks. The press, always fascinated by hints of behind-the-scenes influence in Washington, has fed the public's imagination. "The top lawyers of the capital are a special breed," *Business Week* reported. "They are not only experts in the art of government, but also influential brokers between big business and Federal authority." *True* magazine depicted Washington lawyers as "treading softly but surefootedly along the corridors of power." The *Washingtonian* airily referred to "the Washington legal establishment which as everyone knows runs the Government."

Before he became a Justice, Fortas was considered the prototype of this influential breed. One letter or one phone call from him, or even just the dropping of his name, some clients believed, would work wonders in the high echelons of bureaucracy. While much of this impression was romance, no one knew how much. Most of the victories Fortas won for his corporate clientele in courtrooms and hearing rooms were owed simply to his boldness and resourcefulness as a lawyer. But the very fact of his success served to foster cynicism about his methods. His fellow members of the bar had accorded him due respect, but in some cases only grudgingly. "I don't like the s.o.b.," said another attorney in town. "But if I were in trouble, I'd want him on my side."

Justice Fortas was also in a sense a victim of guilt by association, the association being his close friendship with Lyndon Baines Johnson. Many citizens felt that the President's own personal behavior left something to be desired in terms of taste and discretion. Moreover, in Johnson's early years in the White House, when Fortas was still a private citizen, the shadowy nature of his role as an adviser-without-portfolio aroused some criticism. And when Fortas continued to serve Lyndon Johnson, even after donning his judicial robes, the criticism spread and sharpened.

Among friends, Fortas tartly dismissed the disapproval voiced in some quarters. Whether it really troubled him or not, no one knew for sure. At times he appeared indifferent to other people's opinions. He gave the impression he had his own code of behavior, one tenet of which was to suppress whatever inner concerns and resentments he might harbor. At the Senate hearings on his nomination to be Chief Justice he had withstood twelve hours of grueling and often harassing interrogation without ever losing his grip on himself. He had accepted the unfavorable outcome with dignity and calmly resumed his duties as an Associate Justice.

Now, months later, he was confronted with a new attack based on an episode he had considered over and done with. He had known for months that *Life* had been looking into the Wolfson matter, and late in April he had been put on notice that its story was near completion. When he was asked to grant an interview, Fortas, generally mistrustful of the press, characteristically refused. Instead he decided to issue his own statement to the press after he had read the article. Saturday night, on the eve of the disclosure, some men might have stayed home to brood. Fortas went off to a charity ball, dancing late into the night. Whatever *Life* had to report, he would deal with it the next day. After all, he was the man other people sent for when they were in trouble. Certainly he should be able to get himself out of difficulty.

But it was not to be that simple. The Justice's association with Louis Wolfson would raise issues of a different sort than Fortas or any other Washington lawyer was accustomed to resolving. Apart from the constitutional and political problems, the implications of Fortas's conduct rubbed against the already raw nerve endings of American society.

Not long before Richard Nixon's inauguration, Daniel Patrick Moynihan, the President-elect's most imaginative and articulate adviser, warned his chief: "It has fallen to you to assume the governance of a deeply divided country." Underlying the difficulties the new President would face, Moynihan wrote, was "the erosion of the authority of the institutions of American society." The erosion process was hard to comprehend. "All we know is that the sense of institutions being legitimate—especially the institutions of government—is the glue that holds societies together. When it weakens," Moynihan said ominously, "things come unstuck."

The nation's loss of faith had become pervasive as the decade of the 1960's neared an end. It was evident in the rioting in the cities, in the violent protests that swept the campus and in the emotional response to the demagoguery of George Wallace. Though resentment and discontent were most vigorously expressed by extremists on each political flank, the malaise was spreading to the center. The main causes could be identified as the war and racial antagonism. But what was most disturbing was that the angry reactions to these problems produced more anger in a seemingly endless chain that threatened social dissolution and either political anarchy or repression. From all sides suspicion and resentment were directed not only at institutions, but also at the men who controlled them. Institutions and men were lumped and condemned together as "the power structure," or "the establishment."

The terms were ill defined. But usually, criticism of the establishment was aimed at the conglomerate of public and private forces whose influence on national life had taken on awesome dimensions in the wake of the upheavals of the 1930's. The leaders of the American establishment were not a monolithic group. But most shared similar backgrounds and ideas which blurred individual distinctions. In a broad sense they were liberals. That is, their actions were informed by the belief that public energies should be deployed to improve the human condition. They seemed to dominate the press, the great universities, the munificent foundations and the Federal government, from inside and out. They belonged to both political parties and moved with ease from one Administration to another, or from public position to private and back again. As a group, with occasional additions and subtractions, they had led the nation through the Depression and World War II and on into the second half of the twentieth century. Some of their promises had been redeemed. The Depression had been overcome, the war had been won, and the country had entered an era of material bounty beyond any previous expectation.

Yet somehow all their efforts had begun to sour, or, as Moynihan, himself a redoubtable establishmentarian, phrased it, "come unstuck." Abroad, the wars went on without end. At home, despite relative affluence, life was filled more than ever with anxiety, frustration and noisy desperation. Increasingly the suspicion grew that the nation had been cheated by the system in which it had long placed its trust.

The rhetoric directed against the establishment often verged on cant. The public's disillusionment was vague and amorphous. But the disclosures about Fortas's conduct would offer a focal point for resentment, a concrete example of what some considered a much broader duplicity. Fortas had been a servant of the New Deal, a Washington lawyer, a presidential counselor. Now he sat on the highest court in the land. As much as any man he seemed to symbolize the system that held the reins of power. Indeed, he had been held up as an example of the best that system could offer. When Fortas was named to the Court in 1965, Philip Hart of Michigan, a widely respected figure in the Senate, in urging support of the nomination, declared: "If Abe Fortas has fooled America over these years we ought to quit; we are wrong on everything." At the time Senator Hart was reflecting a view widely shared by those who held influence and power in America. Now they, as well as Fortas, would have to answer for their judgment.

"A PLAGUE OF LAWYERS"

As THURMAN ARNOLD put it, "The world was standing on its head." Commerce and industry ground to a halt, bankruptcy was rife, and farmers saw land they had tilled all their lives vanish under the sheriff's hammer. In the depths of the Great Depression, thirteen million unemployed walked the streets. Some sold apples and some sought escape. When the Soviet government announced openings for 6,000 skilled workers, 100,000 Americans applied.

Despair hardened into violence. After months without a paycheck, miners in West Virginia looted the company stores. Farmers burned bridges and turned over trucks to stop the flow of goods to market. In a once peaceful little Iowa town an angry mob surged into a courtroom in the midst of foreclosure proceedings, dragged the judge from the bench, threw him into the dirt, tore off his clothes and stopped just short of a lynching.

"No one has starved," President Hoover insisted. But in Harlan County, Kentucky, miners' families lived on dandelions and blackberries while their children's bellies ached with dysentery. In Pittsburgh, steel workers recalled to the mills by a brief flurry of orders collapsed from hunger at their machines. And in New York City, the year Herbert Hoover left the White House, twenty-nine persons actually did starve to death.

This was the world that awaited Abe Fortas when he graduated from Yale Law School in June of 1933. The economy had collapsed. Now the social and political structure also threatened to come crashing down. But in the midst of chaos, a trumpet sounded in Washington. In his inaugural address, Franklin Delano Roosevelt issued a call to arms. "This nation asks for action, and action now," the new President declared. ". . . I assume unhesitatingly the leadership of this great army of our people dedicated to a disciplined attack upon our problems."

Some were troubled by the martial tone of FDR's rhetoric. One particularly faithful listener, Eleanor Roosevelt, found it "a little terrifying" that the crowd in Capital Plaza gave its loudest applause when her husband talked of seeking war powers to deal with the emergency. After hearing Roosevelt out, Edmund Wilson wrote uneasily: "There is a suggestion, itself rather vague, of a possible dictatorship."

But most misgivings were drowned out by the early thunder of the New Deal. Four days after his inauguration, with every bank in the nation shut down, FDR sent his emergency banking act to Capitol Hill. The House approved the measure before its members even had a chance to read it, and a few hours later the Senate shouted the bill into law. That set the pace and pattern for the New Deal's First Hundred Days. Before a weary Congress adjourned in mid-June it had passed fifteen major laws, laying the groundwork for the Agricultural Adjustment Administration, the National Recovery Administration and the other acronymic agencies that became the New Deal's hallmark.

As it sought to staff the machinery of reform, the Administration set off the greatest manhunt Washington had ever seen. Never before had such a multitude of jobs become so suddenly available. Having swiftly stripped the ranks of the public servants and politicians who had served him as governor of New York and as presidential candidate, Roosevelt sought new reservoirs of talent. Of these, the richest were the nation's great law schools and law firms. The President's chief recruiter was his long-time friend and adviser, Professor Felix Frankfurter of Harvard Law. Frankfurter and his friends combed the legal profession for talent, and each recruit became in turn a recruiter, passing the word back to his friends at home.

Though Frankfurter, like Roosevelt himself, was a Harvard man, it was only to be expected that Yale would furnish a large portion of the managers the New Deal needed. Yale Law School had pioneered the concept of "legal realism," which envisaged the law not as an abstraction but rather as a practical tool for dealing with social and economic problems. And it was also predictable that Fortas, one of Yale's outstanding products, would be among the first tapped for duty in Washington.

Fortas's distinction at Yale had been foreshadowed by his earlier academic record. His road to New Haven was paved with high scholastic achievement; there was, in fact, no other way for him to get there. His parents had immigrated from England, bringing with them their Orthodox Jewish faith but little else. The youngest of five children, Fortas was raised on Pontotoc Street in a lower middle-class section of Memphis, a bustling Mississippi River city, which had just fallen under the domination of Boss Ed Crump. His family's social horizons were limited mainly to the confines of Memphis's tiny Jewish community, which numbered about 6,000 out of a total population of 160,000. Their economic circumstances were modest at best. Fortas's father, Woolfe, was at different times a shopkeeper, jeweler, pawnbroker and cabinet maker, drifting from one trade to another, mastering none.

Early on, the boy learned to seize whatever opportunities opened to him. He was given violin lessons, quickly took to the instrument and, in his teens, formed a group called the Blue Melody Boys Band which performed at high school dances. His efforts earned him $8 a night spending money and the nickname of "Fiddling Abe." But most of his energies were focused on school. He captained the high school debating team and, though he was bright enough to coast, kept his nose in his books. "With Abe, it was study, study, study," his brother Meyer recalled. "He had a goal to attain." In three years he swept through South Side High, ranking second in his class at graduation, and was rewarded with a scholarship to Southwestern College, a small liberal arts school in Memphis.

At Southwestern Fortas came to be much admired by students and faculty alike, but some of his teachers worried because, one said, "We noticed a strain of unhappiness about him. He took life very seriously on the whole." Fortas was relatively young, just sixteen, when he started. He was one of only half a dozen Jews in a student body of 500. As a child, Fortas had attended synagog regularly. At Southwestern, though, he displayed little interest in Judaism, or in any other organized religion. Some considered him an agnostic. Nevertheless, he remained conscious of his Jewish background, and so did the Presbyterian campus world, where daily chapel was mandatory. Socially, one professor thought, "he just really didn't fit into things. He was an outsider looking in."

These circumstances may have contributed to the reserve that was one of young Fortas's notable characteristics. But they did not prevent him from making an impressive record. Fortas was president of Southwestern's debating and dramatics clubs and director of its orchestra. His grades could hardly be improved on. His undergraduate achievements pointed to a professional career, and his aptitude for debate and interest in public affairs inclined him to the law. In his senior year at Southwestern he applied to Harvard and Yale. Conscious of his youth, and determined to be precise, he listed his age at "nineteen and ten-twelfths." "As far as scholastic records, there is no one better in the class," one of his professors wrote in endorsement. "But it is in the part that he has played in stimulating others to think that the extraordinary power of the man is seen. As far as one can tell, he will be heard from one day."

Harvard and Yale opened their arms, both offering scholarships. Fortas decided on Yale, partly, he said, because its scholarship paid $50 a month more than Harvard's.

Yale Law School, when Fortas arrived in 1930, was a center of intellectual ferment. Robert M. Hutchins, who had been its dean during the 1920's, had led a revolt against the conventional jurisprudence of the times, which rigidly adhered to previous court decisions and tended to give greater weight to property values than human concerns. Hutchins called for a broader view, greater flexibility and increased responsiveness to social and economic inequities. Among other innovations he tested at New Haven was the study of law in collaboration with other academic disciplines, including sociology and psychology. This and other heresies stirred ripples of disapproval among established academicians and jurists. According to one possibly apocryphal but illustrative story, Justice James C. McReynolds, one of the Supreme Court's arch-conservatives, grumbled to Hutchins: "I understand you are teaching your students that the decisions of the Supreme Court are all nonsense."

"Not at all," Hutchins replied. "We simply give them the decisions and let them judge for themselves."

Hutchins left Yale in 1929 to blaze more new academic trails at the University of Chicago. But under his successor, Charles Clark, the revolt of the realists went on. Clark shifted the emphasis in the law school's curriculum from theory and principle to study of the everyday processes and procedures that directly affected the courts, the litigants and the functioning of society.

Joining Clark in the effort to modernize the law and enhance its relevance was an extraordinary group of faculty members whose talents and personalities enriched and enlivened the academic environment. Perhaps the most engaging of these men was Thurman Arnold, who came to Yale the same year Fortas started there as a student. Raised in Wyoming, educated at Princeton and Harvard Law, Arnold was a cheerful iconoclast whose behavior at times bordered on eccentricity. "When he walked into his class smoking a pipe, wearing a hat and leading his dog, he was not producing an act," his colleague William O. Douglas explained. "He was so lost in thought that the amenities escaped him." Arnold's irreverent wit and sweeping imagination turned his lectures into intellectual entertainments. "He could see life," Fortas wrote later, "bounce it about, reshape and deflate it, reduce it to its essential absurdity, inflate it to its potential greatness, toss it over to astonished colleagues and amazed students and recapture it again and bounce it about."

Professor Douglas was less genial, but no less compelling. A hardy outdoorsman, he had hitchhiked his way across the country to study law at Columbia University before coming to Yale in 1929. Still in his early thirties, he was already winning recognition as a specialist in corporate finance. Douglas, Arnold and another high-spirited teacher, Wesley Sturges, who would later be dean of the law school, became close friends. All three were coming into increasing prominence, and they engaged in a good-humored rivalry over the number of times their names appeared in the press. Arnold formalized the competition by devising an intricate scoring system under which points were awarded for mentions in various newspapers, depending on circulation and influence, with the largest award going to whoever got his picture in the *New York Times.*

Fortas flourished under their tutelage. His fellow students found the young man from Memphis self-possessed, serious and intensely conscientious. Thomas Emerson, a senior at Yale during Fortas's freshman year there, recalled that whether he came to the library to study early or late, Fortas was usually there when he arrived and stayed on after he left. A classmate, Gordon Gray, later a special assistant to President Eisenhower, thought Fortas "had the brightest mind in the class." In his senior year Fortas was named editor-in-chief of the *Yale Law Journal,* an honor usually accorded the number-one student in academic rank. "He was a very meticulous editor," said Gray, who worked under him. "He had no hesitancy about throwing back a case note that was sloppily thought out or not too well written."

The pages of the publication were reflective of the times and of Fortas's interests. The *Journal* analyzed such contemporary problems as the gold clause in private contracts and reorganization of bankrupt corporations. In February of 1933 Fortas devoted an entire issue to the credit problems of wage earners. He himself wrote one of the main articles, whose subject had been suggested by Professor Douglas. Entitled "Wage Assignments in Chicago" and bearing the byline "A. Fortas," it was a study of the practice, then commonly resorted to by employees lacking other collateral, of obtaining credit by granting garnishment rights to their salaries. Under this arrangement, if the employee fell behind in his payments, his employer was obliged to hold up his paychecks until the worker had satisfied his creditors. The summer before his senior year Fortas went to Chicago and examined the operations of this system firsthand, under the pressures of the Depression. He concluded that it was manifestly unfair to employees, resulting in their arbitrary discharge, and generally inconvenient for employers. The only remedy, he argued, was a total ban on wage assignments. With a sophistication striking for his years, he rejected as pointless a proposal to require a wage earner to get his wife's consent to an assignment agreement. That idea, Fortas argued, "may confine within reasonable limits the use of wage assignments for the benefit of mistresses, but beyond that its value depends upon an obsolescent conception of the wife's providence."

Fortas had undertaken an ambitious project for a student, and he carried it off superbly. "A factual, functional, classically Yale piece of investigation and analysis at its statistical best," Eugene Rostow later called it. The wage assignment article and his overall supervision of the *Journal* added to his academic laurels at Yale. As his senior year drew to an end, Fortas was asked to stay on at New Haven as a member of the faculty. This invitation was not only a great honor but also, considering economic conditions, an advantageous way to launch his career. But before Fortas could take advantage of the opportunity he was called to Washington, where the legal realism that had been preached in Yale's classrooms was being put into practice.

No sooner had the school year ended than Thurman Arnold and Wesley Sturges were on their way to the capital to join the legal staff of the Agricultural Adjustment Administration, then barely a month old. When they learned that more help was needed, Sturges sent word to Fortas in New Haven. Though Fortas had accepted a position on the faculty, his teaching assignments would not begin until fall. Fortas decided to join the New Deal, if only for the summer. In July 1933 he arrived, beginning a career that would last for nearly thirteen years, carry him close to the summit of power and transform him from a precocious young man into a seasoned public figure.

His first job provided a baptism in bureaucratic infighting. The AAA, said Thurman Arnold, was "a perfect bedlam." With surpluses piling up and prices plummeting, agriculture was worse off than any other sector of the economy. The embittered farmers were feared to be on the point of open rebellion. The AAA had been set up to alleviate their problems mainly by curtailing production, and also by stabilizing prices through marketing agreements with food processors. The new agency was riven by discordant ideas and clashing personalities. Its general counsel was Jerome Frank, a successful corporation lawyer who had found in the New Deal an outlet for his passionate idealism. He quickly surrounded himself with a crackerjack staff, including, besides the Yale contingent, two exceptionally talented Harvard Law products, Adlai Stevenson and Alger Hiss. It mattered little to Jerome Frank that most of his deputies had no previous experience with farming. This deficiency, he believed, was more than offset by their overall intelligence. "What we need," he told associates, "are brilliant young men with keen legal minds and imagination."

To George Peek, a crusty farm expert who had been put in charge of the AAA, this was stuff and nonsense. Peek's opinion of Frank was such that when his appointment was announced, Peek immediately retained a private attorney, whom he paid out of his own salary, to give him legal advice. As for Frank's staff, Peek hardly knew what to make of them. "A plague of young lawyers settled on Washington," he later complained. "They all claimed to be friends of somebody or other and mostly of Felix Frankfurter and Jerome Frank. They floated airily into offices, took desks, asked for papers and found no end of things to be busy about. I never found out why they came, what they did or why they left."

Frank's young lions irked Peek and his sober staff of administrators on matters large and small. Early in his career, Fortas got into a minor scrape over a long distance phone call to Memphis. He had made the call from his office phone, without going through the switchboard. When the ever-vigilant government operator cut in, Fortas told her the call was "official business." But the operator decided the call did not sound at all official, and she reported the incident. The AAA's old records show that her complaint reached the desk of Peek's administrative assistant, who then sent a memo to Fortas's boss, Jerome Frank, informing him that the call cost $7.70 and asking for an explanation. The records do not show who ultimately paid the bill.

Fortas later became involved in another and more prolonged financial controversy with the AAA's higher-ups, this time over his salary. Fortas originally came to the AAA as a temporary appointee, intending to return to Yale for the fall term. But his work was so impressive and the agency's manpower needs so great that he was urged to stay on. As an inducement he was offered a permanent appointment at $4,000 a year. Then, however, the agency balked at keeping its part of the bargain. Someone had ordered a check of the salary scales at other new government agencies, including the Tennessee Valley Authority, the National Recovery Administration and the Farm Credit Administration. The survey disclosed that lawyers with Fortas's limited experience were getting no more than $2,000 a year.

A battle of interoffice memos ensued. The $4,000 figure was described as "gravely out of line." Fortas was offered $3,000 instead. He sent back a note threatening to return to Yale, where, he claimed, he could expect to earn "in the neighborhood of $3,750 a year." At this point Jerome Frank, who had taken a liking to Fortas, stepped into the fray and won assurances that Fortas would get the $4,000. Fortas duly notified Yale that he would not begin teaching there until February of 1934. But still the appointment and the salary failed to come through. Matters dragged on until October of 1933, when Frank sent a stern memorandum to Chester Davis, one of Peek's top deputies, reminding him of the promises made to Fortas and concluding: "I think it proper of me to ask you to do whatever possible to avoid a breach of moral obligation."

Whatever salary Fortas was paid, the government got its money's worth. Like everyone on Frank's staff, he worked at a feverish pace. Fortas's sister Esta reported to the Memphis *Commercial Appeal,* which kept track of the hometown boy's progress, that her brother was toiling "fourteen hours a day." Most of the time he was too busy to write, and, Esta added, "He hasn't had a chance to touch his violin."

His job consisted mainly of negotiating marketing agreements with food growers and processors, and by all accounts he did it well. "Fortas has been doing excellent work on the fruit and vegetable agreements," Chester Davis wrote to George Peek in August of 1933. The work took him around the country. He teamed up with Thurman Arnold to battle the peach canners in San Francisco, audited a milk price hearing in Detroit and checked up on the orange shippers in Orlando, Florida, which he described in a letter to his office as "God's country." Fortas tarried in the Southern sun only briefly, though. Operations were "proceeding smoothly," he wrote, and "a tender conscience does not permit me any longer to act on the Government's money as wet nurse to such a lusty infant."

In February of 1934 he left the AAA for Yale to teach for a semester. The next summer he plunged back into his bucolic

[37]

routine. He spent his working hours keeping track of price and production data on eggs, poultry, red sour cherries and gum turpentine. In October, in the midst of a complicated furor over the price of milled rice, the head of the agency's "rice section" turned over to Fortas a letter on the problem which, he said, "had best be answered by an expert."

But for all his new-found expertise, it must have been clear to Fortas that the AAA was not the place to build a government career. From its beginnings, the agency had been beset by sharp conflicts over policy. George Peek, its director, strongly objected to its most important program, which was designed to cut production and boost prices by paying farmers a subsidy for acreage they did not plant. Eventually these subsidies would become a mainstay of the farm economy. But in 1933 they were a radically new idea, which to Peek and others smacked of socialism. Before the year ended Peek submitted his resignation, after which he publicly denounced Jerome Frank and Felix Frankfurter as "socialists" and "collectivists." Their tactics, he charged, "were unpleasantly reminiscent of those followed in the setting up of totalitarian governments in Russia, Italy and Germany."

Even after Peek's departure the agency remained a tense and divided place. Though the AAA had some success in boosting farm prices, the liberals on its high command, Jerome Frank among them, contended that almost all its benefits were going to the big farmers. They proposed that a greater share of the government largesse be distributed to the tenant farmers, many of whom were being forced off the land as a result of crop control. They also believed that the AAA should protect consumers from being overcharged by food processors, who were permitted to agree among themselves on prices for their products. The battle culminated early in 1935 when Agriculture Secretary Henry A. Wallace, bowing to pressure from the big farm groups and to orthodox economic theory, summarily dismissed Jerome Frank and a flock of his young associates.

Fortas was not around for the denouement. In the summer of 1934 William Douglas had left Yale to work at the Securities and Exchange Commission under its first chairman, Joseph P. Kennedy. Douglas's assignment was to study procedures for reorganizing companies that had gone through bankruptcy. Needing lawyers to help conduct his investigation, Douglas called on his former student, who was already on hand in Washington. In November 1934, about three months before the Frankophiles were purged at the AAA, Fortas left there under his own power to work at the SEC.

His experience was typical of the job mobility in government during those years. Unemployment was still a staggering problem for the nation. But young men in Washington had little difficulty in shifting from one new agency to another, a circumstance that added to the attractions of the New Deal.

Fortas was by now quite at home in the capital's fervent ambience. In some ways the world he worked and lived in was similar to life at Yale. Youthful bureaucrats encountered their former professors everywhere, and many of them went home from their jobs to households that resembled college dormitories. Fortas himself shared a three-story house on 34th Street in northwest Washington with four other young lawyers. All of them had, as one put it, "inconspicuous but very important jobs." Two were clerks to Supreme Court Justices. Thomas Emerson, who had finished Yale two years before Fortas, was with the National Labor Relations Board, and Leon Keyserling, later to become President Truman's chief economic adviser, was a legislative assistant to Senator Robert Wagner of New York.

"If you went into government in those days, and had anything on the ball at all, you moved ahead very fast," said Emerson. "We were all doing far more important things than if we had been in normal practice for twenty years. It was very heady kind of stuff." It added to the headiness that the young lawyers sat down to dinner once or twice a month with such

[39]

distinguished guests as Justices Stone and Cardozo, Senator Wagner, and Ben Cohen, one of the movers and shakers at the White House.

This was fast company, but Fortas moved in it at his own self-assured pace. He carried himself, as he had since he was a teen-age student at Southwestern, with a restraint and gravity that belied his years. He seemed, one close friend thought, "as if he were born an old man." He was certainly bright, but, Leon Keyserling said, "he was not scintillating in the showy sense of the word." What marked his intelligence in a group where intellectual flamboyance was not uncommon were his insight and sense of perspective. He could look beyond his own job and see the underlying political and economic problems. The New Deal moved swiftly, but Tom Emerson noticed that Fortas was "one of those people who kept ahead of it and knew what was happening next."

If Fortas was reserved, he was neither dull nor shy. An excellent dancer, "he was not the sort of fellow who sat in the corner" at the many mixed parties he and his housemates gave. Young women found his puckish sense of humor and Southern gallantries appealing. "He may not be the most interesting man here," one girl remarked to Keyserling, "but he certainly has the best manners."

At least one young woman found Fortas both gracious and interesting. She was Carolyn Agger, a petite, attractive blonde whom Fortas had met when both were working at the AAA. The daughter of a Rutgers University professor, she had graduted from Barnard College and taken a Master's Degree at the University of Wisconsin in economics. She was the same age as Fortas and just as quick and confident. Men who worked alongside her found her "very able and decisive," a woman "who knew what she was doing and had a mind of her own." She was not Jewish, but religion was no problem to Fortas. Their courtship continued after Fortas left the AAA for the SEC, and in July of 1935 they were married.

From the start it was clear that both would continue to pursue their careers. At a point when most young couples ordinarily begin to plan for their children, the Fortases instead planned to further Carol's education. Fortas proposed that she add to her already impressive academic credentials by entering law school. Yale was the natural choice, particularly since Fortas himself continued on its faculty, commuting to and from Washington. Carol enrolled there in 1935 and graduated three years later, second in a class of 125. In her freshman year she took a course in corporate law taught by her own husband. The situation would have flustered most couples, but the Fortases took it in stride. The normally outgoing and aggressive Carol "never said a word" in class and her fellow students soon forgot that she was the professor's wife.

For a young man, Fortas had considerable stature on the Yale faculty. His accomplishments as editor of the *Law Journal* were still well remembered. His involvement in the New Deal added a touch of glamor, so that in one student's romanticized view he came to the classroom "trailing clouds of glory." Confronted with the hero in the flesh and at the lectern, his students' opinions tended to diverge, depending on their own political point of view. "Liberals admired his New Dealish approach," one recalled. "The conservatives didn't." Students who sought a close personal relationship with a teacher were in for disappointment. Fortas "had a distinctive air—not exactly aloof, but of a certain dignity nonetheless. He was not hearty and there was no false bonhomie in his manner. He was not in the least sentimental." But he was "a precise and exacting artist," always in control of the class. Students who could meet him on his own terms profited from his lucid analysis of legal theory, sharpened by his experience on the firing line in Washington.

Though he was the youngest member of the faculty, Fortas was "no shrinking violet" among his colleagues, as one later recalled. At one of his first faculty meetings he "crossed swords" with the senior professor on the staff on some point of the curriculum and "did not come out second best."

He joined in the lighter side of faculty life, too, playing the outfield alongside Thurman Arnold in the annual softball contest with the *Law Journal* staff. A teammate remembered Arnold chasing after a long fly, grabbing at it "with a large, generous gesture," missing it completely, and then discovering that Fortas had dashed up behind him and made the catch. Fortas was also invited to share in the elaborate horseplay of the "Hunt Club," a semi-secret society that conducted ritualistic snipe hunts in New Haven's East Rock Park. Bill Douglas held the title of club mattress bearer and Arnold was its flashlight bearer. Fortas was "an apprentice beater." Without this institution, Fortas later said, "the New Deal never would have succeeded."

Fortas enjoyed the academic environment, and his salary as assistant professor was a welcome supplement to the modest earnings he received from the government. Moreover, it was undoubtedly comforting to know that should he slip in the uncertain footing of the bureaucracy, he had a fall-back position at Yale. But New Haven remained only an outpost. As the time passed and his experience broadened, he was increasingly drawn to the center of power in Washington.

THE CURMUDGEON'S ASSISTANT

In the functioning of government, Tom Corcoran, one of Franklin Roosevelt's favorite troubleshooters, observed, "what really makes the difference is what happens down the line before—and after—the big decisions are taken." For four years at the Securities and Exchange Commission Fortas was one of the men down the line who made things happen. His name never made headlines, and frustration was his frequent companion. But the experience and reputation he gained as a member of the New Deal cadre would serve him in good stead later on.

Those were turbulent years. As FDR sought one strategy and then another to combat the continuing economic crisis, he also frequently switched strategists. Trusted counselors suddenly fell from favor, and occasionally, just as suddenly, returned to influence. Though Fortas was not directly involved in these high-level machinations, sometimes the struggle brushed uncomfortably close. Fortas's position at the SEC was linked to William Douglas, who had brought him to the commission and who was in the thick of the great controversies over economic policy. In 1937 when James Landis quit as SEC chairman to become dean of Harvard Law School, Douglas appeared to be his logical replacement. But Douglas's record as a tough regulator of the securities industry had made him conservative enemies who opposed his promotion. Discouraged, Douglas was preparing to pack up his law books and return to Yale when he received a phone call from *his* friend, Joseph Kennedy. Kennedy, who had originally hired Douglas to work for the SEC, still had the President's ear. "Sit tight," Kennedy now counseled Douglas. Sure enough, a few hours later FDR was on the phone to Douglas, urging him to accept the chairmanship of the commission.

Fortas meanwhile was completing work on the bankruptcy reorganization study, which had been his first assignment at the SEC. The three-year investigation produced a detailed report demonstrating that the so-called protective committees of company officials and creditors who took over bankrupt companies were, in fact, often protecting no one's interest but their own. The majority of investors were left out in the cold. The report called for specific action to correct these abuses, and Congress, in the Bankruptcy Act of 1938, adopted its most important recommendations. The new law required, among other reforms, the appointment in substantial bankruptcy cases of an impartial trustee who would oversee reorganization and make certain that the interests of all investors were considered.

Fortas then moved to the SEC's public utilities division as assistant director; his job was to enforce yet another New Deal reform. This measure was designed to break up the vast nationwide holding companies that dominated the electric power industry and to foster instead the development of regional electric utility companies. The power industry was defiant. Wendell Willkie, then president of Commonwealth and Southern, one of the great holding companies, led the fight against the Administration program. And within the SEC itself opinion differed as to how vigorously the government should proceed against private industry. Fortas found himself stalemated. Prospects for improvement in his situation were dimmed when his sponsor, William Douglas, resigned as SEC chairman to accept appointment to the Supreme Court.

Soon thereafter, Fortas himself left the SEC. He had found another opportunity and another sponsor in Harold Ickes, the Secretary of the Interior, who was also, like Fortas, a good friend of Bill Douglas. Ickes described himself as a "curmudgeon," and this was one of the few statements he made in Washington that no one disputed. A nominal Republican and a veteran of countless political crusades, he had signed on with FDR at the beginning of his first term and had become an Administration workhorse—and lightning rod. Ickes loved nothing better than personal combat and he never missed an opportunity to pick a fight—with the press, with the New Deal's opposition or with his own colleagues in government. Often ridiculed and denounced, he usually gave better than he got. He called the wealthy Wendell Willkie, the 1940 Republican presidential candidate, "a simple barefoot Wall Street lawyer." And when the youthful Thomas E. Dewey announced for the presidency, Ickes jeered that Dewey "has thrown his diaper into the ring."

Fortas joined up with Ickes in the spring of 1939 as general counsel to the Public Works Administration, one of the Depression-born agencies that had been entrusted to Ickes's stewardship. Not quite twenty-nine, Fortas already had five years of experience as a government lawyer behind him. He had cut his teaching ties with Yale and was ready for new challenges.

Ickes gave them to him. Before Fortas could get settled in to his new post at PWA, Ickes hurled him into another bureaucratic breach. The Bituminous Coal Commission, which had been set up to bring some economic order out of the chaotic soft coal industry, had been declared unconstitutional by the Supreme Court. Out of its wreckage was created the Bituminous Coal Division, which was given the task of setting minimum prices in the coal fields and turned over to the Department of the Interior. Ickes appointed Fortas as counsel to the division and ordered him to take charge.

Fortas's first problem was the staff. Morale was low and many of the holdovers from the defunct commission were mediocrities. Fortas cleaned house, despite the objections of Mine Workers Union president John L. Lewis, who had sponsored many of the people Fortas fired. Then Fortas brought in his own men and set about the business of organizing and scheduling hearings. The morale problem was forgotten; Fortas drove himself and his staff so hard there was no time to complain. Norman Diamond, a former law student of Fortas's at Yale who had been brought to the coal agency, remembers another staffer asking him, as they left work late on Christmas Eve: "Do you suppose he'll give us half a day off tomorrow?"

Dealing with industry officials and lawyers many years his senior, in a field essentially alien to him, Fortas nevertheless maintained "great dignity and presence." Despite his youth, Diamond remembered, "no one called him Abe. It was always Mr. Fortas." When the hearings were completed after nearly two years, Fortas and his staff felt "as if we had accomplished a miracle."

Ickes was impressed, too. The Interior Secretary was noted not only for his honesty and vigor but also for his vast ambition. Not content with his department's already extensive responsibilities for the nation's natural resources and overseas territories, Ickes sought to extend his authority into new domains. In 1941 he made Fortas director of the Interior Department's new division of power, which was specially created to help Ickes expand his influence over public power. Ickes's chief rival was David Lilienthal, head of the Tennessee Valley Authority. Lilienthal, who believed public power should be administered by regional authorities, like TVA, rather than by any one central agency, thought Ickes's ambitions ridiculous and jeered at Fortas and his associates at Interior as "Ickophants."

Fortas did well enough there so that in 1942 Ickes moved him up again, this time to the post of undersecretary of the interior. With the nation at war, Fortas as Ickes's chief deputy had a broad range of responsibilities. As supervisor of the division of territories he staved off a threatened famine in Puerto Rico, laid plans for the postwar economy of the Philippines, and carried on delicate negotiations with the Army leading to an end to military rule in Hawaii. When John L. Lewis threatened to call a nationwide coal strike, Fortas, drawing on his background at the Bituminous Coal Division, was Ickes's chief adviser in negotiations with the mine operators and the union.

The coal crisis led to an angry clash with Wayne Morse, who was later to become a U.S. senator from Oregon and at the time was a member of the War Labor Board. Morse thought that the Board, not the Interior Department, should have authority over the Mine Workers Union, and he argued his case out before FDR at the White House, to the indignation of Fortas and Ickes. Later Morse wrote Fortas a letter, charging that by their handling of the coal strike Ickes and Fortas had "written a disgraceful page of American industrial history."

Fortas replied in kind. "Your letter," he wrote Morse, "is as intemperate as has been your entire conduct in the handling of the coal case. After reading it, no one can doubt that you are completely unsuited for any position which requires the exercise of judgment and balance . . . If and when Secretary Ickes and I feel we need guidance as to our responsibilities to the President or to the Government, we certainly will not consult a person who is so obviously irresponsible as yourself."

Though he was rarely so outraged as he was at Morse, the undersecretary told off other government officials, too. Cold sarcasm was his usual style. To a functionary of the War Production Board who disagreed with Interior Department policy on metal production for military use, Fortas wrote that "this unfounded criticism . . . demonstrates an attitude toward the established agencies of Government which makes further discussion most difficult. . . . If there be no lack of objectivity in board officials, then at least there should be enough stamina in persons of such virtue to withstand any misguided proposals we may make."

With his friends in government, Fortas occasionally indulged in bureaucratic humor. Responding to a memo from James Rowe, another early New Dealer then working at the Department of Justice, Fortas wrote: "It took your memorandum of December 7 four days to get over here. I am sure that that is entirely due to delay within your own department. . . . If your agents spent less time checking up on me and giving me information about the activities of the Department of Justice and more time on internal communications, the paper-saving campaign which this department has instituted would be vastly benefited."

On more formal communications Fortas took great pains, and he also took considerable pride in the results. When Ickes's personal assistant, a man named Briggs, made some changes in a letter Fortas had drafted for Ickes, the undersecretary sent his boss a snippy memo. Fortas complained that the changes "do not add to the literary quality of my draft and they certainly do not improve the substance."

Ickes replied that Briggs "has the unpleasant job of trying to see to it that letters presented for my signature are couched as nearly as possible in my language." Some of the words Fortas had used, Ickes said, were on his personal "black list." Briggs didn't relish his editing chores, Ickes said, and added: "If you would feel any happier to have me do the operating I am willing to take it on and I know that Mr. Briggs would be delighted."

The patience displayed by the usually irascible Ickes in handling this incident reflected the warm regard he felt for Fortas. The interior secretary, who was more than old enough to be Fortas's father, had come to rely on his young deputy to handle a multitude of details efficiently and faithfully, thus leaving Ickes freer to involve himself in the broader issues that stirred his ambitions. Occasionally, when Ickes was out of town, Fortas would sit in for him at a cabinet meeting. At one such session, President Roosevelt decided to turn his celebrated charm on the young undersecretary but could not recall his name. Quietly he passed a note of inquiry around the cabinet table.

"Fortas," whispered Attorney General Francis Biddle helpfully.

But that was not good enough for FDR. He dashed off another note to Biddle: "Not his last name, his *first* name?"

Biddle told him. And when it was Fortas's turn to report, FDR asked warmly: "Well, Abe, what's been going on at Interior?"

Fortas's name cropped up again at the White House in the spring of 1943 in connection with the sensitive issue of his draft status. Fortas had been exempted from military service because his job at Interior was considered "essential." But then a new selective service regulation made all childless men eligible for induction, regardless of their job status. Fortas, who was not yet thirty-three and had no children, felt uncomfortable enough to submit his resignation to Ickes and announce his readiness to be drafted. Ickes fought against losing his deputy. He forwarded Fortas's resignation to Roosevelt along with a note of his own in which he said that Fortas had resigned "only because he did not want me or the Administration to suffer as a result of possible attacks upon him for remaining in a civilian post."

Taking his cue from Ickes, FDR refused to accept the resignation and told Fortas he could best serve his country "by continuing to do your job as undersecretary of interior." Not everyone saw it that way, and rumbles of protest were heard from Congress. In September of 1943, five months after his original resignation, Fortas quit again. "I feel that I should not be denied the privilege of joining the fighting forces of my country," he said. "If I stayed, my usefulness would soon be ended by the attacks I know would come. Besides, I'd like to see a little of this fighting." In a farewell salute, Ickes wrote Fortas: "You have been indispensable. You are 'irreplaceable.'"

In October Fortas was inducted into the Navy—almost. Instead of being called to active duty it was announced that Fortas would hold his position at Interior while he led a mission of geologists to inspect oil resources in the Middle East. By this time the press was aroused. Newsmen tried to find out about the mission, but the more questions they asked, the more mysterious it became. No one seemed to know exactly when it would begin or how long it would take. Finally, in mid-November, Fortas washed his hands of this mysterious assignment, left the Interior Department and reported to the Navy training center at Camp Sampson, New York.

One month after he had answered the call to the colors the Navy announced that Apprentice Seaman Fortas was suffering from an eye ailment which it described as arrested ocular tuberculosis. He had spent all but one day of his Navy service in sick bay and according to Navy doctors never should have been inducted in the first place. Thereupon the Navy discharged him and soon Fortas was back at his desk at the Interior Department, his brief military career behind him.

He returned just in time to take on probably the most complicated and sensitive problem he had yet faced in the government. This was the effort to resettle the Japanese-Americans who had been expelled from the West Coast early in the war. The Japanese who lived in the Pacific states had long been discriminated against, much as Negroes were in the South. Following the attack on Pearl Harbor, the press, public officials and local military commanders raised a great outcry against Japanese residents, warning that many were probably spies and saboteurs. It made no difference to these patriots that most of the Japanese were United States citizens. "The Japanese race is an enemy race," declared Lieutenant General John L. DeWitt, the highest ranking Army officer in the area. Even in the second and third generation born on American soil, he asserted, "the racial strains are undiluted."

At the time, of course, the nation was locked in a life-and-death struggle against forces whose racist creed embodied much the same philosophy expounded by General DeWitt. But it was not a moment when such ironies were noticed. Earl Warren, then attorney general of California and normally a rational man, found it "quite significant" that as of February 1942 no "fifth column" activity had been reported in his state.

Warren was not to be fooled by this. "It looks very much to me," he said, "as though it is a studied effort not to have any until the zero hour arrives."

In response to public pressure and the recommendations of the War and Justice Departments, the President authorized the evacuation of the West Coast Japanese, and the Army eagerly hastened to the task. More than 110,000 Japanese, citizens and aliens alike, were driven from their homes and penned up in eight detention camps scattered around the country. A new agency, the War Relocation Authority, was created to supervise the camps, stand guard over disloyal Japanese and arrange for the relocation of the rest—anywhere but on the West Coast whence they came.

If there was a swift and equitable way to carry out this mandate, which is to be doubted, the WRA's sensitive but irresolute director, Dillon Myer, could not find it. He and his agency came under a drumfire of criticism from the House Un-American Activities Committee, the Hearst press, and West Coast veterans' groups and labor unions. The WRA was charged with coddling its wards and with sending subversive Japanese to live in American cities. At the same time the Imperial Japanese Government made propaganda capital out of the alleged mistreatment of the evacuees and balked at repatriating American civilians interned in Japan. The Administration, waging a war for the Four Freedoms, was embarrassed both at home and abroad.

The President decided that the solution required a firmer and more experienced hand. At a loss to know what else to do, FDR turned the WRA over to Harold Ickes with orders to find the best way out of a bad situation. Ickes immediately put Fortas in charge.

Neither Ickes nor Fortas was enthusiastic about the new stepchild. They felt, as Fortas said later, that the original evacuation order was a "terrific mistake. We knew that the most that we could do was to ameliorate the evils which resulted from it." Obstacles loomed on all sides. Dillon Myer's laxity as an administrator tried Fortas's patience. The press kept up its attacks. Demands were heard that the evacuees be detained until war's end, when they should all be shipped back to Japan. A riot had erupted at one detention center and Fortas knew that any further incidents would endanger the whole resettlement program. As it was, efforts to get loyal evacuees out of the detention camps met with angry objections, and not all from right-wing groups. New York Mayor Fiorello LaGuardia, an ardent civil libertarian, complained to Ickes that the arrival of Japanese in his city was "creating a very dangerous situation." New York, the mayor said, was short of police to guard against sabotage. "If Washington, Oregon and California do not want them (the Japanese), what right has the Federal government in placing them in New York City?"

Fortas managed to calm the mayor. But he knew that LaGuardia's point was difficult to refute. Resettlement of the Japanese in any significant number seemed impossible unless they were allowed to return to their homes. Hostility on the West Coast was still intense. Earl Warren, now governor of California, continued to warn against the Yellow Peril. Many of the Japanese, he claimed, were army reservists and others had been trained in sabotage. "Nothing more destructive to our defenses could happen than to release potential fifth columnists," he said. Besides, Warren added, the Japanese might decide to land saboteurs by submarine. If the evacuees were permitted to return, how could one tell the difference between them and the invaders? To Americans who cheerfully confessed their inability to distinguish one Oriental from another, the argument made a great deal of sense.

In the face of such rationalizations, Fortas realized that the only hope for a solution was in reaching an agreement with the Army, which had carried out the evacuation in the first place. By this time it was mid-1944 and the Navy, the Marines and General MacArthur were driving the Japanese forces back toward their home islands and defeat. The War Department found it hard to argue convincingly that the West Coast was still in military danger. Nevertheless, the Army, naturally reluctant to revoke what it had once so vigorously advocated, raised another objection: the returning Japanese might be harassed by West Coast residents. If such incidents occurred, the War Department feared the Japanese might be provoked to retaliate against American prisoners of war and interned civilians. Fortas argued back that the danger could be averted if the Army would publicly vouch for the loyalty of the Japanese and explain that military necessity no longer required their exclusion.

The discussion seesawed back and forth for months. Fortas's best arguments were the continuing improvement in the war in the Pacific and the President's desire to end the public clamor over the situation. But he also found other ways to pressure the military. The Supreme Court was considering a case testing the constitutionality of the exclusion order. Fortas himself believed the Court would uphold the government, as indeed it eventually did. But he realized the Army was worried about the outcome of the case, and he played upon this anxiety to wring concessions from the military. The War Department negotiators also noticed that quite often in the midst of their bargaining with Fortas, the undersecretary took phone calls from important congressmen. From Fortas's end of the conversation it was plain to the military men, as Fortas clearly intended it should be, that he was on excellent terms with the powers on Capitol Hill.

"Abe operated as a man of principle, but also with a certain deviousness," recalled Adrian Fisher, who argued the War Department's side in these negotiations. "He was a very strong force for good. But he also cut a few close corners, and he laid on the political stuff a bit thick."

Ultimately Fortas persuaded the Army to permit the Japanese to return to the West Coast once the Army had determined they were loyal to the United States. The constitutionality of the loyalty check was dubious, but it seemed the most practical way out of an impasse. In December 1944, three years after Pearl Harbor, the exclusion order was revoked, and a shameful chapter in American history came to an end.

In a controversy that aroused intense public feeling Fortas

had fought on the unpopular side and won a significant victory. Once again he had demonstrated his astuteness and resourcefulness, but some of his associates wondered about the absence of passion that characterized his efforts. "He wasn't one of the enthusiasts," said Arthur Goldschmidt, a friend and colleague at Interior. "Or he didn't let himself be an enthusiast. He was a technician really. He took the political issue as given and worked around it, or with it. There are an awful lot of people like that, but most of them seemed more committed than Fortas did." Fortas was plainly more concerned with tactics and results than with displays of idealism. His detachment was largely a matter of style, but the style became such an integral part of him that eventually it gave cause for doubts about the substance of the man.

Four months after Fortas helped make it possible for the Japanese to return to the West Coast, Franklin Roosevelt died and Harry Truman became President. A month later Germany surrendered, and before the summer of 1945 was over Japan, too, capitulated unconditionally. An era had ended, and Fortas began to consider the career possibilities outside of government.

He was one of many early New Dealers who began cleaning out their desks. With Roosevelt gone, the sense of drama and high purpose that had drawn them to Washington was fading into a memory. The New Deal's reforming energies had been shunted aside by the demands of the war, which itself had fostered a semblance of unity and its own brand of idealism. But when peace came the national commitment splintered in a series of squabbles over higher prices, higher wages and shortages of cars, clothing and other items which many assumed to be the fruits of victory. Government no longer offered much in the way of inspiration, or of financial reward either. In the midst of the Depression the civil service salary scale had been enticing. But now, while Federal wages were rigidly limited by Congress, earnings in the outside world were soaring.

Having decided to leave, Fortas was at a crossroad. One

path led back to New Haven where Yale offered him a full professorship, scholarly prestige and relative security. The other would take him into the practice of law in Washington with the potential of much greater remuneration, but also much greater risk. Fortas had his doubts. One day in 1945 Norman Diamond, his old friend from Yale and the Coal Division, dropped by to discuss the future. Both men talked of practicing law. "But if I opened an office," Fortas asked Diamond, "who would my clients be?"

Diamond could not take this seriously. "If you have trouble getting clients," he joked, "I'll starve to death."

But Fortas was genuinely concerned. "He ran scared," Arthur Goldschmidt said. "I never knew anyone who was more worried whether he would make a go of it or not." Fortas was then thirty-five, and in all his adult life he had never worked for anyone except Yale University and the Federal government. Moreover, the future of the postwar economy was uncertain. There was much talk of another depression, which would doom any new enterprise.

The man who persuaded Fortas to put aside his anxieties was his former professor, Thurman Arnold, who since leaving Yale had become a person of stature in Washington. As chief of the Justice Department's antitrust division in the late 1930's, Arnold had spearheaded the New Deal's attack against monopolies. The press had made his name synonymous with "trust buster." In 1943 FDR had elevated Arnold to the U.S. Court of Appeals in Washington, after the Supreme Court the nation's most important judicial post. But the energetic Arnold found judging dull work. He quit the bench in 1945 and set up in private practice. When he heard Fortas was on the brink of leaving the government he urged him to become his partner. Arnold's experience and prestige made this an ideal opportunity for Fortas. He accepted, a decision which Arnold with characteristic grace later called "by all odds the luckiest thing that ever happened to me."

THE WITCH HUNT

IN JANUARY 1946 the firm of Arnold & Fortas opened its doors in modest offices in the Bowen Building on Fifteenth Street, a few blocks from the White House. Its purpose, Fortas wrote later, "was to provide a means for its two partners to make a living. Neither partner quite knew how this was to be done. But both were dedicated to the great cause of economic survival."

A year later the venture gained a third "name partner," Paul Porter, who clearly shared the same sense of dedication. Like Arnold and Fortas, Porter had started in Washington with the AAA. Later he directed publicity for the Democratic National Committee, headed the Federal Communications Commission, presided over the death of the Office of Price Administration and capped his public career by overseeing the U.S. aid program to Greece, with the rank of ambassador. A tall, broad-shouldered Kentuckian, Porter was a storyteller, a backslapper and a superb front man. Not long after Porter joined the firm, Arnold encountered "a cynical friend" who remarked: "Your firm used to be known as Arnold, Fortas & Integrity. Now that you have fired integrity and taken on Paul Porter, your future is very bright indeed."

But before that prophecy was fulfilled, the partners were

caught up in a struggle that tested their integrity and, for a while, seemed to threaten their prosperity. The issue was the conflict between security and liberty which divided a nation haunted by the fear of communism.

Americans had worried about communism for decades, to a greater or lesser extent, depending on foreign upheavals and domestic tensions. In the years right after World War II the threat of Soviet aggression abroad and espionage at home turned the long-festering anxiety into a national phobia. Public concern was fed by conservative newspapers and politicians eager to tarnish the reputation of the New Deal and to discredit the Truman Administration. Truman's own reaction was ambivalent. He publicly scoffed at early allegations of Communist penetration of the government. "I have never believed," he later insisted, "that this Government could be subverted or overturned from within by Communists." Nevertheless, having studied confidential intelligence reports on the activities of Soviet spy rings, the President felt that both the national interest and his own political interest required that he do something about subversion. It was Truman's early haphazard efforts to root out "security risks" from the ranks of government that drew Fortas and his law firm into the courts.

Their initial involvement was more by accident than by design. Morton Friedman, their first loyalty case client, happened to be a friend of Milton Freeman, one of the firm's associates. Friedman had been fired by the War Manpower Commission as a suspected security risk. The normal civil service procedures designed to prevent arbitrary dismissals were denied him; he had no chance to hear the charges against him or answer them. Moreover, he would carry the stigma of disloyalty with him wherever else he sought employment, a punishment that to Fortas and his colleagues seemed manifestly unfair. Since Friedman's dismissal had been upheld by a lower Federal court, his only chance for vindication was an appeal to the Supreme Court. In April 1947, in a brief asking the High Court to review the action taken against Friedman, Fortas eloquently argued that more was at stake than the career of one government employee.

"Assaults upon freedom have a habit of growing beyond a stated objective. They quickly attack not merely a manifestation, but freedom itself. So this crusade, once under way, will not stop with its victims in the Federal service. It will spread and is now spreading over this country, blighting our democracy and bringing fear and distrust to American homes throughout the nation."

The alarm fell on deaf ears. Ordinarily, for the Supreme Court to take a case for judgment on its merits, at least four Justices must agree that the issues raised are significant enough to warrant the Court's time and attention. Only Justices Hugo Black and William O. Douglas, the Court's most stubborn defenders of civil liberties, voted to hear Friedman's appeal. The majority, motivated, Thurman Arnold suspected, "by the principle that one of the functions of the Court is to keep out of trouble," rejected the matter out of hand.

It may already have been too late to stem the tide. As the national obsession with communism deepened, President Truman formalized and expanded government loyalty procedures. The background and beliefs of all two million Federal employes were put under the scrutiny of the Federal Bureau of Investigation. As Fortas had predicted, fear and distrust came to dominate the thoughts of the public and the actions of its leaders, and the country fell under the grip of a witch hunt that prompted comparison with Cotton Mather's purge of the devil's agents in Salem.

Panic spread among the ranks of government workers who had formed left-wing associations, however innocent, during the heyday of the New Deal and the wartime alliance with the Soviet Union. Fearing dismissal and disgrace, many turned to Arnold, Fortas & Porter for help. They were frightened and bewildered. "They had worked for the government for ten or fifteen years," one member of the firm recalled. "And then suddenly they'd get a loyalty questionnaire asking about something that had happened fifteen years earlier."

The partners early on decided take all the loyalty cases they could handle, free of charge to their clients. At the start, many of the loyalty clients were, like Morton Friedman, friends of members of the firm or at least friends of friends. But the firm's willingness to help them reflected more than personal sympathies. It was also, as Fortas later observed, a product of "the background and ideological identification of the members of the firm. We were 'liberals.' We were 'New Dealers.' " What was now under suspicion and attack, the partners realized, was the intellectual climate that had shaped the attitudes of many New Dealers, Arnold, Fortas and Porter themselves included. Confronted with the economic and social disarray revealed by the Great Depression, Fortas wrote, "many of the young and not-so-young people of conscience" had searched for "ultimate and absolute answers." Some were intrigued, at least briefly, by the Utopian promises of communism. "Happily," Fortas noted, "there were vastly more flirtations than affairs, more engagements than marriages." But in the postwar era any dalliance was considered damning, the distinctions between revolution and reform were blurred, and suspicion cast a wide net.

Some of the loyalty cases that came to the firm could be handled relatively quickly, but others presented more complicated and time-consuming problems. Though Arnold, Fortas & Porter was not alone among Washington law firms in aiding suspected security risks, it was carrying the largest share of the burden. Soon the firm was so swamped with loyalty work that the partners began to wonder whether they could afford to keep taking such cases. "We have to," Fortas remarked at one policy discussion. "If we don't do it, nobody else will."

Weary of the case-by-case battle, the hard-pressed partners sought a broad ruling from the courts that would eliminate the worst features of the Administration's new loyalty program. The dismissal of Dorothy Bailey, a job-training expert for the Labor Department, seemed to present just such an opportunity. Miss Bailey had been tried by one of the special

boards that had been established to consider charges of disloyalty. The procedure had many of the trappings of due process,
with the crucial exception that the boards were free to convict
on the basis of secret information furnished by unidentified
informers. At Miss Bailey's hearing she presented a flock of
affidavits attesting to her loyalty. The evidence against her,
the details of which were never divulged, came from sources
whose identities were known only to the FBI. Her lawyers
suspected that the charges of Communist sympathies stemmed
from malicious gossip by her enemies in a governmental employees' labor union.

Contending that Miss Bailey's right to a fair trial had clearly
been violated, Arnold, Fortas & Porter appealed to the Federal District Court. "It seemed incredible," Thurman Arnold
wrote later, "that a citizen of the United States could have her
entire career ruined and her livelihood taken away on a record such as this." But the District Court upheld the loyalty
board action, and so did the U.S. Circuit Court of Appeals.
Finally, the Supreme Court agreed to hear the case. But one
Justice disqualified himself from participating, and when the
decision was handed down in 1951, the remaining eight Justices divided four to four. The effect of the split decision was
to uphold the lower court rulings and Miss Bailey's dismissal.

Bitterly disappointed but still determined to overturn the
loyalty board procedure, the partners found another test case.
Their new client was Dr. John P. Peters of Yale Medical
School, an expert on nutrition, who was occasionally called in
as a consultant by the surgeon general's office. Since Peters had
no civil service status, Thurman Arnold pointed out, if the
government suspected his loyalty, all it needed to do was to
stop consulting him. "But those were the days of the numbers
game in loyalty cases," Arnold wrote. "Each department head
prided himself on the number of scalps he could tie to his belt
as a result of loyalty convictions." Dr. Peters was haled before
a loyalty board, tried and acquitted. Whereupon a second
board was convened, reviewed the first board's decisions and

convicted Peters, relying, as in Dorothy Bailey's case, on evidence provided by unknown witnesses.

Once again Arnold, Fortas & Porter fought their way up through the tedious channels of judicial appeal, to the District Court, which sustained the loyalty board, to the Circuit Court, which sustained the District Court, and finally, to the United States Supreme Court. But the ultimate decision by the High Court sidestepped the basic issue of a defendant's right to confront his accusers. The Justices overturned Peters's conviction on the technical grounds that the government had no business setting up a second loyalty board to hear his case after one loyalty board had already cleared him. This unsatisfying victory left Peters's reputation in doubt and left the government free to continue using secret testimony against its employees.

While the loyalty board struggle dragged through the courts, Arnold, Fortas & Porter was fighting on other fronts. "Everyone here who can investigate is investigating," Thurman Arnold wrote to a friend in June 1951. "Everyone who can't investigate is being investigated. Our firm is trying to do its part in the conflict." Its most dramatic part was the defense of Owen Lattimore against the sustained attack of the Senate's two most reckless demagogues and the Department of Justice. A little-known Johns Hopkins professor and government consultant on Far Eastern affairs, Lattimore had suddenly become security risk number one by the reckoning of Senator Joseph McCarthy. In March of 1950, soon after McCarthy had vaulted from obscurity by charging that the State Department was infested with card-carrying Communists, he branded Lattimore as the leading Russian espionage agent in the United States. And he offered to rest his whole case against the State Department "on the guilt of this one man."

Lattimore was in Afghanistan at the time on assignment for the United Nations. Back in Washington, his wife, Eleanor, remembered meeting Abe Fortas at a dinner party, where she had been impressed by his ideas on dealing with Red-baiting attacks, and she rushed to his office. Fortas and his partners agreed to help. Eleanor Lattimore recalled that they asked her only one question about her husband: "Will he fight?"

Fortas himself fought with one eye on the news media. He put together a mimeographed fact sheet for the press on Owen Lattimore, replete with anti-Communist quotations from his writings. He also saw to it that Drew Pearson learned that Lattimore had helped several enemies of the Communist government of Outer Mongolia resettle in the U.S. The "inside story," as Pearson told it to his nationwide radio audience that next Sunday night, was that Lattimore "was giving aid and comfort to these Mongolians until the day when they may go back to the Far East and oust the Communists." Next, Fortas obligingly arranged a press conference for Lattimore's suddenly famous Mongolian friends. Then he dashed off a letter to Lattimore, who was on his way home, filling him in on the unfolding battle.

> This may seem somewhat insane to you, but I assure you that we're operating in a situation characterized by insanity, and a certain amount of drama is not only desirable, but also completely unavoidable. You will realize that every newspaper in this country has assigned its top men to the story and that they will leave no angle unexplored. . . .
>
> It may be necessary that you get down in the gutter in which we are now operating as a result of Senator McCarthy's personal attack on you. But if we can place the Senator in the gutter where he belongs before your return, it may be that the best strategy, both from your personal viewpoint and in terms of the national interest, will be for you to address yourself in your statements before the Senate committee to the underlying issues which have made possible this attack upon you.

The language of the letter may have been imprecise, but there was no mistaking its aggressive tone. In the face of Fortas's well-orchestrated counterattack, McCarthy backed down a bit. Lattimore became only "one of the top Communist agents" in the country. Moreover, the senator declared himself no longer certain that Lattimore had actually engaged in espionage.

When hearings got under way before a special Senate committee, the shy, bookish Lattimore, under coaching by Fortas and Porter, proved an effective witness in his own behalf. Just as important, Committee Chairman Millard Tydings conducted the hearings with a firm and even hand (for which McCarthy never forgave him—that November Tydings was defeated in a reelection bid largely because of smear tactics inspired by McCarthy). The case against Lattimore collapsed and the Tydings Committee cleared him.

Vastly relieved, Lattimore went home to Ruxton, Maryland, to write *Ordeal by Slander,* in which he retold his victory over McCarthy and expressed his thanks to his attorneys, who had worked without a fee. His story, Lattimore wrote, would have been "different and more tragic if it had not been for the law firm of Arnold, Fortas & Porter, and particularly for Abe Fortas who after weeks of exhausting work on the 'case' still had wisdom and patience left to give me counsel on the book."

As it turned out, however, Lattimore's ordeal was only beginning. With Red China emerging as a major threat, Lattimore's connection with past U.S. Asian policy made him too good a target to overlook. A year and a half after Lattimore had been cleared by the Tydings Committee, Senator Pat McCarran, head of the Senate Internal Security Investigating Committee, whose inquisitorial zeal was exceeded only by Senator McCarthy's, took up the chase. McCarran had his investigators pore over the back files of *Pacific Affairs,* a scholarly journal Lattimore had edited for seven years. Then he took eight volumes of testimony, most of it unfriendly, about Lattimore's beliefs and activities. Finally Lattimore himself took the stand. Committee staff members cross-examined him for twelve days, exploring every crevice of his professional career. The hearings, Thurman Arnold said later, "were a masterpiece of hypocritical ingenuity . . ." The questions "were not asked in order to obtain information, but for the purpose of entrapment."

The predictable result was that Lattimore was indicted for perjury. The Justice Department charged that he had lied when he told the McCarran Committee he believed he had never done or said anything to promote the interest of communism. In effect, Lattimore was accused of giving the committee an insincere appraisal of his own ideas.

Federal District Judge Luther Youngdahl struck down the heart of the indictment as being too vague. But the Justice Department refused to give up. Two years later, in July 1954, it filed another perjury indictment against Lattimore along the same lines as the first but supplemented by specific examples of Lattimore's allegedly pro-Communist views. "There was no possible way to prepare a defense," Thurman Arnold contended, "because it covered political and economic writings of thirty-five years and involved the proof before a jury selected by lot of the rightness or wrongness of international policy."

Along with the indictment the Justice Department took the almost unprecedented step of filing an affidavit of prejudice against Judge Youngdahl. Ordinarily such charges of bias are based on some action of the judge outside the courtroom. But here the government was accusing Youngdahl of prejudice solely because of his rulings from the bench on the previous indictment. Its apparent intention was to embarrass Youngdahl publicly so he would disqualify himself. Youngdahl, who had been a liberal Republican governor of Minnesota before his appointment to the bench, stood his ground. He dismissed the affidavit of prejudice; then he dismissed the indictment too, for much the same reasons he had thrown out the first. Forcing a defendant to stand trial for perjury "under charges so formless and obscure," Youngdahl ruled, "would be unprecedented and would make a sham of the Fifth Amendment."

Not until the Justice Department appealed Youngdahl's

ruling and lost, in July 1955, did it abandon its prosecution of Lattimore. His ordeal had lasted for five years. He had not been convicted of anything, but his adversaries had succeeded, as Arnold wrote bitterly, "in getting him pilloried from coast to coast."

For Arnold, Fortas & Porter it had been a long and lonely fight. Because of the temper of the times and the relentlessness of the prosecution, few others rallied to Lattimore's support. Even the usually stalwart American Civil Liberties Union wavered and proposed to file a brief in the case, which Arnold felt would undermine rather than strengthen Lattimore's defense. Arnold dictated an angry letter to the ACLU:

> If the American Civil Liberties Union management does not realize that the new indictment of Owen Lattimore is a fundamental assault upon civil liberties, it will certainly be beyond my capacity to demonstrate the point. . . . I have no intention this time to engage in a debate with you. The only thing I want is for the American Civil Liberties Union to stay out of this case."

When he had finished, Arnold wondered if he had been too harsh. He showed the letter to Fortas, who handed it back and said, "If anything, it's not tough enough."

If the ACLU was wishy-washy, other lawyers were openly hostile to the firm because of its involvement in the Lattimore case and other unpopular causes. Paul Porter liked to tell the story that one day at Burning Tree Country Club he encountered another Washington attorney who remarked, "Paul, I understand your firm is engaged in defending homosexuals and Communists."

"That's right," Porter replied cheerfully. "What can we do for you?"

More seriously, the firm came under increasing pressure from some of its clients to drop the Lattimore case. One client, Joe Pew, head of the Sun Oil Company, did in fact take his business elsewhere in protest. But the partners stood fast. "We were so deeply involved we would have looked like a bunch of damn fools if we had done anything else," one said. "It never seriously occurred to us to pull out."

The Lattimore case was one of the final convulsions of McCarthyism. By 1955 McCarthy himself had been discredited by the Senate, and the witch hunt had lost most of its momentum. Arnold, Fortas & Porter had given heavily of its time and had risked its reputation and its future. "It wasn't as tough on us as it would have been on an establishment firm that depended mainly on trusts and estates," said one member of the firm. "On the other hand, we didn't have that many big clients. All we had to do was lose two or three to be in trouble."

Arnold, Fortas & Porter emerged from the age of McCarthyism with its business and prestige intact. If anything, the firm scored a net gain by stamping itself with the seal of liberal respectability, which helped to attract clients and bright young lawyers to serve them. And while the firm's heart was always in the struggle against the witch hunt, the fundamental goal of making a living was never out of mind.

THE BIG MONEY

ARNOLD & FORTAS started from scratch, without "a single client or any prospects," as Fortas recalled it. "Yet somehow by the mysterious process of life and law the venture went forward, and increasing numbers of partners and associates joined it."

The firm's progress was not really that mysterious. The times were favorable and the partners were aggressive and resourceful. In the postwar years new corporations were springing up and old ones were flourishing as never before. But both the new entrepreneurs and the old had to contend with the rain forest of Federal regulations that had sprung up during the New Deal and war years. As Fortas pointed out, "Lawyers who were veterans of the New Deal and Government service were presumed to be qualified to find their way through the maze."

All three partners were particularly well qualified as guides to the bureaucracy. Arnold for five years had been the government's top anti-trust specialist. Porter had headed the Federal Communications Commission, now entrusted with overseeing the growth of the economy's newest giant, the television industry. Fortas's position at the Interior Department had given him broad reach throughout the upper levels of government.

Fortas was quick to put his background to use. Soon after he left the Interior Department, he was given a $12,000 retainer to represent the territorial government of Puerto Rico in its major legal dealings on the mainland. In the past these matters had been handled by the Federal government's own lawyers in the Interior and Justice Departments, and the new arrangement raised some eyebrows in Washington. It was no secret that as interior undersecretary Fortas had been deeply involved in Puerto Rican affairs. Moreover, when he was still working for Harold Ickes, Fortas had gone on record in opposition to private attorneys representing the Puerto Rican government, or any other public agency, as "unsound and unwise." If a private attorney representing a government agency took on another client who also had dealings with that agency, Fortas argued, "it is obvious that the situation would be embarrassing for both the lawyers and the government."

"That was good counsel," Marquis Childs wrote in a column in May 1946 chiding Fortas for exempting himself from his own rule. "The interweaving of private and public business is dubious. No matter how good the intentions, the public customarily gets the short end of the bargain."

Fortas later claimed that he was dragooned into taking Puerto Rico's legal work by his friend Luis Muñoz Marin, later the island's first elected governor, who wanted the benefit of his expertise on certain "specialized problems." One of his partners contended that the firm's efforts on Puerto Rico's behalf, which continued for more than twenty years, were "a labor of love," and a losing proposition. But whatever the long-term balance sheet was, Puerto Rico's business must have been welcome at a time when the firm was scrambling to find clients. And the arrangement reflected Fortas's determination to deal with the world on his own terms, an attitude that would contribute substantially to his success.

In the firm's early days Fortas was overshadowed in the public mind by his two partners. Both Thurman Arnold and Paul Porter had pursued their government careers in the spotlight

of publicity, while Fortas for the most part had operated behind the scenes. Like most people, G. Duane (Bud) Vieth, who
joined the firm in 1949 straight out of the University of Iowa
Law School, had "heard a lot more about Arnold and Porter
than about Fortas."

Within the firm itself, however, Fortas had no trouble holding his own. "It was quite apparent to me soon after I got
here," said Vieth, "that Fortas was a man of extraordinary
ability. He could take a case in any area of law and do an excellent job with it." In preparing a case Fortas almost made
a fetish out of thoroughness. When the three top partners discussed an antitrust suit involving the United Fruit Company,
Thurman Arnold recalled: "I said I'd try that case carload by
carload, Paul would probably try it bunch by bunch, but only
Abe would try it banana by banana." His standards were high,
particularly when it came to legal prose. Milton Freeman
showed him a brief which Fortas pronounced one of the best
pieces of work he had ever read. Then, Freeman recalled, "He
sat down and rewrote the whole thing." Fortas demanded not
only technical precision, but also stylish flair. "Take it back
and put some poetry into it," he told an associate who had
produced a stuffy brief.

Fortas handled mostly appellate cases, considered to be
more intellectually demanding than trial law, where success
often depends on showmanship. Yet Fortas was quick enough
on his feet to put on an impressive show when the occasion
demanded. In 1952 he came before the Second Circuit Court
of Appeals in New York to argue for Otis & Co., the investment house, which had been ordered by a lower court to pay
$3.1 million to Kaiser-Frazer Corporation as a result of a mis-
fired stock deal. As is customary, the court limited the time for
argument. Before he began, Fortas told Milton Freeman to
pass him a note when he had five minutes left. Freeman
watched the clock while Fortas soared to the heights of foren-
sic eloquence. At the appointed moment, Freeman handed
him the warning note. Fortas interrupted himself in mid-pas-

sage, stared at the slip of paper and sorrowfully told Judge Augustus Hand, cousin of the celebrated Learned Hand: "Your honor, I am informed my time is almost up."

But Judge Hand was spellbound. "Please go on, Mr. Fortas," he urged.

Fortas swept ahead for another forty minutes. When he was finally through, Freeman said: "It didn't make any difference what the other side said." Three months later Judge Hand wrote a decision that reversed the lower court judgment and saved Otis more than three million dollars.

Apart from his handling of individual cases, Fortas was the driving force behind the firm's overall success. "Right from the start, to the extent that any one partner managed the firm, he managed it," said Bud Vieth. "To the extent that any one partner was responsible for most of the business getting, he was responsible for it." He was quick and incisive. An associate recalled meetings at which Fortas, after hearing everyone out, would then "analyze the whole thing in one-two-three order, saying: 'You should do this about that.' " He had a way with clients, too. "After they had dealt with him a couple of times most of them felt they couldn't breathe without consulting Abe," one member of the firm said. "He made himself indispensable."

His manner did not inspire affection. "There was little spontaneity in the man," a colleague said. "He was always calculating. If he was having a conversation, he'd be constantly thinking ahead to what the other guy might say next." He set a rigorous pace and some considered him a martinet. Young lawyers quaked when he lectured them, and one member of the firm supposedly broke out in a rash when Fortas entered the room.

But he could be generous with praise for those who met his standards. John Ely, a Yale Law School junior, spent a summer at the firm laying the groundwork for the *Gideon* case, which Fortas later argued successfully before the Supreme Court. When Ely returned to school that fall, Fortas wrote him a letter lauding Ely's work as "first-rate on any basis,"

and took the trouble to send a copy of the note to Ely's dean.
His friends maintained that Fortas was a warmer man than
most people thought. "Fortas is a no-nonsense kind of guy,"
said Bud Vieth. "If you were someone who could take care of
yourself it was strictly a business relationship. But he never
took advantage of anyone who was vulnerable. And he looked
out for people who needed looking out for."

Even those at AF&P who felt no personal fondness for Fortas had to concede that the firm was flourishing under his
leadership. By the early 1950's, after little more than five years,
it had achieved such dimensions of prosperity, *Harper's* magazine reported, "that envious colleagues have begun to make
wry jokes about it." According to one bit of professional humor, neighboring lawyers had abandoned their own practices
so they could spend all their time chasing after the thousand-
dollar bills "which fluttered unnoticed out of the door of the
Arnold, Fortas & Porter suite."

To accommodate its expanding roster, the firm soon moved
out of that office building suite into a group of refurbished
Victorian homes on the edge of DuPont Circle. Here, in an
atmosphere of cozy sophistication, the big money kept rolling
in from some of the country's biggest corporations. Starting
with Coca Cola, its first important business client, the firm
before long was serving major companies in every field, including Lever Brothers, Western Union, American Broadcasting Company, Philip Morris, Federated Department
Stores and Braniff Airlines. By the mid-1960's, AF&P had become one of the three largest law firms in Washington.
Though members of the firm did not divulge details in public, other Washington lawyers calculated that most senior
partners at AF&P were earning close to $200,000 a year.

Sharing in this prosperity, and significantly contributing to
it, from an office on the miniature AF&P campus diagonally
across from her husband's building, was Carolyn Agger. After
Yale and stints at the National Labor Relations Board and
the Justice Department's tax division, she had entered private
practice with a law firm whose Washington office was headed

by Randolph Paul, probably the top tax lawyer of the day. Carol Agger became his protege. Later, after Paul died and Adlai Stevenson joined the firm, she stayed on as its chief tax expert despite her husband's efforts to persuade her to join him at Arnold, Fortas & Porter. But in 1961 when Stevenson became United Nations ambassador her firm closed its Washington office and she brought its tax staff with her to AF&P, where she became head of the tax law section.

She remained a strong and independent personality, a distinctive combination of femininity and feminism. Slim and chic, she loved bright clothes, admitted to owning 150 pairs of shoes and rarely was seen without a hat and gloves. She also puffed on long black cigars, insisted on being referred to around the office by her maiden name, and in her professional dealings with men asked and gave no quarter.

The Fortases lived elegantly only about ten blocks from their office in a comfortable Georgetown home which they shared with three French poodles and a housekeeper. On Thursdays and Sundays, the cook's days off, the two lawyers enjoyed dabbling in the kitchen together. Neither had great taste for the Washington social whirl, nor were they much given to lavish entertaining at home.

Music remained Fortas's chief outside interest and his greatest pleasure. "It is one of the things I cannot do without," he told a friend. Now he could afford to indulge his boyhood avocation in grand style. He had been given a 200-year-old Guidantus violin, and on Sunday evenings a mixed group of amateur and professional violinists and cellists would gather at his home for performances of what Fortas called "the 3025 N Street No Refunds Quartet." Musicians of renown who visited Washington sat in with the group and were entertained at the Fortas home. Memphis's erstwhile schoolboy fiddler now included among his friends such artists as Isaac Stern, Rudolf Serkin, David Oistrakh, Van Cliburn and Pablo Casals.

As a result of his friendship for Casals and his own ties to Puerto Rico, Fortas played a part in arranging the annual

Casals festival on the island. Once, on the eve of the festival's start, a seam broke in Casals's cello and nothing would do but for Fortas personally to take it to an expert in New York for repairs. As Fortas liked to tell the story, he boarded a plane, strapped the cello into an adjoining seat and ordered one martini for himself and another for the cello. Then he gulped down both drinks himself. "I was nervous," he explained. "Carrying a man's cello is like carrying his wife."

In search of relaxation the Fortases fled Washington whenever they could. In the winter they skied and skated in Canada. In summer they hid away in their sprawling country house on Minuteman Hill overlooking Long Island Sound in Westport, Connecticut. Garbed in baggy trousers, old shoes and a sweater, Fortas ran errands for Carol in town and hauled manure for her garden. He usually prevailed upon some of his music-loving cronies to visit him for a week or two, much of which time was given over to chamber-music sessions sometimes lasting eight hours a day with a break only for lunch. It was, he assured friends back in Washington, a splendid way to relax.

Hardly a sentimentalist, Fortas could nevertheless be genuinely compassionate. One of his spare-time concerns was with the humane treatment of animals, which he called "an essential ingredient of civilization." He served as unofficial legal adviser to the Animal Welfare Institute, helped to found the Society of Animal Protective Legislation, and drafted legislation setting humane standards for slaughtering animals and using them in medical experimentation. For his efforts he was awarded the Animal Welfare Institute's Albert Schweitzer medal, an honor which he accepted with a speech lamenting the "sheer practical idiocy of man's inhumanity toward other creatures."

More relevant to his legal practice was Fortas's special interest in psychiatry, which he had pursued since the 1940's. He was a trustee of the William Alanson White Psychiatric Foundation, wrote articles for its journal and believed strongly that a lawyer ignorant of psychiatry "was not a complete lawyer." His interest in the field probably led to his assignment in 1954 by the U.S. Court of Appeals in Washington as attorney for a small-time criminal named Monte Durham in a case that dealt with the complex problem of insanity as a defense in criminal cases. In the past the courts had generally held that a defendant could be found innocent by reason of insanity only if he did not know the difference between right and wrong. Fortas believed this doctrine to be based on an obsolete conception of mental illness. Even if a person could distinguish right from wrong, Fortas believed, his behavior could be controlled by a mental disorder that would override that distinction. In finding Durham innocent by reason of insanity, the Circuit Court laid down a new and more flexible doctrine that "an accused is not criminally responsible if his unlawful act was the product of a mental disease or defect."

Fortas's success in the *Durham* case established him as one of the few prominent Washington lawyers with a serious interest in criminal law. Soon after, Chief Justice Warren appointed him to a special bar committee to recommend changes in the rules of procedure in Federal criminal cases. In June of 1962, as a further sign of recognition, Fortas was selected by the Supreme Court to represent an impoverished prisoner whose appeal for a new trial had raised a fundamental constitutional issue. Like other lawyers appointed by the High Court to represent indigents, Fortas would not receive a cent for his services. But such assignments are considered a mark of professional esteem. The reward in prestige from this particular case was rich indeed, because it led to one of the most significant criminal decisions of modern times. Fortas's client was Clarence Earl Gideon, a fifty-one-year-old ne'er-do-well who was serving time in a Florida prison for breaking and entering a poolroom. Gideon, who had no money to hire a lawyer, had asked the judge at his trial to appoint one to defend him without fee. The judge, in accordance with the laws of Florida, had refused. Eventually Gideon filed a pauper's appeal to the Supreme Court. His contention, laboriously printed in pencil, was that the Constitution guaranteed the right of every defendant in a criminal trial to a free lawyer.

Twenty years earlier, in the case of *Betts vs. Brady,* the Supreme Court had rejected that very proposition. It held instead that the right to free counsel existed only under "special circumstances," if, for example the defendant was very young or illiterate or mentally ill. But over the years the doctrine of *Betts vs. Brady* had come under increasing criticism from legal authorities as inconsistent and unjust. When the Court agreed to hear Gideon's appeal, four justices had already declared, in commenting on previous cases, their belief that *Betts vs. Brady* should be overruled. Only one more vote was needed for a majority that would reject the old precedent and give Gideon a new trial.

But as Anthony Lewis pointed out in *Gideon's Trumpet,* the challenge facing Fortas was greater than simply winning a majority. The Supreme Court reverses itself on great constitutional questions only rarely. The broader the support for such a turnabout, the better it is for the Court's prestige. Fortas felt obliged "not just to try to win the case, but to get as many Justices as possible to go along with what I considered the right result. If you assume *Betts vs. Brady* was going to be overruled," he said afterward, "it was right for the institution of the Supreme Court, and for the law, to have as much unanimity as possible."

For help Fortas called on his firm's considerable resources. One partner drafted a memorandum which laid out the basic issues of the case. Another, Abe Krash, who had earlier done much of the research for the *Durham* brief, directed an exhaustive study of relevant cases and law review articles. Many memos later, by the end of the summer, a draft brief was presented for Fortas's consideration. He was impressed but by no means completely satisfied. He spent a week in the library cramming and two more days in a New York hotel room drawing up a detailed outline, which he turned over to Krash for the final draft. "I want this to be a little jewel," Fortas told him.

When the case came up for argument in January of 1963, Fortas stood before the High Court for more than an hour dispassionately insisting that it was impossible for a man to have a fair trial unless he had a lawyer to speak for him. He recalled that when Clarence Darrow was prosecuted for jury fixing, "the first thing he realized was that he needed a lawyer —he, one of the country's great criminal lawyers." And he reminded the Justices of the infinite difficulties of enforcing the special circumstance rule of *Betts vs. Brady*. Having read the major cases on right to counsel, Fortas said: "I hope I may be forgiven for saying that my heart is full of compassion for the judges having to review the record and look for 'special circumstances.' "

Fortas knew that Justice Hugo Black passionately believed that the right to counsel, along with all the rest of the Bill of Rights, should be automatically applied to the states as a result of the Fourteenth Amendment to the Constitution. But he also realized that most of the other Justices vigorously disagreed, and he sought to steer clear of this controversial ground. Black, stubborn in his convictions, refused to let the matter rest and demanded to know where Fortas stood.

"I like that argument that you have made so eloquently," Fortas told him respectfully. "But I cannot as an advocate make that argument because this Court has rejected it. I hope you never cease making it." Laughter from the Justices, Hugo Black among them, broke the tension in the courtroom.

In March 1963 the Court handed down its opinion. Mr. Justice Black, who had dissented from *Betts vs. Brady* twenty-one years before, was given the honor and satisfaction of writing the judgment that overturned it. In his Southern tones and blunt language Black declared: "That government hires lawyers to prosecute and defendants who have the money hire lawyers to defend are the strongest indications of the widespread belief that lawyers in criminal cases are necessities, not luxuries. The right of one charged with crime to counsel may not be deemed fundamental to fair trials in some countries, but it is in ours." The Justices differed among themselves on matters of detail. But there were no dissenters. On the main issue, the Court spoke with one voice.

It was a famous victory. Clarence Gideon was given a new trial and with the help of a free, court-appointed lawyer was found innocent. The Supreme Court's ruling in his case was acclaimed by the bar and the press. Fortas's role was dramatically documented in the widely read *Gideon's Trumpet*. His success enhanced his standing as a man of scholarship and liberal principles dedicated to human values.

Fortas had excellent credentials for the part, but the fact was that most of his time and energy were expended on very different purposes. As Arnold, Fortas & Porter's corporate clientele increased, so did Fortas's identification with big business. Federated Department Stores, Greatamerica Corp., Franklin Life Insurance Co., Braniff Airlines and the Madison National Bank of Washington made him a member of their boards of directors. He was spending more of his days in board rooms, and fewer in courtrooms.

Occasionally, Fortas revealed an ironic awareness of the demands this sort of law practice imposed upon him. Once, in the midst of a heated legal discussion with another attorney, he was interrupted by a phone call from an important business client. As cranky and weary as he was, Fortas nevertheless listened patiently, from time to time murmuring appropriately sympathetic comments. Still the client rambled on, until Fortas took the phone from his ear and turned to his visitor. "This is my life," he said wryly, "this is my life."

Fortas was obviously free to do as he pleased with his life, but his law firm was in the public arena, and the policies of some of its clients outraged his liberal friends. The talent and resources that had challenged McCarthyism and won Clarence Gideon his freedom also sought loopholes in the antitrust laws, battled against labor unions and tried to prevent the government from regulating cigarette advertising. Joseph Rauh, a former New Dealer and later an official of Americans for Democratic Action, complained about Arnold, Fortas & Porter: "Their good works in the past didn't stop them from representing every stinking interest in town."

As Fortas looked at it, this was all part of a lawyer's job. His firm had amply demonstrated its commitment to social welfare and conscience. Why, then, shouldn't it be free to make money where it could? In defending the practical principles on which he and Thurman Arnold had founded their partnership, Fortas later wrote: "There is nothing dishonorable in representing a commercial client for money, or in representing a rapist out of a sense of duty to the law and our legal system." Both he and Arnold believed it proper that a law firm should take on a certain amount of "social service, nonremunerative activities." But, he contended, "It does not follow that the firm is obliged to assess the social implications of the activities of those seeking its services." A lawyer was free to choose not to represent a particular corporation, if he did not want to. But he "should not elevate his personal predilection into a principle of universal application to others."

Arnold, Fortas & Porter's obligation to its clients, Fortas felt, was clear: "If the interest of a client required the lawyer to advocate a position or seek a result which he personally disliked or even which he considered contrary to society's welfare, it was the lawyer's duty to do so with all his mind and heart, subject only to the restrictions and proprieties which the rules and conventions impose."

The liberal criticism of the firm, however, was directed not only at clients but also at tactics. It was gossiped around town that Fortas and his top partners used their personal prestige to gain special advantages for their clients. This was a general indictment lodged against all powerful Washington law firms which the muckraking journal *Hard Times* described as "a new estate of government, all the more powerful because of its isolation from inspection and its insulation from criticism."

The tales of influence wielding and string pulling were ridiculed by most Washington lawyers. "Trying to get something fixed by influence in Washington is like trying to rob

Tiffany's at high noon," said Lee Loevinger, who was a member of the FCC before turning to private practice. "It's just barely possible that it can be done, but it's certain to attract lots of attention."

Nevertheless, the popular suspicions were fostered by the name-dropping, romantic style cultivated by some Washington attorneys to impress their clients and justify their fees. No one could deny that the top private attorneys were usually on good terms with the people who counted in government. "Paul Porter and Thurman Arnold and Abe went to see the big shots, because they knew them," said one junior member of the firm. "Now I don't know what difference it made, but it got them in the door."

It was almost impossible for anyone to tell how much difference it did make. But many in Washington considered it reasonable to assume that lawyers possessed of such privileges and contacts did themselves and their clients more good than harm. That assumption applied particularly to Fortas, when he was at the height of success in the 1960's. For while every prominent Washington lawyer had friends in high places, no one else had such a good friend in such a high place as Abe Fortas had in Lyndon Baines Johnson.

A FRIEND IN NEED

HISTORY cannot be readily anticipated. So no drums rolled and no one recorded for posterity the moment when Lyndon Johnson and Abe Fortas first encountered each other. Their handshake commenced a collaboration that eventually would carry both men to the heights of power, influence the fate of nations and become itself the focus of heated public debate. But in 1939, when the two met, these events were still sleeping some years in the future. Johnson was then just a hard-driving young congressman and Fortas just another link in the personal network he was constructing in the varied agencies of the government.

This is not to say that Johnson treated Fortas or any of his other contacts lightly. "He deliberately cultivated all the young New Dealers—young men on the White House staff and the young lawyers around town like myself," Tom Corcoran recalled. "Gradually these guys found they were working for Lyndon Johnson. He got more projects and more money for his district than any other man in Congress."

The project then closest to Representative Johnson's heart first brought him into contact with Fortas. This was the development of the Lower Colorado River, near Austin, which promised rich benefits in electric power and flood control to

Johnson's constituents. The work was under the supervision of the Interior Department's Public Works Administration, where Fortas was general counsel. Johnson, eager to expedite the project, sought Fortas's help in solving the legal problems that stood in the way of its completion.

Though Fortas soon left the PWA and moved ahead in the Interior Department, he and Johnson kept in touch. They had a number of mutual friends. Fortas's colleague at Interior, Arthur Goldschmidt, had known Johnson back in Texas, and it was Goldschmidt who introduced the two men. Alvin Wirtz, a liberal Austin lawyer who had been the chief sponsor of Johnson's early political career, was Fortas's predecessor, once removed, as undersecretary of interior. And Johnson was also on good terms with Fortas's old friend William Douglas, who was now on the Supreme Court, and with Fortas's boss, Harold Ickes. The Johnsons and the Fortases encountered each other at cocktail parties and dined at each other's homes. The Johnsons liked to drop by the Fortases for steak supper of a Sunday evening, with LBJ usually bringing his own choice Texas cuts.

During office hours, Congressman Johnson did not hesitate, when the occasion presented itself, to seek his friend Fortas's aid for himself and his constituents. Not long after Fortas became undersecretary of interior, Johnson sought his help in finding a job for a lawyer friend. After getting two letters from Johnson on successive days, Fortas "rechecked" the situation and wrote to "Dear Lyndon" that "it is still true that no vacancy on the Federal Petroleum Board is expected. I regret the circumstances."

LBJ had better luck a few months later when he relayed to Fortas a complaint from a group of independent oil companies in Texas. The independents were furious about a wartime order issued by an Interior Department agency which sharply restricted the business hours of the service stations they supplied. "I don't want to be persistent," Johnson wrote, "but I think you ought to have the enclosed mimeographed sheets which are being circulated by certain people in the oil industry to all members of Congress." Unless the order was revised "right soon," Johnson warned, the department was likely to be in for "a good deal of trouble."

The next week Fortas reported to Johnson that the order had been revoked, and soon afterward Fortas was rewarded with a heartfelt letter of gratitude from one of the independent dealers. ". . . We are deeply appreciative of your untiring efforts in this connection and I know you did work for the petroleum dealers, as Lyndon has told me on several occasions that you were putting up a stiff fight for us." Fortas sent Johnson a copy of the thank-you note, adding: "Whether or not you inspired it, I appreciate it, although it's not entirely deserved."

No matters of great consequence were involved in this early give and take between Johnson and Fortas. But such contacts taught the two men to trust and respect each other and helped to preserve their friendship even after Fortas left the government for private practice. It was then, at the most critical moment of his political career, that Johnson once again called on Fortas for help.

The crisis arose during Johnson's tumultuous campaign for the United States Senate in 1948. Restless as always, Congressman Johnson had dreamed of moving up to the Senate for years. He tried for the first time in 1941, when the death of Texas Senator Morris Sheppard created a vacancy. With Alvin Wirtz, who resigned from the Interior Department, at his side, and with the tacit backing of FDR, Johnson waged a bitter and expensive campaign against Texas Governor Pappy O'Daniel. "Pass the Biscuits" Pappy was a master of homespun invective, and also, it turned out, had some helpful enemies. When ninety-six per cent of the vote had been counted Johnson held what seemed to be an insurmountable lead of 5,000 votes. But O'Daniel, an apostle of temperance, got some last-minute assistance from the liquor industry, which was happy to see the governor go to Washington rather than remain in the statehouse. Liquor lobbyists helped local politicians "find" enough votes in outlying Texas counties to wipe out Johnson's lead. Defeated and depressed, Johnson visited his friend in the White House, who offered some practical advice. "Next time," FDR told his protege, "sit on the ballot boxes."

The next time was 1948. Senator O'Daniel, whose folksy charm had worn thin even in Texas, prudently decided not to seek reelection. Another former governor, Coke Stevenson, emerged as Johnson's most formidable adversary. Johnson whirled around the state in a helicopter called the *Johnson City Windmill* while the taciturn Stevenson plodded from town to town in an old Plymouth. Slow and steady won the July primary; Stevenson had forty per cent of the vote to thirty-four per cent for Johnson. Since neither had a majority, a runoff was scheduled for September.

Johnson had been forced to relinquish his relatively safe seat in the House to run for the Senate. Defeat in the runoff would leave him jobless, facing political oblivion. Desperation spurred his already frantic campaign pace and he drove himself mercilessly from one massive rally to another. Seeking to win conservative support, Johnson proudly cited his vote for the Taft-Hartley Act, which President Truman had vetoed as anti-labor; he depicted the staunchly conservative Stevenson as "the silent whip of the labor bosses," and portrayed himself as the intended victim of the "Communist labor czars." Stevenson, who yielded to no man in his opposition to organized labor, replied in kind. Disgusted with the mutual slander, the United Steelworkers Union in Texas advised its members not to vote for either man.

As the battle drew to an end, Johnson cried to his supporters: "We're comin' round the mountain and don't anyone slow down." But on election day, August 28, it was by no means clear that he had come far enough. For days, as ballots were counted, the two candidates seesawed in the lead. On September 3 Stevenson appeared to have won the nomination by 114 votes, but the next day there was dramatic news from the Panhandle town of Alice, seat of Jim Wells County. Alice's Thirteenth Precinct "discovered" 203 previously uncounted votes. The tabulation gave 202 votes to Johnson and 1 to Stevenson, enough to give Johnson victory by 87 votes.

Stevenson, however, detected the not-so-subtle hand of the celebrated political finagler George Parr, known as the "Duke of Duval County." The Duke, who had been convicted of Federal income tax evasion and had served time in prison, was the absolute ruler of Duval and surrounding counties, including Jim Wells. His power was derived from the illiterate Mexican-Americans who worked for him. The Duke paid their poll tax and delivered their votes to the candidate of his choice. "I was beaten by a stuffed ballot box," Stevenson charged. "And I can prove it."

With two ex-FBI men in tow, Stevenson rushed to Alice, demanding to see the voting list for the Thirteenth Precinct. The list was locked in the vault of Parr's bank. Stevenson called in the Texas Rangers. He was allowed to look at the lists, but they were snatched away before he could copy down the names. Finally the ballot boxes were opened for inspection; they turned out to be empty. Meanwhile Johnson's supporters railroaded an endorsement of Johnson's victory through the state party executive committee and the state convention.

Stevenson turned to the Federal courts. His lawyers, rousing District Judge T. Whitfield Davidson in the middle of the night, persuaded him to issue an injunction prohibiting Johnson's name from going on the November ballot pending a Federal investigation into Stevenson's charges of fraud. No matter what the investigation turned up, it seemed certain that the judge's final decision would come too late for Lyndon Johnson to get his name before the voters.

But Johnson's field marshal, Alvin Wirtz, had laid plans to meet almost any eventuality. When Stevenson first challenged Johnson's victory, Wirtz had alerted his and Lyndon Johnson's friend Abe Fortas. Now, with Stevenson's injunction staring him in the face, Wirtz reached Fortas by phone in Dallas, where he was taking depositions in an antitrust case. "Lyn-

don's here in Fort Worth and he's in trouble," said Wirtz.
"Come over right away."

Fortas first sent Johnson to ask the Fifth Circuit Court of
Appeals, which included Texas in its jurisdiction, to set aside
the injunction. But the Fifth Circuit was in summer recess
and would not act until mid-October. The only place left to
appeal was the U.S. Supreme Court. The High Court also was
still out for the summer. But during recesses each of the Justices has the authority to hear emergency appeals from his assigned judicial circuit. The Fifth Circuit was the responsibility of Justice Hugo Black, who like Johnson himself was a
Southerner with strong ties to FDR and the New Deal. Moreover, Black was familiar with the rough and tumble of state
politics, having served in the Senate before Franklin Roosevelt named him to the Court. But even though Black might
be personally sympathetic to Johnson's cause, Fortas realized
that Supreme Court Justices are customarily reluctant to use
their emergency power to act alone unless the matter before
them verges on life and death. Fortas's fundamental task
would be to convince Black that Lyndon Johnson's problem
was of such overriding urgency that its solution could not be
postponed until the full Court reconvened in the fall.

When the lawyers for Stevenson and Johnson gathered in
Black's oak-paneled chambers at the Supreme Court, Fortas
argued vigorously that time was a critical factor in the case.
Texas law required that the names of all party nominees be
posted by October 3, and it was already September 28. Moreover, Fortas pointed out, no matter what the outcome of the
suit, Coke Stevenson could not get his name on the ballot. His
sole aim seemed to be to destroy Lyndon Johnson's candidacy.
Unless Judge Davidson's order was overturned, there would
be no Democratic candidate at all on the Texas ballot, a
circumstance, Fortas declared, that would be "perfectly ap-
palling."

Dan Moody, another former Texas governor who spoke for
Stevenson, challenged Black's jurisdiction to rule on the in-

junction Judge Davidson had issued. The injunction, Moody contended, was justified under a post-Civil War statute designed to give Federal protection to the voting rights of Negroes.

Fortas replied that it was Davidson who had overstepped his jurisdiction. Johnson's right to be on the ballot was "irrevocably and incontestably vested" under the laws of Texas. The whole case, Fortas insisted, was nothing more or less than "a political controversy."

Black called a recess, ate his lunch and made up his mind. Summoning the lawyers back to his chambers, the Justice quickly disposed of the dispute over his jurisdiction. The Constitution gave him the power to act, he maintained. Moreover, the controversy before him was, he declared, "a matter of supreme importance, not only to Texas but beyond the borders of Texas." He could find no statute that empowered a Federal court to intervene in a state election. To permit this to happen "would be a drastic break with the past." Therefore, pending consideration by the entire Court, he declared Judge Davidson's injunction "no longer in effect."

Johnson had won his battle. The next month, when the full Court got around to the case, it upheld Black's decision. The November election, in what was then still the one-party South, was little more than a formality. Though Stevenson urged his supporters to vote Republican, Johnson swamped his GOP opponent by more than 350,000 votes. His critics, remembering the dubious 87-vote margin in the primary, would refer to him ever afterward as "Landslide Lyndon." But those numbers made no difference to Johnson now. The Senate gateway to power was open and he would never forget that it was Abe Fortas who had turned the key.

Another man who helped, of course, was George Parr, the Duke of Duval. Not long after the election he was given a presidential pardon for his income tax sins by Harry Truman. Some years later Parr was convicted of mail fraud and appealed to the Supreme Court, where Fortas argued his case and won a reversal of his conviction.

In the 1950's, as Johnson and Fortas gained national prominence, the one as leader of the Senate Democrats, the other as a singularly successful Washington lawyer, the ties between them grew stronger. Outwardly they seemed an unlikely combination: Johnson, blustery and often bawdy, was a larger-than-life prototype of the rip-snorting Texas politician. Fortas, self-controlled and surgically precise, was the well-honed model of a modern corporation counsel. But their differences complemented each other neatly, and in certain basic traits they were much alike. Both were demanding, ambitious and aggressive. Though they welcomed the glare of public attention when it suited their purposes, their collaboration was conducted in the shadow of privacy. What passed between them for the most part remained between them.

Still, it was clear that their association was mutually advantageous. Fortas's close connection with the most puissant figure in the Senate enhanced his own prestige. Moreover, his ties to Johnson kept his hand in the inner workings of government. "Fortas liked being an effective force in the affairs of men," said one of his law partners. "He got great satisfaction out of important people coming to him, esteeming his knowledge."

As for Johnson, he learned to rely on Fortas's hardheaded approach to law and politics. "He had this great sense of meticulousness about any decision or question that was put to him that would be of great comfort to a flamboyant guy," said Arthur Goldschmidt. "Fortas was the kind of guy you would go to if you had a knotty problem, because you knew it would be analyzed without any body English. I don't think he'd let questions of ideology or his personal views enter it."

Fortas offered Johnson something besides astute advice. By reputation and personal association Fortas was linked to liberal ideas and organizations, and these connections had potential importance for Lyndon Johnson's political future. Johnson was no more willing to remain forever in the Senate, even as majority leader, than he had been to stay in the House.

[87]

He wanted nothing less than the presidency, and he came to realize he needed liberal support to get it.

In 1956 Johnson went to the Democratic National Convention as Texas's favorite son, cherishing the hope that the delegates would deadlock and turn to him as a standard bearer. But his candidacy never was taken seriously. The convention nominated Adlai Stevenson on the first ballot. Johnson got only eighty votes, all but two from Mississippi and Texas. His fundamental problem, Johnson realized, was that his party regarded him as essentially a Southerner and thus too parochial and too conservative to stand successfully for the presidency. With his eye on 1960, he sought to transform himself into a national politician who would appeal to the Democratic Party's liberal constituency. A major part of his program was to get Congress to pass civil-rights legislation, something it had not done since the Reconstruction era. In 1957 and again in 1960, Johnson steered two civil-rights bills through the Senate, helped by Fortas's behind-the-scenes advice.

It was a sticky business. Johnson dared not back really strong legislation because he feared such action would damage his standing with his Southern colleagues. Anyhow, he believed a tough civil-rights bill would be filibustered to death on the Senate floor. Compromise was the order of the day. With the help of Fortas and another astute Washington lawyer, Dean Acheson, he watered down a section of the 1957 bill which originally subjected violators of Negro voting rights to criminal contempt proceedings before a Federal judge. Johnson's change provided for trial by jury instead of by judge. The bill passed the Senate that way but in the House the liberals revolted. They were skeptical that a Southern jury would convict a fellow Southerner of a civil-rights violation no matter what the evidence. So Johnson compromised the compromise. He proposed that a judge sitting without a jury could handle cases that called for sentences of no longer than forty-five days, and the bill finally passed both houses of Congress.

As it turned out, and as civil-rights leaders had predicted at the time, neither the 1957 nor the 1960 bill made it substantially easier for Negroes to vote in the South. Congress did not pass effective voting-rights legislation until 1965. But the two earlier laws did give Lyndon Johnson talking points in his drive for the 1960 Democratic presidental nomination. Time and again, in appealing for support from liberal leaders in the Democratic Party, he boasted of his role in pushing through this legislation.

Some former New Dealers, including, besides Fortas, Tom Corcoran and Dean Acheson, gave him their backing. They had been close to Johnson during his years in the Senate and they considered him a responsible liberal in the tradition of Franklin Roosevelt. They raised money for him and tried to build a base of support outside the South. Fortas's liberal friends were "startled," he later said, by his support for Lyndon Johnson's candidacy. "But I told them that I knew the man—that if he were to do only one-tenth of what he actually did but spent more time telling people about what he'd done and what he believed in, people would be falling all over themselves to get behind him."

But neither Fortas nor LBJ's other old comrades from New Deal days had much influence with the dominant forces in the Democratic Party. At the convention in 1960, as in 1956, Johnson was unable to extend his delegate strength outside the Southern states. His candidacy was buried on the first ballot, under an avalanche of Kennedy votes. Indeed, Johnson was viewed with such suspicion by Democratic liberals that his selection by John Kennedy as vice-presidential candidate met with angry protest and nearly set off a floor fight.

Kennedy's political judgment was vindicated on election day when Johnson's presence on the ticket helped the Democrats win the electoral votes of key Southern states, notably Texas, which made the difference between victory and defeat. Johnson's contribution to victory, however, did little to increase his authority as Vice President of the United States. In that lofty but hollow position he encountered the same frustrations that had tormented most of his predecessors.

[89]

John Kennedy sought to improve LBJ's morale by keeping him active. He dispatched him as a good-will envoy overseas, where Johnson put his personal mark on diplomacy by letting out a cowboy yell to test the echo at India's Taj Mahal and inviting a Pakistani camel driver to visit him at his Texas ranch. Kennedy made Johnson chairman of the President's Committee on Equal Employment Opportunity, whose purpose was to curb discrimination by government contractors. Johnson called in Fortas to draft a tough executive order giving the committee power to cancel contracts, and Fortas became an ex-officio adviser to the agency. Staff members with problems to solve and decisions to make were told to "check it with Abe."

None of this could alter the dreary reality that Lyndon Johnson had less power at his command than at any time since he had become a congressman. While an admiring public fixed its attention on the vigorous young President, his glamorous First Lady and their appealing children, the Vice President plunged into despondent obscurity. "Whatever happened to Lyndon Johnson?" became a familiar wisecrack in Washington.

When Johnson ultimately did get his name in headlines, it was for the wrong reasons. While he had been in the Senate, Johnson had befriended a sharp, hustling page boy from Pickens, South Carolina, named Bobby Baker. Johnson had made Baker secretary to the Senate's Democrats, in which position he served as LBJ's chief scout, compiling head counts before crucial votes and snooping on the opposition plans. But Baker was busy on his own behalf, too. He got into real estate, insurance and other business ventures, some of which were connected with the friends he had made on Capitol Hill. All of this first came to public notice in September of 1963 when a Washington food-vending-machine company sued Baker for $300,000. The suit charged that Baker had used his influence to persuade a big defense contractor to take its business away from the vending firm and give it instead to a firm in which Baker had an interest.

The Vice President's name inevitably was drawn into the affair. His early sponsorship of Baker was well known and there was plentiful evidence of their friendship. Baker had named two of his children Lynda and Lyndon Baines, and Johnson had described Baker as "one of my most trusted, loyal and competent friends." Baker, Senator Johnson had said, was "my strong right arm. The last man I see at night, the first I see in the morning." As had become customary in a Johnson crisis, Fortas was called in, and he agreed to defend Baker against the suit brought by the vending company. But the court case was only a small part of the difficulties now confronting Baker. His net worth had climbed from $11,000 in 1954 to more than $2 million in 1963, and it appeared that his financial success had been aided by his friendships with important senators. Suddenly the press, the Senate Rules Committee and the Justice Department were all investigating Baker, and a major scandal loomed.

The disclosures of Baker's freewheeling operations seemed likely to hasten the decline in Johnson's political fortunes that had begun with his accepting the vice presidency. "He seemed to have faded astonishingly into the background," Arthur Schlesinger wrote later, "and appeared almost a spectral presence at meetings in the Cabinet Room." From the first, many members of the President's entourage had regarded him with hostility and treated him coldly. Now some considered him more of a liability than an asset to the New Frontier. Johnson began to worry that when Kennedy sought reelection in 1964, he would choose someone else for Vice President.

Adding to the burden of Johnson's problems was his inability to control Democratic politics in his own home state and political base. The bitter warfare that Texas Democrats had waged against each other on and off for more than twenty years had broken out again. Conservatives, led by Governor John Connally, a long-time Johnson supporter, were pitted against the liberals, whose champion was Senator Ralph Yarborough. Johnson, unable himself to end the hostilities, appealed to the President to exert his personal influence on the rival camps. Mindful of the importance of Democratic unity in Texas with its twenty-five electoral votes, Kennedy agreed. With the First Lady at his side, the President flew to Texas and arrived in Dallas on November 22, 1963.

Kennedy's assassination enveloped the nation in tragedy and probably altered the course of history. No one, of course, was more drastically affected than Lyndon Baines Johnson. The equations by which he had calculated his future suddenly shifted in value. Old problems faded in importance, while new ones loomed large. But at least one factor remained constant. As President of the United States, Johnson would still be Abe Fortas's client and friend.

CHAPTER FOUR——PART TWO

c/o 1600 PENNSYLVANIA AVENUE

THOUGH Lyndon Johnson had always yearned for power, he
was unprepared for the tragic suddenness with which power
came to him in Dallas. Shaken and harassed, he sought counsel where he could. In the interests of continuity, he made a
point of soliciting the support of the men who had been closest to John Kennedy. "I need you more than he did," he told
the Kennedy staffers, with a measure of truth, and most agreed
to stay on at the White House, at least for a while. But Johnson like his predecessor needed his own men around him. His
official staff was not yet large enough or seasoned enough to
meet his needs. It was only natural, then, that he should turn
for help to Fortas.

Kennedy's death ultimately transformed Fortas's life nearly
as much as it did Johnson's. The relationship between the
two took on added dimension and urgency, a process that began within hours of the assassination. No sooner had Johnson
returned to his Washington home from Dallas than the new
President had Fortas on the phone to take up his most immediate problems, in which Fortas would soon be directly
involved.

Uppermost in Johnson's mind was the need to deliver an
address that would establish himself firmly in the public

mind as President. "This is a sad time for all people," he had declared on arriving at Andrews Air Force Base outside Washington. "I will do my best," he pledged. "That is all I can do. I ask for your help—and God's." There was little he could add to that until after Kennedy's funeral. Then he planned a full-scale nationally televised address to a joint session of Congress in which he would seek to calm the nation and establish the tone of his new Administration.

Johnson asked a number of people to write drafts of the speech, including John Galbraith, Charlie Murphy, a former ghost writer for Harry Truman, and Horace Busby of his own staff. Their work he turned over to John Kennedy's own chief speech writer, Ted Sorensen, who on the night of Kennedy's funeral composed his own version. Johnson gave Sorenson's draft his enthusiastic approval, but other advisers objected that Sorensen's prose sounded too much like Kennedy. Johnson may well have felt that way himself. At any rate, later that night he turned the draft over to Fortas'who jiggered words and phrases around to give the text a Johnsonian tone. "I corned it up a little," he said later.

The finished product was widely acclaimed. One particularly felicitous phrase, "Let us continue," set the theme. Johnson delivered a moving affirmation of Kennedy's goals, with special emphasis on the need for congressional action on civil-rights legislation. From his seat in the Johnson family's personal box in the House's executive gallery, editor Fortas joined in the applause.

More than oratory was needed to deal with the sense of shock and anxiety produced by the assassination and its bizarre aftermath. Many Americans had been appalled at the Dallas Police Department's cavalier handling of the suspected assassin after his arrest. When Lee Harvey Oswald was mortally wounded in police headquarters, forty-eight hours after Kennedy's murder, the national tragedy threatened to become an international disgrace. For a while Johnson considered the idea of appointing a commission made up entirely of Texans to conduct an inquiry. Fortas helped persuade him that such a parochial group would have difficulty getting public confidence. Then he helped lay the groundwork for the broadly based national commission, headed by Chief Justice Earl Warren, which eventually investigated the tragedy.

Never before had Fortas been so busy on Lyndon Johnson's behalf as in the days following the assassination. His activity, however, created its own limitations. In October Fortas had agreed to defend Johnson's former assistant, Bobby Baker, in the lawsuit brought against him by the vending-machine company. But two weeks after Johnson became President, Fortas withdrew from the Baker case to avoid a possible conflict of interest. "In the crisis of transition I have undertaken certain assignments which involved conferences with some officials of the government who may be concerned with the Baker case," he explained. "In these circumstances I could not effectively represent Mr. Baker without embarrassment."

Fortas did not specify what these assignments were. But at the time he was serving as liaison man between the White House and the Justice Department on the investigation of Kennedy's assassination. Meanwhile, the Department was conducting a criminal investigation into Baker's affairs that was to culminate in 1966 with his indictment for fraud, larceny and tax evasion. Apart from the possible conflict of interest, which was real enough, Fortas's representation of Baker would serve as a reminder of Baker's close ties to the former Senator Johnson. With Baker under increasing fire, that was a connection Johnson preferred to have forgotten.

Though he dropped out of the lawsuit against Baker, Fortas continued to advise Johnson on other aspects of the troublesome situation. Particularly embarrassing to the President was the testimony before the Senate committee investigating Baker of Don Reynolds, an insurance man who had taken Baker into his business. Reynolds had sold Johnson $200,000 worth of life insurance. In return, Reynolds said, Johnson's chief of staff, Walter Jenkins, had prevailed upon Reynolds to buy $1,208 worth of advertising on the television station Johnson owned in Austin, Texas. When Reynolds's testimony was made public in January of 1964, Fortas advised Johnson against letting Jenkins appear before the Committee to answer Reynolds's charge. Instead, the President issued a statement of his own in which he recounted the purchase of the insurance policies but did not mention Reynolds's purchase of television time. Later, Fortas helped persuade Baker's new lawyer, Edward Bennett Williams, to make an out-of-court settlement with the vending company whose lawsuit had touched off the whole controversy. The parties sealed their agreement in secret only a few weeks before the 1964 presidential election.

As Johnson's tenure in the White House lengthened, the indications of his closeness to Fortas proliferated. Social-minded Washington noted that the Fortases were among the first private citizens to play host to the new President and First Lady, at a dinner dance attended by more than 100 guests. Georgetown residents observed that the presidential limousine was parked outside Fortas's home many an evening while the President stopped in for a chat. Lawyers at Arnold, Fortas & Porter remarked on how often Fortas was called away from meetings to take phone calls from the White House. "People there practically lost track of him," said one lawyer. "He was living on the telephone or at the White House."

Not that the firm was suffering. To the contrary, its business was flourishing, but under the circumstances the prosperity made some of the partners a bit uncomfortable. "Unfortunately," one said later, "a lot of people assumed the firm was growing so rapidly because Johnson was in the White House. I don't deny that a lot of people came here because they thought we had some special association. But Fortas had always had an extraordinary ability to get clients, including the period when Eisenhower was President."

Still, the notion persisted that Fortas's ties with the White House might bring his firm's clients some special advantage in solving their varied problems with the government. Some members of the press noted, for example, that Arnold, Fortas & Porter represented Philip Morris while the controversy over cigarettes and health was at its height. And they wondered if it was only a coincidence that Lyndon Johnson omitted any mention of the dangers of cigarette smoking from a major presidential message on the state of the nation's health.

Fortas himself generally kept silent about his relationship with the President. But in what seems to have been a Puckish departure from his customary discretion, he listed himself, in the 1965–66 edition of *Who's Who in the South and Southwest,* as "presidential adviser," and gave his address as "care of the White House, 1600 Pennsylvania Avenue, Washington, D.C."

The subjects on which Lyndon Johnson sought Fortas's counsel and heeded it were numerous and varied. Culture was one. Fortas tried unobtrusively to elevate the doggedly middlebrow standards that prevailed at the Johnson White House by arranging for Rudolf Serkin, Isaac Stern and others of his virtuoso friends to perform at official functions. A connoisseur of fine sculpture and painting as well as great music, Fortas once took time out from his weightier responsibilities to negotiate a dispute between the President and the celebrated sculptor Jacques Lipchitz. Eric Goldman, who was the President's special consultant on intellectual and cultural matters, had commissioned Lipchitz to design a bust of Johnson for a medallion to be presented to a group of young scholars. When Johnson got a look at the sample of Lipchitz's avant-garde work, he pronounced it "the goddamnest thing," and refused to have anything more to do with him.

For three days Goldman tried vainly to change the President's mind, while Lipchitz sulked and hinted darkly around town that he was the victim of presidential anti-Semitism. Finally, Fortas, a friend of Lipchitz and an admirer of his work, "effectively intervened," as Goldman put it. Johnson agreed to two brief sittings which he and Lipchitz endured with pained politeness. When confronted with the finished work Johnson grumbled: "Looks like I've been dead three weeks and maybe ought to be." But he agreed to let it pass. The incident may have contributed to Eric Goldman's ap-

[97]

praisal of Fortas as "the man who throughout the Johnson Administration was probably the greatest single influence on the President."

Having seen Johnson through a successful transition to the presidency, Fortas was called on to help the President prepare for the 1964 election. As the campaign began, the prospects seemed bright for the President and his party. In his first months in the White House Johnson had taken firm control of the reins of power. The Republican opposition was beset by bitter internal rivalries that were to culminate in open warfare on the floor of the 1964 convention, seizure of control by the party's ultraconservative faction, and the nomination of Barry Goldwater. Still Johnson was wary of the dangers of overconfidence. Moreover, he was painfully aware that he had inherited his office by tragic accident from John F. Kennedy, whose brief presidency was fast becoming a national legend. He was determined not only to win, but to win a victory impressive enough to overshadow the Kennedy myth and settle all doubts about his right to the presidency.

To help with overall strategy Johnson established an informal senior advisory board whose members included Jim Rowe, a friend from New Deal days, Clark Clifford, who had mapped the strategy for Harry Truman's upset victory in the 1948 election, and Fortas. According to campaign chronicler Theodore White, one or the other and sometimes all three were involved in every major decision and speech of the campaign. They devised the complicated scheme by which Johnson disposed of Robert Kennedy as a vice-presidential possibility. First the President told Kennedy, well in advance of the nominating convention, that he did not want him as a running mate. When the attorney general balked at taking himself out of contention voluntarily, Johnson publicly proclaimed a transparent formula for eliminating "any member of my cabinet or any of those who meet regularly with the cabinet" from consideration for Vice President. Later Kennedy wisecracked: "I'm sorry I took so many nice fellows over the side with me."

During the campaign, Fortas gave special attention to combating Republican efforts to make the Johnson Administration's morality, or rather the lack of it, a political issue. By nominating Barry Goldwater they had yielded the middle ground in national politics to the Democrats. Goldwater's right-wing rhetoric alarmed a number of Americans who feared he meant to undo many of the reforms of the previous three decades. The Republicans found it difficult to attack Johnson's handling of the economy, which was booming, or of foreign affairs. Except for the still smale-scale conflict in Vietnam, the nation was at peace. With almost no other issue left to them, Republican leaders desperately sought to fire suspicions that Lyndon Johnson was not nearly so scrupulous or so ethical as he should be.

Their most obvious target was the Johnson family personal fortune, a subject on which Fortas had become expert. During his years in Congress Johnson had acquired several television stations in Texas and had made them the foundation of a financial empire that extended into real estate and banking. The broadcasting licenses were in Lady Bird Johnson's name, but there were many indications that Lyndon Johnson took an active role in the business. His interest in an industry subjected to Federal regulation raised ethical questions Lyndon Johnson realized he could no longer ignore when he became President. But the Johnsons were reluctant to sell outright their lucrative television stations and decided instead to place them in trust until the President left public office. In the early days of Johnson's presidency, Fortas drew up the agreement, which he later described as "the tightest, toughest trust arrangement ever drawn up for a public official." Critics pointed out that the principal trustee, A. W. Moursund, was a long-time friend and business associate of Johnson's, but Fortas contended that anyone who objected to that arrangement "just doesn't know Judge Moursund."

Still, the extent of the family's holdings attracted the interest of a number of publications, including the Washington *Star,* the *Wall Street Journal* and *Life* magazine. When ques-

[99]

tions on the subject were raised at the White House, reporters were generally referred to Fortas for answers. In an effort to curb speculation, Fortas arranged for the reputable accounting firm of Haskins & Sells to compute the net worth of the Johnson family. The accountants came up with a figure of $3.4 million. But critics contended that the figure was misleading, since it was based on the original purchase price of the properties, most of which had increased substantially in value over the years. In August 1964 *Life* produced its own accounting of the Johnson family wealth, which it estimated at $14 million.

Whatever the correct figure was, it was hard for the Republicans to capitalize on it. They could find no hard evidence that the President had ever used his political power for financial gain. The legal maneuverings involving the Johnson family's various corporate entities defied description in a stump speech or a TV spot commercial. *Life* compared unraveling these transactions to a Western movie "where the cowboys ride off in a cloud of dust to the south, the herd stampedes northeastward, the Indians start to move westward but, once out of sight, circle toward the north, the rustlers drift eastward and the cavalry, coming to the rescue, gets lost entirely."

The Bobby Baker case also offered potential ammunition for the Republican morality crusade. But so far, despite all the allegations and innuendos, Baker had not yet been indicted, much less convicted of anything. Meanwhile, whenever the subject came up, Johnson sought to emphasize his remoteness from his one-time assistant. Still, gossip and rumor imputing sleazy behavior to the President or his associates persisted, and Fortas was given major responsibility for checking and rebutting the stories. As the campaign moved into its final weeks, one Democratic worker felt as if he were part of "a damn vice squad" of which Fortas was "squad leader." Then, just a month before election day, a sordid incident involving one of the President's closest assistants seemed to provide the Republicans with just the sort of evidence they had been looking for.

On the night of October 7, Walter Jenkins, the President's chief of staff, took a break from his rigorous campaign duties to attend a party given by *Newsweek* magazine to celebrate its move into new Washington offices. After a few drinks Jenkins left the party, crossed the street to the YMCA and entered the basement men's room, a known hangout for homosexuals. Within the hour he was arrested, together with an aged Army veteran, and charged with disorderly conduct. Jenkins posted bail, was released and went home to hope that no one would find out what had happened. Five years before, as it later became known, he had been arrested in the same place under similar circumstances, but had managed to escape public attention by forfeiting his bail money and not standing trial.

This time he was not that fortunate. Rumors of the arrest soon began to spread in the capital, and on October 14 the Washington *Star,* acting on a phone tip, checked police records and confirmed the story. When the *Star* called the White House for comment, the President and his press secretary, George Reedy, were out of town campaigning. An aide passed the word to Jenkins, who did what years of working for Lyndon Johnson had taught him to do. He called Fortas.

"I'm in terrible trouble," Jenkins said. "I have to see you."

A few minutes later Jenkins arrived at Fortas's home in a condition approaching shock. Fortas took him upstairs to his study, where Jenkins poured out his story.

"What is the charge specifically and is it true or is it not?" Fortas asked.

But Jenkins, Fortas said later, "could not at that moment put one word consecutively after another." Fortas moved quickly. He had Jenkins sent to a hospital, tried vainly to reach his wife, then called Clark Clifford and told him to meet him at the *Star.*

Though it is overshadowed in the capital by the richer and larger *Washington Post,* the *Evening Star* has a well-deserved reputation for aggressiveness and accuracy. Now its editors had a substantial scoop on their hands and they were understandably reluctant to give it up. Fortas told the *Star's* editors he did not know whether the Jenkins story was true "or whether it is the kind of desperate thing that sometimes happens in Washington." But the *Star* had proof of the story's accuracy from police records. Fortas argued that the *Star* and other Washington papers "don't ordinarily publish information about incidents of this kind." But the editors pointed out that, considering Jenkins's relationship to the President, this was hardly an ordinary incident.

Fortas then threw himself and Jenkins on the mercy of the editors. Jenkins, he said, was a broken man who had ruined his health in the service of his President and his country. He had a wife and six young children; surely compassion demanded that the *Star* delay its scoop until Fortas could prepare Mrs. Jenkins for the shock that was to come. Besides, Fortas added, to print the story now would serve no useful purpose. Jenkins was in the hospital and whenever he left there he would not return to the White House. This was a remarkable assertion for Fortas to have made since he had not yet talked to Lyndon Johnson about Jenkins. But the *Star's* editors must have been convinced that Fortas could speak for the President on such matters. At any rate they agreed to hold the story. Fortas and Clifford then hurried to the offices of Washington's other two newspapers, the *Post* and the *Daily News,* where they made the same appeal, strengthened by the *Star's* demonstration of forbearance, and won the same agreement.

But the story was too hot and too widely known to keep for long. That same evening United Press International broke the news, and Walter Jenkins's misfortune swiftly became a matter of public knowledge. For the moment, the Johnson camp was stunned. For years Jenkins had had access to closely guarded information on the nation's security. The alarming possibility was raised that he might have been blackmailed by foreign agents since his original arrest in 1959. Given that kind of ammunition it seemed conceivable that Goldwater and the Republicans could reverse the course of the election.

That night Fortas reached Johnson by phone in New York,

where he was campaigning, and the two agreed on a cautious strategy. The White House announced that Jenkins had resigned. It ordered the FBI to determine whether Jenkins had breached national security, a question which the Bureau subsequently answered in the negative. Privately Johnson commissioned a fast telephone survey to test public reaction to the episode. The results indicated that voters have better judgment than politicians ordinarily give them credit for; most said that the disclosures about Jenkins would have no bearing on their choice for President. As one housewife told an interviewer: "I never was going to vote for Jenkins."

Lyndon Johnson went on to defeat Barry Goldwater by a record margin, sweeping into office with him top-heavy Democratic majorities in both houses of Congress. In the glow of Johnson's great personal triumph, Walter Jenkins's personal tragedy was all but forgotten. Harder to forget, and to forgive, for the public was Fortas's attempt to prevent publication of a story which, however unsavory, was a matter of public record and a legitimate piece of news. The mere fact of his presence at the *Star's* office, along with another of the President's close advisers, amounted to pressure which any editor would have found difficult to resist. Under the circumstances, it was both unnecessary and unseemly. Fortas and Johnson, both aggressive men, reacted to nearly every problem by trying to intervene one way or another. The lesson of the Jenkins affair is that sometimes the wisest and most responsible thing to do is simply nothing. By itself, Fortas's role in the Jenkins case was not of great consequence. But it was one of the early indications of a pattern of behavior that eventually undermined the public's faith in both the President and his friend.

THE OFFICE SEEKS THE MAN

ABE FORTAS's friendship with Lyndon Johnson and his influential role in the early months of Johnson's presidency fostered the widespread belief in Washington that sooner or later Fortas would take a high position in the government. The only question seemed to be what position. It was to take all Johnson's vaunted skill at manipulation to find the answer.

In the summer of 1964 when Robert Kennedy resigned as attorney general to run for the U.S. Senate in New York, Johnson urged Fortas to take his place. Fortas declined. Though no official announcement was ever made, as often happens in Washington, numerous unofficial accounts were published of the offer and the declination. The President, according to one version, "moved heaven and earth" to persuade Fortas to accept and kept after him for weeks. But Fortas made clear to the President he was "simply not interested." He had a multitude of reasons.

It would be too great a drain on his time and energies to supervise the Department of Justice along with the other chores the President assigned him. Carol Agger was adamantly opposed to his assuming extra responsibilities, and the prestige of high public office did not attract him. "I've been through all that," he said. Fortas was well into his fifties, a period in life when a prudent man takes stock of himself and tries to budget his remaining years. He wanted time for his music, and he was not yet prepared to sever his relationship with Arnold, Fortas & Porter. "We've got a lot of fine young lawyers who marry fine young wives and have fine young babies," he told *Esquire*. "I have my responsibilities here." Though he did not mention it to interviewers, he also had his own financial situation to consider. The attorney general of the United States was then paid only $35,000 a year, a substantial comedown from the $200,000 level that Fortas enjoyed at the law firm.

Another drawback that Fortas did not bring up in public was the loss of his independence. For twenty years no man had been his boss. His relationship to Lyndon Johnson was friend to friend. It was one thing to help a friend as a favor, but it would be quite another thing to be directly subjected to the will of this very demanding President.

Apart from his own reservations, Fortas could make a case that his appointment to an official position would limit his services to Lyndon Johnson. As a private citizen, free from the inhibitions of protocol, he could roam far and wide into whatever area most troubled the President at any particular moment. During the 1965 civil war in the Dominican Republic, Fortas was pressed into service as an intermediary. When fighting broke out in that tiny country between supporters of liberal ex-President Juan Bosch and right-wing forces, Johnson, fearful of another Communist takeover in the Caribbean, ordered in the Marines. Embittered by the attitude of the U.S. ambassador, Bosch told his side of the story to an old friend of Fortas's, Chancellor Jaime Benítez of the University of Puerto Rico. While the fighting raged, Benítez got in touch with Fortas by telephone. Fortas relayed Bosch's views to Johnson and helped arrange for the dispatch of John Barlow Martin as the President's special emissary to the embattled country. Later Johnson sent Fortas himself to Puerto Rico to establish a secret liaison with Bosch. This was certainly not the sort of assignment he could undertake as attorney general.

In the face of Fortas's many objections, the President decided not to press the appointment on him. Instead, he gave the job to Nicholas Katzenbach, Robert Kennedy's deputy at the Justice Department. As for Fortas, Johnson decided to wait for another vacancy.

That opportunity did not simply present itself; Lyndon Johnson created it. The occasion was the death of his ambassador to the United Nations, Adlai Stevenson, who was stricken by a heart attack in London in the summer of 1965. Johnson's ensuing actions can best be understood against the background of mounting national tension and LBJ's own sense of personal frustration. Only months before, he had won election by the greatest popular margin in history. He had made clear from the first that he intended to use his mandate to carry out the most sweeping social and economic reforms the nation had seen since the New Deal. Yet some of the liberal leaders, who in Johnson's view should have been his strongest supporters, were turning into his severest critics. They were not yet great in number but they were passionate and articulate, and the attention they commanded in the press and in the universities threatened the President's grip on the country.

Their grievance was the rapidly escalating conflict in Vietnam. It was a war whose complexities Johnson could not fully fathom. He wanted only to stamp it out and carry on with building the Great Society at home. But the harder he stamped, the more his liberal critics harassed him. Johnson badly wanted more time. If he could keep the liberal disaffection from spreading until he somehow finished the war, he could salvage his presidency.

In this regard Adlai Stevenson had been of great value. Twice defeated for the presidency, he had remained a poetic figure for whom millions reserved respect and affection. As long as he served the Administration at the United Nations he gave the stamp of credibility to Johnson's promise to bring peace and justice to Vietnam. His passing was an untimely blow, and Johnson urgently sought a replacement of comparable stature.

No one on the scene could fully match Stevenson's prestige at home or abroad, but the man who came closest in Johnson's mind was Supreme Court Justice Arthur Goldberg. Goldberg's skill as a negotiator, sharpened in countless labor bargaining sessions, would serve him well in the diplomatic world. Of more political significance was Goldberg's excellent standing among the various liberal factions whose good will Johnson needed. His years as the chief legal adviser to the CIO and the steelworkers union had earned Goldberg the trust of the labor movement. As the most prominent Jew in public life he had the admiration of the liberal financial backers and intellectual leaders in the Jewish community. Also, it was remembered that Goldberg had been called to public service, as secretary of labor, by John F. Kennedy, whose memory still had a powerful hold on liberal loyalties.

Arthur Goldberg considered his position at the Court, which Kennedy had conferred upon him in 1962, the signal honor of his life and the crowning accomplishment of his career. But such sentiments did not deter Lyndon Johnson. One of his first acts as President had been to persuade Chief Justice Earl Warren, much against Warren's better judgment, to head the investigation into John Kennedy's assassination. He had warned Warren that the uncertainty over Kennedy's slaying threatened the nation's stability and security and insisted that the Chief Justice was the only man who could lead a credible inquiry. He used much the same approach on Goldberg, calling upon him, in Goldberg's words, "to join in the greatest adventure in man's history—the effort to bring the rule of law to govern the relations between sovereign states. It is that or doom," said Goldberg. "I have accepted as one simply must."

Justice Goldberg owed Johnson nothing and wanted nothing from him. His position on the Court was his for life no matter how Lyndon Johnson or any other President felt about it. As for the post at the United Nations, Goldberg must certainly have realized that past ambassadors had exerted little authority or influence. Adlai Stevenson's own tenure there had been marked by continual frustration. His seduction by the President can be credited either to an unsurpassed nobility of spirit or to an equally expansive conceit that permitted him to believe Lyndon Johnson's assurances that the nation's fate depended on his succeeding Adlai Stevenson.

At the White House, when the public announcement was made, Goldberg said: "I shall not, Mr. President, conceal the pain with which I leave the Court after three years of service. It has been the richest and most satisfying period of my career." Then he left for three frustrating years at the United Nations, an experience which did nothing to improve his reputation or self-esteem. Later he made a vain effort to win elective office as governor of New York. At one point in his fitful campaign against Nelson Rockefeller an admiring voter told Goldberg: "I wish you were still on the Supreme Court." Goldberg wistfully replied: "So do I, sometimes."

Stevenson died on July 14. Two days later Johnson had Goldberg's resignation in hand. Then he set out after Fortas.

No appointment a President makes approaches in enduring significance his selection of a Justice for the Supreme Court. The President himself is limited by the Constitution to eight years in office, and when he departs his executive retinue goes with him. But Justices serve for life, resolving great national controversies long after the President who appointed them has left the political scene. In 1965 the Justices of the Supreme Court included two, Hugo Black and William O. Douglas, who has been appointed by Franklin Roosevelt more than a quarter of a century earlier. Yet the lifetime tenure of Justices also limits a President's power to shape the High Court to his taste. No President ever knows how many appointments he will be able to make or when they will occur. Franklin Roosevelt went through his entire first term, his bold reforms hamstrung by a conservative majority on the Court, before he had a chance to appoint his first Justice. Moreover, once a Justice takes his seat he becomes his own man, free, as many Presidents have learned to their intense dismay, to chart his own course.

Having witnessed Dwight Eisenhower's shock at the liberal decisions of Chief Justice Warren, Lyndon Johnson was determined to avoid such surprises for himself. This made Fortas's appointment particularly appealing. There was no other candidate Johnson knew so well, trusted so completely and could rely on so confidently to lend support to Johnsonian policies. From Johnson's point of view it would be more advantageous to have Fortas at the Court than running the Justice Department as attorney general. The judiciary proceeded at a more deliberate pace than the agencies of the executive branch, thus allowing Fortas more time to spend on the President's infinite problems. Still another factor made the vacancy appear tailor-made for Fortas. Goldberg had vacated what had come to be considered the Jewish seat on the Court. The precedent was of dubious logic and validity but of substantial political importance. It had been established by Woodrow Wilson's appointment of Louis Dembitz Brandeis in 1916 and Lyndon Johnson was not about to become the first President in half a century to break that tradition.*

Beyond all these considerations, Johnson realized that for most lawyers the Supreme Court was the pinnacle of professional attainment; it was a rich prize to bestow upon a friend. Johnson may well have recalled Franklin Roosevelt's appointment of Felix Frankfurter to the High Court. Frankfurter had been as close to FDR as Fortas was to Johnson. In the early days of the New Deal he had politely declined Roosevelt's offer to become Solicitor General of the United States. But in 1939, when FDR told Frankfurter he was nominating him to be a Supreme Court Justice, Frankfurter was overwhelmed with gratitude. His only regret, he told the President, was that

---

* Though Brandeis was the first Jewish Justice, by the time he resigned, in 1939, Felix Frankfurter had been appointed to the Court. Brandeis himself was replaced by William Douglas, and Frankfurter's seat became the so-called Jewish seat.

his mother was not alive to hear the news. It was Frankfurter's seat on the Court, filled by Goldberg on Frankfurter's retirement, that Johnson now offered to Fortas.

Fortas was a very different man from Felix Frankfurter, and much harder to persuade. The President first broached the matter to him at the White House on July 16 while Fortas and his wife were dining with the Johnsons on the Truman Balcony. "Abe was moved, quiet, grateful," Lady Bird Johnson wrote later. But he went home to think it over. Practical considerations weighed heavily upon him. He had just purchased a $250,000 home in Georgetown, he had a $100,000 mortgage to pay off and he and Carol had ambitious plans for redecorating. And he still felt his obligations to his law firm.

On July 19, 1965, Fortas wrote Lyndon Johnson a letter in his own hand in which he reiterated his desire to remain in private practice and his belief that he would be of more help to the President if he were unencumbered by official duties. With a "heart full of gratitude," he turned the job down.

Two days later, when Fortas met with Lady Bird Johnson to discuss plans for the proposed Johnson Library at the University of Texas, she asked about his decision. "With a wry smile," Fortas talked to her about the difficulties of leaving the law firm, where so many people depended on him. And he added: "If the President were faced with any real troubles, I would want to be around to help him. And if I were on the Court, I could not." Mrs. Johnson, a persistent and practical woman, told him that if his refusal was not irrevocable, "he had better let Lyndon know right away."

Meanwhile word of Johnson's offer to Fortas leaked out. When newsmen questioned Bill Moyers, the White House press secretary, he reminded them of Fortas's well-known reluctance to give up his law practice. But then he added, significantly, the White House press corps thought, that Fortas was highly regarded by the President, by lawyers and "by everyone with whom he has worked." Moreover, Moyers pointed out, he himself had once told the President he was not interested in a government post; yet, as everyone could see, "I'm here."

Nowhere was speculation more intense about what the President would do than at the Supreme Court in the chambers of the lately resigned Justice Goldberg. The two young men who had only recently arrived to serve as Goldberg's clerks for the forthcoming year, and who knew they would almost certainly be retained by his successor, pressed Goldberg for news. Goldberg told them that the President was insistent on appointing Fortas, whom Goldberg himself considered to be an excellent choice. "The President says he's going to appoint Abe and Abe says no. The President won't even consider other names. He's going to wear him down," Goldberg predicted. "He'll wait until the end of time."

But Johnson soon grew tired of waiting. Never a patient man, the pressures of the presidency had made him more importunate than ever. On July 28, two weeks after Stevenson's death, he phoned Fortas and invited him to the White House to attend a press conference. "I'm going to be making a statement on Vietnam," he said. But as soon as Fortas arrived in the oval office, his host made clear that he had more on his mind that day than the war. With mock solemnity, he quickly reviewed Fortas's objections to the Supreme Court appointment. As he understood it, LBJ said, Fortas was concerned about young lawyers at his firm who depended on him and about the mortgage payments on his house. Johnson paused to allow these arguments to eliminate themselves by their own frivolity. "As to the rest of it," Johnson said firmly, "you better let me be the judge of where you can help me best."

Finally, the President reminded his friend there was a war on. "I'm sending fifty thousand boys to Vietnam," Johnson said. "I want you to go to the Supreme Court." It was a masterful flourish, evoking images of battle, young men called upon to risk their lives, and their beleaguered Commander-in-Chief. Now he had given Fortas his marching orders and he expected Fortas, like Arthur Goldberg, to be a good soldier and obey.

Triumphantly the President led his guest into the East Room, where he sat off to the side while the President launched into a text he had prepared for the television cameras. First, he sought once again to justify the strange conflict in Vietnam to the nation. "This is a different kind of war," the President acknowledged; but the fact remained, "this is really war." With great stakes in the balance—the control of the vast Asian continent and the security of the United States itself—great sacrifice was called for. The 50,000 additional troops he was dispatching that day, he made clear, were only part of a continuing buildup of American strength in Indochina. Then he spoke of his hopes for peace, his readiness to meet the enemy at the conference table and the latest instructions he had given his new United Nations ambassador, Arthur Goldberg, to enlist the resources of the UN in bringing the fighting to an end.

Finally the President unveiled his surprise: "The distinguished American who was my first choice for the position now vacant on the Supreme Court has agreed to accept this call to his vital duty." The President described Fortas as "a scholar, a profound thinker, a lawyer of superior ability and a man of humane and deeply compassionate feelings toward his fellow man"—an appraisal, he was confident, that was widely shared in the nation. As everyone knew, "on numerous occasions" Fortas had declared he would not accept appointment to any position. "In this instance," Johnson declared, "the job has sought the man. Mr. Fortas agrees that the duty and the opportunity of service on the highest court of this great country is not a call that any citizen can reject."

Fortas's own remarks to newsmen after the presidential announcement were appropriately muted. He felt "a little overwhelmed." Yes, the position had been offered to him before. "I had reminded the President that I was not seeking any government post, judicial or otherwise. The President was kind enough to say it was a place where I could perform superior service."

For all his well-justified confidence in his powers of persuasion, Lyndon Johnson did not choose to strain them by inviting Carol Agger to share in his surprise. At the moment that the President was announcing her husband's nomination, she was protecting the interests of a client at the offices of the Internal Revenue Service. She had been given no warning and the news stunned her. "She refused to believe it," an IRS official said. Her later public reaction was carefully noncommittal: "All such drastic changes in one's life take considerable thought." One thing that would not change, though, was her career. As propriety demanded, Fortas's name would be dropped from the name of the law firm he had helped found, but the new Justice's wife would continue to practice there. "I have been in the law all my life," she said, "and I don't expect to give it up now."

In the Congress, the President's decision provoked some protest. Fortas himself had confided to friends his concern that his close relationship to the President might make him vulnerable to attack, and, sure enough, this was the line his critics took. Republican Congressman Durward C. Hall of Missouri charged that Fortas had been "a quiet participant in some of the more dubious transactions of the Johnson Administration." He specifically mentioned Fortas's efforts to prevent publication of the Walter Jenkins story and his brief stint as Bobby Baker's lawyer. Senator John Williams, Republican of Delaware, known as a stickler for propriety, acknowledged Fortas's legal ability, but complained: "Contrary to the President's claim that he had looked all over America to find the best qualified man for the job, it is quite obvious that he did not look far beyond his inner circle of friends."

These few dissenters were drowned out by a chorus of praise. In Fortas's home state, the *Chattanooga Times* pointed approvingly to the nominee's "deep commitment to the rule of law in the affairs of free men." In New York the

Republican *Herald Tribune* said: "From the standpoint of letting nothing get in the way of choosing the best man, the appointment merits high marks." The *New York Times* forecast "a significantly useful career on the Supreme Court," and the *Washington Post* saw "every reason to believe" that the nominee would serve the court "with great distinction."

Moreover, when the Senate Judiciary Committee convened to consider the nomination, it had before it the laudatory endorsements of Fortas's prominent friends and clients. Former Army Secretary Kenneth C. Royall praised Fortas's "wisdom and excellent judgment." Coca Cola's senior vice president, Benjamin Oehlert, called him a man of "the very highest character and principle."

The committee itself, though its members included some of the Senate's most determined conservatives, seemed little disposed to challenge the President's judgment. The only testimony offered against the nomination was an attempt to depict Fortas as a fellow traveler during the 1930's. He was accused of having joined Red-tainted organizations and of having worked alongside Communists at the Agricultural Adjustment Administration. The 100 or so lawyers on the AAA's legal staff during Fortas's tenure included a handful identified years later as Communists or Communist sympathizers. These included John Abt, Lee Pressman, and, according to Whittaker Chambers, at least, Alger Hiss. Had this been brought up when Senator McCarthy was in his prime, it might have stirred a fuss. But in 1965 the Judiciary Committee had little interest in such innuendoes.

When Marjorie Shearon, editor of a publication called *Challenge to Socialism,* testified about Communist activities at the AAA, Senator James Eastland asked: "What has this got to do with the nominee?"

"Well, if your powers of deduction do not make it have anything to do with him then it probably doesn't," said Miss Shearon. Still, she insisted, there was something wrong. "A man who is as clever as Mr. Fortas is said to be," she argued, could not have associated himself with Communists "and not been aware of what he was doing."

"What was he doing?" demanded Senator Roman Hruska. "I haven't the slightest idea," said Miss Shearon.

Fortas's own recollections were hazy. He was "not sure" whether he had ever belonged to the Southern Conference of Human Welfare, one of the organizations cited by Miss Shearon. He might have joined the International Juridical Association; but if he had, he could not remember attending any meetings. "That was the day when joining was mighty easy," he testified, "and we were all quick to do it." As for Alger Hiss, he knew him only "in the sense that we served in the same Government agency. As a matter of fact," he added with a measure of indignation, "in all these years when I have successively had to read things about myself and Alger Hiss, and so on, it has occurred to me that maybe I ought to have a cause of action against the U.S. Government."

He might well have let the matter drop there; no one seemed to have taken Miss Shearon's allegations seriously. But Fortas could not resist an inclination to artful elaboration. He depicted his AAA career as a period of youthful innocence, and a very brief one at that. When he came there, he said, "I was a boy fresh out of Tennessee three years before." His service was limited, he testified, to the summer of 1933, "and then the following Christmas holiday and so on." That summary hardly squared with the AAA's records which show that Fortas worked full time for the agency for nearly a year, between July 1933 and November 1934, with time off to teach for a term at Yale. His memory might have failed him about this long-ago period, but it would have been easy enough to refresh his recollection by examining his own biography in *Who's Who,* which listed him as "assistant chief, legal division, AAA, 1933–34."

But the senators plunged ahead into areas of more immediate interest. Some were worried about a trend in Court decisions, which, said John McClellan of Arkansas, "favors the criminal rather than protects society." The doctrine seemed to be gaining hold that the poor defendant deserved special treatment in the courts. Where did Fortas stand? As the defender of Clarence Gideon, Fortas of course affirmed his belief in a poor man's right to counsel. "But," he added reassuringly, "I would utterly reject any suggestion that the scales of justice should be weighted by one ounce or a fraction of an ounce in his favor because he is poor. Justice," said Fortas, "is not like the progressive income tax."

Next, Senator Hruska asked about Fortas's role in the Walter Jenkins case and Fortas offered his version of the events beginning with his phone call from Jenkins and culminating with the agreement of the *Evening Star's* editors not to run the story. "I shall always honor these men at the *Star*," Fortas said. "I shall always as a human being feel grateful to them."

Hruska pressed on, reaching the issue that nagged at everyone's mind. Over the years, he observed, Fortas had formed "a very close friendship and relationship" with the President, extending into "professional, business and political dealings." Hruska presumed that before long various aspects of the President's program would reach the docket of the Supreme Court. There was no way to soften the key question, so Hruska put it bluntly but politely: "Is there anything in your relationship with the President that would militate in any way against your being able to sit on that bench and pass judgment on cases that came along and thus would affect your ability to function in the true judicial fashion and tradition?"

Fortas was obviously well prepared to deal with this subject. "The short answer to that," he said forthrightly, is "absolutely not." In a lighter vein, he added that there were two things that had been "vastly exaggerated" about himself. "One is the extent to which I am a presidential adviser, and the other is the extent to which I am a proficient violinist. I am a very poor violinist but very enthusiastic, and my relationship with the President has been exaggerated out of all connection with reality." It was hard to persuade the public and the press of this, Fortas complained archly, because all his denials were taken as fresh affirmation of their suspicions. Nevertheless, he assured the committee, there was "no possibility" that his relationship with the President "could in any way enter into any judgment that I might make."

That settled that. The hearing adjourned in less than three hours, with Senator Sam Ervin's concluding observation reflecting the generally amiable tone of the proceedings. The senator, an inveterate teller of tales from the North Carolina hill country, remarked on a distinction between the judiciary and the Senate. If the facts of a case were known, Ervin said, a court's decision could be safely forecast. "But the U.S. Senate operates on a different basis. You can't foretell what it will do because it is like Josh Billings's mule that don't kick to no rule whatsoever."

In this case, however, the Senate's reaction was predictable. Fortas's nomination received the unanimous endorsement of the Judiciary Committee, and soon thereafter it was approved by a voice vote of the Senate. On October 4, 1965, in the courtroom where he had often distinguished himself as an advocate, Lyndon Johnson's first choice took the oath of office and became, somewhat against his will, Mr. Justice Fortas.

ON THE BENCH—AND ON CALL

THE SUPREME COURT seemed to present an alien setting for a man of Fortas's worldly background. The Court is the most cloistered of government institutions. The Justices need not answer to any constituency; their office is designed to shield them from lobbyists, legislators and even the President. They meet behind the walls of a great marble structure which one Justice called "almost bombastically pretentious." The building itself contributes to judicial detachment. Its broad corridors are quiet, even when tourists troop through, and bronze gates guard the way to the Justices' chambers.

But for all its outer serenity, the Court, as Mr. Justice Holmes observed, is a storm center. Ultimately, nearly every important national controversy is fought out among its members, each of whom carries the weight of the Court's immense authority on his own conscience. Fortas, accustomed to combat most of his life, readily adapted to this new arena. Putting aside his well-advertised reluctance to join the Court, he set about establishing himself as one of its important figures.

Fortas first had to contend with the tradition of seniority which is deeply rooted in the customs of the Court. Seniority dictates the rigid seating arrangements of the Justices at their high mahogany bench, where Fortas took his appointed place at the extreme left of the Chief Justice. It also governs procedure in the conference room where the Court conducts its secret deliberations. The junior Justice serves as doorkeeper and message taker for the rest, and when cases come up for discussion is the last to give his views. Once the issue is settled, the Chief Justice, or the senior Justice in the majority, decides who will write the Court's opinion, a choice sometimes influenced by expertise developed over years on the bench.

Fortas, however, was no ordinary junior Justice. He had come to the Court with the celebrity and status of a presidential adviser. He could discuss matters of state from personal experience gathered at Lyndon Johnson's side. Moreover, the other Justices had ample firsthand evidence of his proficiency in the law. Justice John Marshall Harlan, himself considered by many to be the Court's preeminent legal craftsman, confided to law clerks that he rated Fortas as the most brilliant advocate to appear before the High Court in his time.

The new Justice's influence at the Court was heightened by the close relationship he developed with the Chief Justice. Earl Warren had thought highly of Fortas as a lawyer, and his favorable opinion was reinforced when the lawyer became his colleague. The same astuteness and self-assurance that had inspired the trust of Fortas's corporate clients won him the confidence of the Chief. Warren soon took to visiting the new Justice's chambers to consult with him on fine points of the law and, some observers thought, assigned him a larger share of important opinions than some of his seniors on the bench.

Several of Fortas's colleagues were exceptional men in one way or another. Harlan was widely respected for his polished scholarship, Douglas for his intellectual range and energy, Black for his religious dedication to the bench. Fortas's own work on the Court was distinguished by an intuitive flair for the law, enriched by practical experience and supple intelligence. His imagination was not confined by the ordinary bounds of jurisprudence. "He had the kind of intellectual wit that some composers and artists have," one of his law clerks said. "He could see things out of conventional focus." His view did not always win majority support. But whether he was in the majority or not, Fortas often proposed fresh and provocative solutions to timeworn problems. Dissenting from a ruling upholding the conviction of a chronic alcoholic for public drunkenness, Fortas argued that "criminal penalties may not be inflicted upon a person for being in a condition he is powerless to change," a principle, he maintained, that is "the cornerstone of the relations between a civilized state and its citizens."

Though he was appropriately solemn when occasion demanded, Fortas had a playful turn of mind that recognized the law's absurdities. He once chided a law clerk who was sermonizing about a case: "Your trouble is that you have no sense of Halloween." He enjoyed mocking pomposity. On the bench, for his own amusement he occasionally composed doggerel lampooning the other Justices and the lawyers who appeared before the Court. Discussing antitrust clients in an after-dinner speech to a lawyers' group, Justice Fortas reminisced: ". . . There are few things in a lawyer's life more rewarding than a substantial corporation whose officers are threatened with criminal prosecution. Here we have an ideal combination: A long purse, moral indignation, a protracted trial and a reasonable amount of fear."

The bite of Fortas's wit was evident in his written opinions. He saw himself as a "wordsmith," and the vigor and color of his language called attention to his judgments. In his first written opinion as a Justice, he sarcastically disposed of the conviction of a civil-rights demonstrator for obstructing a sidewalk. If the sidewalks in Birmingham, Alabama, could really be so easily blocked, Fortas wrote, "a general alarm for the people of Birmingham would be in order. Their use of sidewalks would be hazardous beyond measure." In an antitrust case he accused the Court's majority of bolstering their argument by concocting an artificial category which he likened to a "strange, red-haired, bearded, one-eyed man with a limp classification." Fortas generally drove his points home with crisp staccato sentences, but at times, particularly when he was intensely involved in a case, he became prolix. Dissenting from a decision that allowed the Georgia legislature to pick the winner of a gubernatorial election in which neither candidate had received a majority of the popular vote, Fortas unreeled this multifaceted sentence:

"Our understanding and conception of the rights guaranteed to the people by the 'stately admonitions' of the Fourteenth Amendment have deepened, and have resulted in a series of decisions, enriching the quality of our democracy, which certainly do not codify state's rights, governmental theories or conceptions of human liberties as they existed in 1824, the date when Georgia adopted its present system of choosing a governor."

During formal arguments of cases in open court, Fortas's aggressive manner and testy questions sometimes seemed designed mainly to fluster. When the Georgia election case was argued, Fortas startled the attorney for the state by questioning him about Georgia's pre-Revolutionary War constitution, a document which the lawyer had never even seen. Nor, it seemed, had anyone else but Fortas.

To an attorney in an important criminal case who contended that confessions were the most effective way to get convictions, Fortas retorted that he supposed Communist countries were exceedingly efficient in convicting criminals. "But I equally suppose," he told the lawyer, "that you join me in horror at convictions obtained without counsel or fair trial."

Fortas's remarks on criminal justice were scrutinized with particular care by the press and the bar. This was the most pressing issue before the High Court during Fortas's first year on the bench, and the Court was sharply divided on the subject. While Justices occasionally shifted ground on individual cases, the Court that Fortas joined could be roughly divided into two main camps. On one side were the four conservatives: John Harlan and Potter Stewart, both appointed by Dwight Eisenhower; Byron White, who was John Kennedy's first appointment to the Court; and Tom Clark, the last of the Truman Justices. On the other side, providing the main thrust behind the liberalism of the Warren Court, were the two Roosevelt appointees, William O. Douglas and Hugo Black, and two other Eisenhower appointees, William Brennan and Warren himself.

Briefly stated, the liberals were determined to use the power and prestige of the Supreme Court to bring about social and political equality and to protect individual rights. They were prepared to remedy what they conceived to be grave injustices, even in areas traditionally reserved to the Congress or to local governments, where their conservative colleagues urged restraint. Accordingly, the liberals had pushed the Court into proclaiming various manifestations of racial discrimination to be unconstitutional and into insisting that legislative bodies reapportion themselves to comply with the principle of one man, one vote. More recently the liberal drive had carried into the emotion-laden area of criminal law enforcement, where efforts to protect the rights of suspects and defendants clashed sharply with mounting public anxiety over violence and lawlessness.

The current controversy had its roots in the *Gideon* decision, which Fortas himself had successfully argued before he joined the Court. In *Gideon,* the Court had declared that every criminal defendant had an absolute right to a lawyer at his trial. But it did not make clear whether or not a lawyer was also required before the trial, when a suspect was in the hands of police whose efforts to obtain evidence might easily jeopardize his rights. The Court sought to answer this question in 1964 in the case of Danny Escobedo, a young Mexican-American. Escobedo had been convicted of murder on the basis of a statement wrung from him by police after they had denied his request to see his lawyer. In a five-to-four decision, written by Arthur Goldberg, the Court threw out Escobedo's conviction. Once a suspect became the focus of investigation, Goldberg declared, he was entitled to a lawyer. Otherwise, he said, "the trial would be no more than an appeal from his interrogation." Goldberg was not impressed by arguments that broadening the right to counsel would discourage confessions and hamstring law enforcement. "If the exercise of constitutional rights will thwart the effectiveness of a system of law enforcement," he declared, "then there is something very wrong with that system."

Nevertheless, the decision created uproar and confusion among local lawmen. To clear the air, during Fortas's first year as a Justice the Court agreed to consider four cases touching on the questioning of suspects, grouped under the heading of *Miranda v. Arizona*. The drama surrounding the forthcoming decision was heightened by Goldberg's resignation. Since his eight former colleagues were assumed still to be split four-to-four on the issue, Fortas's position was expected to be decisive. The first strong indication of where he stood came during arguments on the cases in March of 1966. "The trouble, I must say, is that I hear so much reference to the problem as one of how to convict people who commit crimes," Fortas remarked from the bench. "We are not dealing here just with the criminal and society. It is a problem of the state and the individual in the large, total sense." As Fortas hammered away at the prosecutors' arguments, the lawyers on the defense side took heart. One scribbled an epigram on a piece of paper and passed it to a friend: "If God be Fortas, who can be against us?"

Any lingering doubts about Fortas's views were swept away on the next to the last Monday of the term when the decision on *Miranda* was announced. By a five-to-four vote, with Fortas providing the margin of victory, the Court affirmed its ruling in *Escobedo* and went beyond it. Not only were police obliged to furnish a lawyer to a suspect who asked for one, Chief Justice Warren wrote, but they must also advise him of his right to a lawyer and his right to remain silent before they attempted to question him.

In the wake of *Miranda,* Fortas led the Court into another area of criminal law, hitherto ignored by the Federal courts— the treatment of juvenile offenders. For years the juvenile courts had been given wide freedom to disregard the standard procedures for adult trials so these courts could concentrate on rehabilitation rather than punishment of wayward children. This was the theory. In practice, as Fortas observed, often "the child receives the worst of both worlds: He gets neither the protections accorded to adults nor the solicitous care and regenerative treatment postulated for children."

In Fortas's second year on the Court the Justices considered the appeal of a fifteen-year-old Arizona boy named Gerald Francis Gault who had been committed to a state industrial school for six years for making lewd remarks over the phone. It was an offense for which an adult could have been jailed for no more than two months. Moreover, the boy had not been advised of his right to a lawyer and his right to remain silent under questioning by officials. During the arguments, counsel for Arizona explained that juveniles were not given these and other criminal safeguards because they were not formally charged with crimes.

"You can call it a crime or a not-crime or you can call it a horse," Fortas snapped. "He's still deprived of his liberty."

Assigned to write the opinion, Fortas threw himself into the task. Ordinarily, as is the custom with many Justices, Fortas's law clerks did much of the research and submitted a first draft which served as an outline for the opinion. But on the *Gault* case, one of the clerks said, "Fortas did the whole thing himself, down to the footnotes." What emerged was the most celebrated opinion Fortas would write on the Supreme Court, a sweeping indictment of the high-handed paternalism of juvenile court procedures coupled with a broad guarantee of constitutional rights to young offenders. Fortas said that juveniles were entitled to a lawyer, to cross-examine witnesses and to protection against self-incrimination. "Neither the Fourteenth Amendment nor the Bill of Rights is for adults only," Fortas wrote. "Under our Constitution the condition of being a boy does not justify a kangaroo court."

This was ringing liberal rhetoric, and for the most part Fortas marched in step with the liberal Justices on the Court. He joined them in reversing convictions of Negro demonstrators and upholding Federal power to prosecute murderers of civil-rights workers. He agreed that the poll tax and loyalty oaths for teachers were unconstitutional.

But Fortas's view of the world and the law was too complicated to fit any one rubric. He did not hesitate to break ranks with his customary liberal allies on occasion and follow his own predilections. In the field of antitrust law, the Court's two senior Justices, Black and Douglas, still nurtured the New Deal's hostility to concentration of economic power, and viewed business mergers with suspicion and disapproval. Fortas, having spent twenty post-New Deal years helping big corporations grow bigger, insisted that some mergers could be "distinctly beneficial" to competition. "He has an understanding of how our business world works and has to work, and he's not about to tear it apart," Carol Agger once explained. "A doctrinaire liberal would say everything big is bad; he doesn't." Dissenting from a decision delaying the proposed merger of the Pennsylvania and New York Central railroads, Fortas wrote what he considered the quintessential statement of his economic position: "We should be conservative and restrained, I think, when all we can say is no. The courts may be the principal guardians of the liberties of the people. They are not the chief administrators of its economic destiny."

Freedom of the press was another area where Fortas's background led to disagreement with his liberal colleagues. Black and Douglas had long maintained that the First Amendment guaranteed absolute protection against libel suits and censorship, and their views, particularly on libel, were gaining increasing influence among the other members of the Warren Court. In 1964, in the landmark case of *New York Times v. Sullivan,* the Court ruled that comment on public officials, even if it was factually wrong, could not be held libelous unless it was malicious or published with reckless disregard of the truth. The majority was determined to protect what Justice Brennan called "a profound national commitment to the principle that debate should be uninhibited, robust and wide open . . ."

Fortas was all in favor of free debate, too. But he took a nar-
rower view of First Amendment freedoms than the liberal Justices, in part because he took a much less sanguine view of the
press. It was not hard for him to think of examples of sensationalism and irresponsibility. The headlines given to Senator
McCarthy's reckless charges and to the Walter Jenkins case
were still fresh in his mind. The liberals argued that a free
press protected the public interest. But Fortas believed that
the public also needed protection against the excesses of journalism.

A collision on this issue came during Fortas's first term as a
Justice. By a fascinating coincidence the case also brought before the Court two of the principals in what would later become the climactic chapter in Fortas's public career. The ap-
pellant was *Life* magazine, which in 1968 would delve into
Fortas's relations with Louis Wolfson. The attorney for the
other side was Richard M. Nixon, who between political campaigns was practicing law in New York.

In April of 1966 all concerned were absorbed with the matter at hand, which was laden with complications. The case cen-
tered on a story *Life* had published about the Broadway hit,
The Desperate Hours. The play, later made into a film, was
partly inspired by the experience of James Hill and his
family who in 1952 had been held hostage in their suburban
Philadelphia home by escaped convicts. The circumstances
were altered and touches of violence added for dramatic effect. The real thing had been grim enough; Hill had turned
down offers to sell his account of the incident and moved his
family to Connecticut to avoid publicity. *Life's* story was published in 1955, complete with photos of scenes from the play
reenacted in the Hills' former home. Hill sued Time Incor-
porated for invasion of privacy, charging that the story made
it seem as if the play were a factual reconstruction of his family's ordeal. The New York courts awarded him $30,000.

Life appealed, contending that the verdict infringed on its
right to publish a story of legitimate news interest. Hill happened to be a client of Richard Nixon's law firm. When the

case reached the Supreme Court, Nixon, who saw the chance to express his views on a matter bound to attract wide public attention, decided to make the argument himself. This was his debut before the Supreme Court, and he had prepared for the occasion, he said, by reviewing every decision under New York's privacy law, which had been enacted in 1903. The passage of time, however, had blurred his recollection of the law in his native state of California. When he slipped on a technical point, Earl Warren, calling on his own experience as state attorney general, was quick to correct him.

In presenting his case, Nixon praised *Life's* overall reputation for reliability, the better to demonstrate the injury its story had done to his client. *Life* was "newsy," generally accurate and, Nixon told the Court, "the most popular picture magazine in America today." He stressed the point so much that Fortas interrupted to say that he did not believe that the magazine's quality was at issue before the Court. Nixon's main point was the right to privacy, which, he argued "was of paramount importance." Without this right, Nixon asked, "how is an individual to remain an individual in our mass communications society?"

Forced to choose between freedom of the press and the right to privacy, the Justices wrestled with the problem all spring. Unable to reach a decision, they asked that the case be reargued after the summer recess. Nixon, taking time off from stumping for Republican congressional candidates, and *Life's* attorneys reappeared and refought their battle. Finally in January of 1967 a judgment was announced in favor of freedom of the press and of *Life*. In effect, the Court extended its doctrine on libel of public officials to privacy suits by people who get into the news even unintentionally. Damages could be collected, the Court said, only if the press was malicious or reckless. "Exposure of the self to others in varying degree is a concomitant of life in a civilized community," Justice Brennan wrote for the majority. "The risk of this exposure is an essential incidence of life in a society which places a primary value on freedom of speech and of press."

In a bitter dissent Fortas charged that *Life* had been sloppy about checking a file of news clippings that revealed the differences between the play and the actual experience of the Hills. "The truth was in a folder on the desk of the author of the story," he said. "It was deliberately disregarded by his editor." Though he, too, believed in freedom of the press, Fortas contended: "For this Court totally to immunize the press—whether forthrightly or by subtle indirection—in areas far beyond the needs of news, comments on public persons and events, discussion of public issues and the like would be no service to freedom of the press but an invitation to public hostility to that freedom."

In dealing with obscenity, Fortas was able to find more support for his conception of First Amendment freedoms and limits. In 1957 the Court had decided that obscene materials were not protected by the First Amendment and could be banned. The question remained: What was obscene? For nearly a decade, as the mores of the country changed rapidly, the Court struggled to find a satisfactory answer. Then, in Fortas's first term, it took the case of Ralph Ginzburg, an imaginative New York purveyor of erotica, who had been given a five-year jail sentence for sending obscene publications and advertisements through the mails. In rejecting Ginzburg's appeal the Court established the principle that evidence of "pandering," advertising openly appealing to erotic interest, could tip the scales against a distributor of borderline materials. Fortas, according to his clerks, helped develop this legal formula and urged it upon Justice Brennan, the Court's specialist in obscenity and the author of the *Ginzburg* opinion. In the opinion, Brennan noted indignantly that Ginzburg had sought vainly to have his material postmarked in the towns of Intercourse and Blue Ball, Pennsylvania, finally settling for the less provocatively named community of Middlesex, New Jersey. Also, Brennan charged, the advertising for Ginzburg's publications was permeated by the "leer of the sensualist." He concluded that such "titillation by pornography" supported the finding that Ginzburg's publications were obscene under the law.

The *Ginzburg* decision was part of an effort by the Court to focus obscenity law on the distribution of materials rather than the materials themselves, thus relieving itself of the futile task of serving as a board of censors. The Court's progress in this direction has been awkward and uncertain, but the over-all impact of *Ginzburg* and ensuing rulings has been to relax restrictions against books and films whose distributors avoided offensive merchandising tactics.

At the time, though, the decision was bitterly attacked by civil libertarians, and by Black and Douglas, the Court's two foremost defenders of the First Amendment. "I believe the Federal government is without any power whatever under the Constitution to put any type of burden on speech and expression of ideas of any kind," Black wrote. The First Amendment required the recognition "that sex at least as much as any other aspect of life is so much a part of our society that its discussions should not be made a crime." Said Justice Douglas: "I do not think it permissible to draw lines between the 'good' and the 'bad' and to be true to the constitutional mandate to let all ideas alone."

Fortas sympathized with the views of his liberal colleagues as a matter of philosophy. But judges were not meant to be philosophers; their job, he told his law clerks, was to deal with reality. Unless the Court imposed some limits on obscenity, Fortas believed, public revulsion would be so great that Congress might eventually step in and perhaps even revise the First Amendment. Fortas considered that his approach offered the most realistic defense of free expression. Black and Douglas, because of their devotion to an abstract ideal, were guilty, in Fortas's own pungent phrase, of "whoring after principle."

In their formal dealings with one another the Justices of the Supreme Court are governed by rituals of courtesy. Each weekly conference opens with handshakes all around. When one Justice refers to another in a written opinion he uses the phrase "my brother." Nonetheless, the Justices are, of course, men of varying tastes and temperaments, and some are more nearly brothers than others. Fortas's own relationships with his brethren were shaped by a combination of personal preferences and judicial attitudes.

Fortas's friendship with Earl Warren was fostered by Warren's strong personal ties to the American Jewish community. Warren had a number of close Jewish friends and political associates and he had long been an active worker for Jewish causes. His record on the Court had made him something of a hero to Jewish liberals. Fortas had taken little interest either in the Jewish religion or in secular Jewish organizations before coming to the Court. Early in Fortas's first term, Warren mentioned to the new Justice that he naturally would be excused from the Court's weekly conference, which coincided with an important Jewish holy day. Fortas, who had not observed the holiday in the recent past, saw no reason to change and attended the conference anyway. Warren's strong sense of propriety was disturbed. Later on, when Fortas was on the point of declining an award from an important Jewish organization, Warren remonstrated with him and persuaded him to change his mind. The head of the organization, a friend of Warren's, would be offended if Fortas rejected the proffered honor. Besides, Warren pointed out, Fortas's public position carried with it a responsibility to the Jewish community. Gradually, partly because of Warren's influence, Fortas saw the light. He accepted speaking invitations from Jewish organizations and took an increasing interest in the state of Israel.

Fortas accepted this sort of advice more readily from Warren than he might have from others because of Warren's warmth and sincerity. In their approach to the law the two men differed sharply, as Fortas fully realized. He once contrasted the "straight, uncluttered, unsubtle" way the Chief worked with his own reliance on "ins and outs and intricacies" intended to cover everything "right back to the invention of money." Still, he pointed out to a friend, "we mostly come out the same place—with the same answer." Though some lawyers complained that Warren's legal scholarship left something to be desired, Fortas, according to his clerks, respected Warren as a "unifying influence on the Court, a man who, apart from his own role in specific cases, made the Court function as a unit."

Fortas was also on excellent terms with William Brennan, a hard-working, good-humored Irish Catholic. Both liberal, both flexible, they operated as middlemen on the Court, often teaming up to decide closely contested issues. While Fortas frequently disagreed with the conservative views of Justice Harlan, he admired Harlan's ability and enjoyed his company. Harlan had a summer home in Connecticut near Fortas's, and the two visited back and forth. On occasion Harlan's daughter, an accomplished pianist, joined them, Fortas brought out his violin, and she and he would offer an impromptu recital, to Harlan's delight. Fortas had less in common with the two youngest Justices, Potter Stewart, who was fifty when Fortas joined the Court, and Byron White, who was forty-eight. He did not consider them important personages in the power structure at the Court, and he could at times be almost oblivious to their feelings. Once Fortas offered to join an opinion Stewart had written if Stewart would make a certain change. Stewart made the revision, but Fortas wrote a dissent anyway, without bothering to tell Stewart about it.

On the Court, as before, Fortas and Douglas were close friends. Fortas considered his former teacher to be a near genius, the superior in intelligence of everyone on the Court, himself included. He once paid tribute to Douglas in glowing words that suggest as much about Fortas's own intellectual values as they do about Douglas. "His mind is a cutting instrument of fabulous sharpness," Fortas wrote. "His intellect is a well-ordered, highly organized machine. For this man of intense sentiment, sentiment which cannot be sharply and effectively deployed is slop. To himself, to friend and foe alike, Mr. Justice Douglas is a harsh critic who lies in wait for the slothful, the untidy, the drooling, the soft and sappy. The unerring leap to the jugular, the fantastic speed, the cleanliness of the kill—these are the marks of Douglas's mind."

With Justice Black, it was a very different story. When Fortas joined the Court, Hugo Black's three decades of unrelenting effort had already won him recognition as one of the major forces in the Court's history. Reared in rural Alabama, Black had been one of the rampant young lions of populism in the United States Senate. His appointment to the Court in 1937 met with a cross-fire of criticism. Black's Senate record as an aggressive New Dealer, particularly his wholehearted support of FDR's proposal to pack the Supreme Court, antagonized conservatives; his membership in the Ku Klux Klan during his early political career shocked liberals. Black shrugged off their disapproval and committed himself, heart and mind, to the Court. He was as belligerent a Justice as he had been a senator. So much so, that in 1946 Justice Robert Jackson wrote an extraordinary public letter to the Senate and House Judiciary Committees denouncing Black for his "bullying." Now as he sat at Earl Warren's right hand, nearing his eightieth year, his white hair almost vanished, Justice Black was as indomitable as ever, and if anything more irascible.

Over the years his dissents had become increasingly shrill and bitter when other Justices read meanings into the Constitution that Black insisted were not there. Though he had long spearheaded the Court's efforts to guarantee constitutional rights, Black was vehemently opposed to judges going beyond the Constitution, whose language was unalterably clear, at least to Black. "The Constitution is my legal bible," he once declared. "Its plan of our government is my plan and its destiny, my destiny."

Each time a new Justice came to the Court Black hoped to find a supporter for his own views. He had been disappointed by Arthur Goldberg, whose interpretation of the Constitution was far too loose to suit Black. Fortas, Black hoped, would be different; as an attorney he considered him a precise and sound man of the law. But Black soon found out that Fortas was not prepared to play the role of disciple. Early in Fortas's first term he dissented from one of Black's opinions so persuasively that two Justices changed their votes and Black found himself in the minority. The case, arising from a claim against the Small Business Administration, was not of great importance, but Black always hated to lose.

More significantly, Black detected in Fortas a tendency, particularly on criminal matters, to interpret the Constitution's guarantee of due process of law as a guarantee of fairness. Fairness was one thing, Black believed; due process was something else. Simply because a statute or a court ruling produced a result which a Justice regarded as unfair did not render it unconstitutional. To hold otherwise, Black contended, was to permit judges "to roam at will in the limitless areas of their own beliefs."

The roiling struggle against segregation in the South added to the friction between Fortas and Black. Despite his persistent advocacy of racial equality and freedom of expression, Black was troubled by the sit-in demonstrations that spread across the map of the Old Confederacy in the early 1960's. He believed that the demonstrators were often overly aggressive and violated the rights of others. A sit-in demonstration in a segregated public library in Louisiana was just the sort of thing Black disapproved of. The demonstrators were arrested, but when they appealed to the Supreme Court their conviction was reversed by a five-to-four vote. Fortas, writing for the majority, criticized Louisiana officials for prosecuting the demonstrators. Black was furious. Shaking with anger, he delivered a thirty-minute tirade from the bench, warning that such decisions would lead "misguided" demonstrators to believe they would be "automatically turned loose, so long as whatever they do has something to do with race."

Fortas's ability to turn a phrase and to propound novel formulas helped him win support for overriding Black's strict standards. But at times Fortas rushed to judgment without reconciling the internal contradictions of his reasoning, leaving himself vulnerable to counterattack. Late in his first term, when Fortas circulated his opinion on an important First

Amendment case among his colleagues, Black denounced it as the worst piece of work he had seen in that field in a dozen years. He told the other Justices he would need all summer to write an adequate dissent. Rather than go through that, the Court scheduled the case for reargument the next term. The second time around, Fortas was unable to win a majority for his view. Another Justice was assigned the opinion, with which Black agreed, and Fortas was forced to express his ideas in a dissent.

The rivalry with Black, sometimes approaching a feud in intensity, continued throughout Fortas's career on the Court. Fortas respected Black for his contributions to the Court and for his combative spirit, but he refused to give any ground. "I'm a justice of the Supreme Court," he told his clerks. "I'm not supposed to argue with people, I'm supposed to write my opinion. If Justice Black doesn't like it, let him write his own opinion." Which in fact is what Justice Black usually did. Even when the two Justices were in general agreement on a case, they often wrote separate concurring opinions rather than sign what the other had written.

Though Fortas and Black were well matched in ability, the battle between them, in one sense at least, was an unequal contest. Hugo Black concentrated every fiber of his being on the Supreme Court. This was a commitment Fortas could not make as long as Lyndon Johnson was President of the United States. Fortas had resisted appointment to the Court because, he told the First Lady, his status as a Justice would prevent him from helping Lyndon Johnson if the President faced "real trouble." But, perhaps because Johnson's troubles were so serious and so numerous, Justice Fortas continued to answer the President's calls for help.

One of Fortas's law clerks observed that he had "a tremendous ability to compartmentalize his life, to keep his various roles and interests separate and independent." Nevertheless, it was difficult even for him to prevent the demands of the President who appointed him from affecting his work at the Court. Fortas often took a huge pile of petitions and briefs from the

Court to read at home. But after evenings when he had been summoned to the White House he would return to Court the next morning, his homework unfinished. More than once his clerks noticed that he was "bleary-eyed" after White House social affairs which often included an epilogue of conferences lasting until the small hours of the morning.

The clerks who worked for Fortas when he was first appointed to the Court were well aware of the reputation he had made at his law firm for piling assignments on himself and his subordinates, but they found they were able to keep pace with the Justice with little strain. "He was doing his fair share of the work, which he could handle pretty easily," one of them said. "But he wasn't putting his all into it. Had Lyndon Johnson not been President he probably would have worked us to death."

Fortas served the President on an informal and irregular basis. "He might be around on every issue for a month," said Joseph Califano, who was himself Lyndon Johnson's top special assistant on domestic affairs. "Then you might not see him for two months." The time the Justice spent at the White House could be made up. But the psychological distraction of his responsibilities there were harder to overcome. "When you've been involved in questions of war and peace," one law clerk said, "it's hard to come back and concentrate on whether some injured sailor should get $3,000 or $4,000 in a compensation case."

The close relationship between the President and the Justice inevitably caused considerable gossip and speculation. *Newsweek* reported that "few important Presidential problems are settled without an opinion from Mr. Justice Fortas." The magazine quoted a "well placed insider" to the effect that "the first person the President consults on anything is Abe Fortas." *Time* asserted: "No one outside knows accurately how many times Fortas has come through the back door of the White House, but any figure would probably be too low."

When he discussed his association with the President at all, which was rarely, Fortas tended to minimize and generalize.

The President, he once said, "has done me the honor on some occasions of indicating that he thought I could be of help to him and to the nation in a few critical matters." He was careful to add that whatever these matters might be, they had "nothing whatever to do" with any case that might come before the Supreme Court.

Lyndon Johnson liked to shop around for opinions, depending on the problem at hand, and Fortas was one of a number of men outside his official circle of advisers whom he consulted from time to time. "The President got different things from different people," said Joe Califano. If Fortas was consulted on matters of closest personal concern to the President, such as the trust arrangement for his investments, it was because of their intimacy bred out of long friendship. His involvement in the President's problems was closely linked to his social relationship with the President. "Work and play were all one with Lyndon Johnson," according to Califano. "With few exceptions friendship and the ability to work with him were all merged together and all mixed up. He would have you down to watch movies on Sunday, to go to the ranch, to swim in the pool with him, because he had an enormous feeling of friendship in response to the fact that you were working hard for him."

At White House social functions Fortas was not only a frequent guest but also sometimes an entertainer. "My name is Fortas, I'm a violinist," he once introduced himself to the President's guests. At a party for the National Council on the Arts, Fortas borrowed an antique violin from a member of the Marine Band and played a duet with Isaac Stern. On another occasion he teamed up with Alexander Schneider to play a bit of Mozart, at which point Lyndon Johnson leaned over to another guest, George Meany, president of the AFL-CIO, and asked: "Do you reckon Abe has a union card?"

Fortas was as close to the First Lady as he was to the President, and she too relied on his judgment. "There is almost nobody in the world that I can talk to," Lady Bird Johnson wrote in *A White House Diary*. "To Abe, I feel I can." In

May of 1967 the troubled First Lady unburdened herself to Justice Fortas on the subject that then dominated much of her thinking: How to get her husband out of the presidency, and when. She considered the prospect of another campaign "like an open-ended stay in a concentration camp." Fortas "was quiet and a little sad, but very understanding." He told Lady Bird that he thought Johnson had done enough in his public life; that by next March, if the situation in Vietnam was improving, he could announce he would not seek reelection. But Fortas stressed that the announcement must wait until March to avoid undercutting Johnson's authority as President. With less prescience, he contended that the President could not afford to withdraw at all unless the war in Vietnam was going better.

In his dealings with the President himself, Fortas once defined his main contribution as "analytical help," drawing a fine distinction between that and advice. His function at White House conferences, as he described it, was merely to analyze and summarize what other men had to say. But the man who sums up an argument, as Fortas himself had often demonstrated at Arnold, Fortas & Porter, can decide its outcome. Moreover, Fortas's contacts with the President were not confined to large-scale gatherings. "I'm sure that the President had many, many private conversations with Fortas, after all things were done, so to speak," said Califano. "You could send Lyndon Johnson a memo on policy and he would call you back the next day and give you all sorts of thoughts."

The most critical subject on the White House agenda during those years was Vietnam. Fortas's role in policy discussions on the war was later said to be a source of considerable irritation to Lyndon Johnson's ambassador to the United Nations, Arthur Goldberg. According to another Administration official Goldberg "felt the deepest irony and anger" at the fact that Fortas had achieved far greater influence on Vietnam issues than Goldberg, while sitting in the very Supreme Court seat Goldberg had been persuaded to surrender.

On most issues that came up at the White House, Fortas

sought to remain objective and detached. Califano, who dealt with him mainly on domestic problems, thought that Fortas was "never an advocate in the sense of pushing hard on matters, of saying that we ought to go this way or that way." But on Vietnam, Fortas abandoned his neutrality, or so it seemed to those advisers who disagreed with him, and he lined up with the hawks.

Some associates of Fortas believe that his attitude toward the war stemmed more from his sense of loyalty to Lyndon Johnson than any strong personal conviction about U.S. policy in Vietnam. "He saw that the President was under terrific attack and he felt that as a friend it was his duty to give him psychological support, by backing his policies," said one friend. Whatever Fortas's motives, neither hawk nor dove doubted his special rapport with the President. Air Force Undersecretary Townsend Hoopes, who often opposed Fortas in Vietnam discussions, wrote of one session: "Fortas continued to play the curious role he had assumed on other occasions in the running debate on Vietnam—as spokesman for those private thoughts of Lyndon Johnson that the President did not wish to express directly."

As important in Fortas's mind as the strategy on the battlefield was the impact of the war at home. He was disturbed by the bitter criticism directed against the President by opponents of the war, and he feared that the protest movement was disrupting the country. In 1968 Fortas published a slim 20,000-word booklet, *Concerning Dissent and Civil Disobedience,* in which he laid down legal ground rules for peaceful protest. A demonstrator's right to free speech should be fully protected, Fortas believed. "But he is not entitled to immunity if he directly and willfully incites violence or insists upon deliberately disrupting the work or movement of others." Those who refused to enter military service because they regarded the war as immoral, Fortas conceded, deserved sympathy and respect. "But," he argued, "in fact their claim that their profound rejection of a particular war should prevail over the state's needs is hardly consistent with the basic theory of organized society. By participating in the particular war, the state takes the position that the war *is* justified and moral. ... The state cannot acknowledge an individual's right to veto its decision that a particular war is right and necessary."

Within the councils of the Administration, as the long and agonizing debate over Vietnam reached a climax, Fortas sided with those who insisted that the war was indeed necessary and argued that more bombing and a bigger military buildup would bring the Communists to their knees. Early in 1968, after the Communist Tet offensive had wrecked most illusions about military victory in Vietnam, Fortas helped draft a defiant presidential address in which Lyndon Johnson declared: "Make no mistake about it—I don't want a man here to go back thinking otherwise—we are going to win." In March of 1968 when the President held a series of meetings with his closest advisers that culminated in the decision to stop the bombing of North Vietnam above the twentieth parallel, Fortas was a member of the minority that persisted in urging heavier bombing and no letup in the ground war.

Fortas got more personal satisfaction out of another foreign policy crisis that engaged his attention for a briefer period of time. In the late spring of 1967, with tensions between Israel and the Arab states nearing the breaking point, Fortas served as a go-between for Israeli diplomats in negotiations with the White House. It is not clear whether the Israelis, who were discouraged at the treatment they had received at the State Department, sought Fortas out or whether he was acting at the direct suggestion of the President. At any rate, he became increasingly sympathetic with the Israeli position and increasingly skeptical of Secretary of State Dean Rusk's assurances of support to Israel. Shortly before Israel launched the six-day war against the Arabs, Fortas advised its representatives that Rusk would probably do nothing to help them. When the fighting broke out he followed its progress closely and was relieved and pleased when the Israelis won their stunning victory.

On domestic policy, Fortas was consulted on "most major

crises" that the Administration faced, according to Califano. "Johnson got from Fortas the kind of extra insurance that a President needs. Fortas was shrewd, wise and very knowing in the ways of Washington. The President didn't always follow Fortas's advice, any more than he always followed anybody else's advice. But it was a very important factor, in my judgment." Fortas was more of a tactician than a policy maker, Califano said. "Often it would be very late in the game. A speech was ready to be delivered tomorrow and we were ninety-five per cent sure where we wanted to land and the idea was let's make sure that it's pluperfect."

At the height of the bloody Detroit race riot of 1967, Fortas was called to the White House where the President was awaiting a formal request from Republican Governor George Romney of Michigan before sending in Federal troops to put down the violence. "There we were with Detroit in terrible trouble," Califano recalled. But Governor Romney, who then viewed himself as a potential presidential candidate, "did not want to put himself in the position of making a legal finding that he couldn't control what was going on. Fortas was very good at a lot of the human judgments involved," Califano said. "You sit around and you plot it out. What do you do? What kind of statement should we issue? It's very fast-moving."

Fortas was also called on to help in the President's efforts to curb inflation by holding down price increases. One of his clerks recalled his spending nearly an entire day on the phone during the White House effort to roll back prices in the steel industry. And stories circulated in Washington that Fortas occasionally used his influence with the President to recommend friends for important government positions. The *New York Times* reported that he had tried to get Bill Moyers appointed undersecretary of state, and had urged that another man be given a Federal judgeship.

Fortas denied the stories, but they contributed to growing concern, expressed in the press and the Congress, that his association with the President violated the doctrine of separation of powers. It was a question open to debate. Certainly Fortas's role was not without precedent in American history. Woodrow Wilson, who appointed Louis Brandeis to the Supreme Court, consulted with him confidentially on diverse matters, including the operation of the railroads during World War I, U.S. policy toward the Soviet Union and the strategy Wilson should pursue at the Paris Peace Conference. During the New Deal era, Brandeis, whom Roosevelt referred to as "Isaiah," remained an important influence on policy through his contacts with key members of the Roosevelt Administration.

A closer parallel was the relationship between Franklin Roosevelt and Felix Frankfurter. Like Fortas, Frankfurter had been a friend and confidant of the President who appointed him long before he became a Justice, and he continued to counsel him afterward. Frankfurter, a man of boundless energy and wide interests, at one time or another contributed phrases for Roosevelt's speeches, recommended candidates for appointment to Federal office, including the Supreme Court, and proposed tax policies for the Treasury Department. When the United States was still at peace with the Axis, Frankfurter suggested that the President send troops to Ireland to protect it from German invasion. Frankfurter, by all accounts, was far more aggressive than Fortas in foisting ideas on the President, particularly in the period before the United States entered World War II, when Frankfurter was eager that Roosevelt do everything possible to aid Great Britain against Nazi Germany.

"Frankfurter made Abe look like a piker, as far as substantive matters are concerned," said Joseph Rauh, who was one of Frankfurter's law clerks at the time. Like Frankfurter, Rauh was an ardent foe of Hitler when isolationist sentiment was still strong in the country. "I remember in the days before Pearl Harbor—we were the hawks then—prompting Frankfurter with ideas to sell Roosevelt. And I remember him telling how he trapped FDR while he was getting his hair cut and made him listen. The President couldn't get away because he was stuck in a barber chair."

The extent of Frankfurter's lobbying activity was not disclosed until after his death and Roosevelt's. But if either man had been compelled to defend their relationship he undoubtedly would have pointed to their long and close friendship and to the great crisis that confronted the nation and its Commander-in-Chief. Whether or not this rationale satisfies the demands of the Constitution, it could equally serve Lyndon Johnson and Abe Fortas.

"I would think that any President with all Lyndon Johnson's problems would turn to the wisest minds he could find to help him," said Califano. "I think if Johnson felt he had a decision to make and that among the ten or fifteen judgments he wanted was the judgment of Abe Fortas, he would call Abe Fortas and ask him for it. Now if you're Abe Fortas and you're on the receiving end of a phone call—and we're not talking about lawsuits before the Supreme Court; we're talking about a war in Vietnam, we're talking about economic problems, we're talking about racial tension—you're going to answer your President."

For his part, Fortas summarily rejected criticism of his activities at the White House as unrealistic. Occasionally, when he read an article accusing him of overstepping his bounds, he would toss it aside with a cryptic reference to "sons of bitches living in ivory towers." It was all very well for political theorists to talk about checks and balances, Fortas told his clerks. What did they know about the real world? He was a Supreme Court Justice whose friend happened to be President of the United States. Lyndon Johnson needed his help. If the purists didn't like it, that was too bad. When Lyndon Johnson stopped being President, that would be time enough to begin playing by their rules.

THE PLEASURE
OF THE PRESIDENT

LYNDON JOHNSON had risen to national prominence by mastering the Senate of the United States. Neither a stirring orator nor a polished debater, he was adroit at parliamentary maneuvering on the floor and overwhelming in man-to-man encounters in the cloakrooms. Once, for the benefit of Arthur Schlesinger, Jr., he depicted the Senate as a football team and played out a one-man scrimmage in which Majority Leader Johnson raced around the gridiron as blocker, tackler, passer and receiver. In the main, of course, he was head coach and strategist.

In the White House, Johnson's manipulative skills were enhanced by the authority of the presidency. The Senate is traditionally jealous of its prerogatives and often defiant of the Chief Executive, but during Johnson's first years as President, on foreign policy, on civil rights and on a host of Great Society economic and social measures the Senate time and again submitted to his will. In the final summer of his presidency, Johnson sought to wring one further concession from the Senate: approval of Abe Fortas as Chief Justice of the United States, a position second in significance only to the presidency itself. But this struggle was to prove more difficult than the President had reckoned. His own influence had been undermined by events at home and abroad. And the issue, as his opponents readily perceived, was a momentous one. At stake, besides the high office of Chief Justice, was the future control of the Supreme Court.

The opportunity to elevate Fortas to the leadership of the Court arose because Earl Warren decided to retire after fifteen years as Chief Justice. Warren's decision was in large measure a personal one, but it also reflected, as did the struggle over his successor, the national condition in the summer of 1968.

In March of 1968 Warren had observed his seventy-seventh birthday. Federal judges with ten years' service can retire at full pay at age seventy, but retirement is not mandatory at seventy, or indeed at any age. Many judges have remained active close to or beyond the limits of physical endurance. On the Supreme Court, the most notable example of longevity was Oliver Wendell Holmes, who waited until he was ninety-one to retire. Chief Justice Stone had to be helped from the courtroom after reading his last opinion and died a few days later, at seventy-three. Among the Justices of the Warren Court, Felix Frankfurter remained on the bench until he was seventy-nine, and Hugo Black, who was five years Warren's senior, seemed determined to stay on until he had set a record for length of service on the Court.*

As for Warren, at seventy-seven he still appeared robust, and his doctors had assured him, he said, that his health was as good "as a person of my age has any right to expect." But Warren realized that the pressure of his duties at the Court was bound to take its toll. After more than fifty years in public service the Chief looked forward to a period of leisure that he would be vigorous enough to enjoy. The question was not whether to retire, but when, and political circumstances made 1968 seem a propitious year for him to leave.

---

* Illness forced Black to retire in September 1971. He died a week after submitting his resignation. Black was 85 years old and had served on the Court for thirty-four years, only seven months short of a record.

For more than thirty years before his appointment as Chief Justice Warren had sought and held elective office. He had been governor of California and a candidate for Vice President of the United States, and he had nurtured ambitions for the presidency. He was thus an experienced student of the political scene, and by June of 1968, although the presidential election was still six months away, it was plain to even the most unsophisticated observer that the Democratic Party was already at a serious disadvantage.

For months the Democratic Chief Executive, Lyndon Johnson, had been presiding over a series of disasters. In January 1968 the Communist Tet offensive in Vietnam had badly shaken the nation's faith in the Administration's ability to end the Indochina war successfully. Johnson's promises about Vietnam aroused increasing skepticism, and the excesses of his personality grated on the public's sensibilities. The growing disaffection with the President had taken root in his own party. Senator Eugene McCarthy had led the initial insurgency, which, in the New Hampshire presidential primary, won a stunning victory. A few days later Senator Robert Kennedy, heir to his slain brother's reputation and support, announced his candidacy for the presidential nomination.

Unwilling any longer to contend against these opponents and resentments, Lyndon Johnson astounded the country by announcing he would neither seek nor accept the nomination of his party for reelection. In a dramatic television address Johnson also proclaimed a scaling down of the bombing in Vietnam and urged the citizenry "to guard against divisiveness and all its ugly consequences." But a few days later the assassination of Martin Luther King, the Negro leader who symbolized the civil-rights movement's commitment to nonviolence, made a mockery of the President's plea. The cities of the country exploded. In Washington a pall of smoke from looted and burned buildings hung over the White House and Federal troops were called in to put down the disorders.

Johnson's withdrawal opened the way for the candidacy of his loyal Vice President, Hubert Humphrey. He plunged into the race with characteristic ebullience, promising to revive "the politics of happiness, the politics of joy," a pledge that soon came to seem so incongruous as to be almost grotesque. On June 4 Senator Robert Kennedy, who had just kept his hopes for the nomination alive by winning the California primary, was mortally wounded in a Los Angeles hotel, and the widespread shock and grief recalled the reaction to his brother's assassination five years before.

The enormous political impact of this series of events can best be understood by comparing the outlook in June of 1968 with the prospects a year or so earlier. Then Lyndon Johnson appeared, like most incumbents, a reasonably good prospect for reelection. If he should falter Robert Kennedy offered the Democrats a strong alternative. But now both these candidates were removed from the race and the party itself was ridden by discord. By contrast the Republicans, having learned their lesson about divisiveness in the 1964 presidential campaign, presented a united front. They seemed almost certain to nominate Richard M. Nixon, who had somehow restored himself as a strong contender for the presidency.

Earl Warren has never discussed what influence these developments had on his thinking as he pondered his retirement. "I left politics fifteen years ago," he said afterwards, "and I would not like to have my retirement from the Supreme Court interjected into politics . . ."

Still, it must have been difficult for Warren himself to keep the one apart from the other. Warren had first encountered Nixon many years before in California politics when their ambitions had clashed and left a residue of antagonism. But more important than any lingering personal animosity was the future of the Court that Warren led. Its string of decisions enlarging the rights of criminal defendants had made the Warren Court more controversial than ever. Public uneasiness about the Court had been intensified by the violence and disorder of recent months and the opening rhetoric of the presidential campaign. Nixon, never a champion of the Warren Court, joined the attack on the Court's ruling as he barnstormed around the country and allied himself with some of the Court's bitter enemies. Warren could be certain that if, as seemed quite possible, political fortune gave Richard Nixon the chance to name his successor, Nixon would select a Chief Justice committed to turning the Court in a sharply different direction from the course it had taken under Warren.

A far more attractive alternative for Warren was to place the choice of the next Chief Justice in the hands of Lyndon Johnson. The Chief and the President were on warm personal terms. Warren, along with Fortas, had enjoyed the pleasures of the White House pool. On the evening of Warren's seventy-fifth birthday, Johnson had arrived unbidden at Warren's home, bearing good wishes and gifts, including a photograph inscribed to "the greatest Chief Justice of them all." Though Warren had entered public life as a Republican, the social and political philosophy reflected in his opinions was far more in harmony with Johnson's Great Society goals than it was with traditional Republican doctrine. Warren could count on Johnson's nominating a Chief Justice who would keep faith with the doctrines of the Warren Court. In fact it would not have been difficult for Warren to guess that Johnson would select his good friend, and Warren's, too, Abe Fortas.

On June 13, as the Court was nearing the time for its summer adjournment, Warren called on Lyndon Johnson at the White House to tell him of his intention to retire. Returning to his chambers, the Chief Justice made his decision a matter of record. He was leaving the Court, he wrote the President, "not because of reasons of health or on account of any personal or associational problems, but solely because of age." The Chief Justice felt it was his duty, he said, "to give way to someone who will have more years ahead of him to cope with the problems which will come to the Court."

Considerably more interesting than this letter of explanation was the brief formal notification that Warren sent along with it to the White House. The Federal statute on judicial retirement does not state specifically how much, if any, notice retiring judges must give the President. There was no recent precedent for the office of Chief Justice, since Warren's two immediate predecessors, Fred Vinson and Harlan Stone, had both died in office. Most Associate Justices who had resigned or retired in recent years had given a specific date when they would leave. But Warren chose to go about his leave-taking differently. "I hereby advise you of my intention to retire as Chief Justice of the United States," he wrote to Johnson, "effective at your pleasure." Warren later explained that he had left the date open out of concern for the Court. "There always ought to be a Chief Justice of the United States," he said. "There is a lot of administrative work . . . and if I selected a particular day and the vacancy was not filled it would be a vacuum." No matter what the Chief's reasons were, the effect of his open-ended retirement, as critics quickly pointed out, was to provide Lyndon Johnson with extra leverage in naming his replacement.

This was an advantage that the President would eventually try to put to use. But for the time being he made no public announcement of the Chief Justice's plans while he devoted himself to planning the succession. His initial decision was an easy one. The President, according to Joe Califano, "reached fairly rapidly in his own mind the decision to make Fortas the Chief." Three years before, Fortas had acceded to the President's wishes, given up his practice and joined the Court. There was no better way to reward his loyalty then and since than to promote him to the highest position within the President's appointive power.

Besides, in his three years on the Court, Fortas had added luster to an already distinguished professional reputation. His qualifications, Johnson believed, could not be challenged. He was, in the President's words, "judicious and compassionate," a friend to business and labor alike, an advocate of the underdog, an efficient administrator. "There may be a better man for the job," the President remarked to an interviewer. "But if there is, I don't know him. There is not a human being living who could get him to do a thing that is not right."

Johnson realized that the nomination would be criticized

because of his friendship with the nominee. "Sure he's a friend of mine," he said. "But am I supposed to nominate someone who is unfriendly?" Anyhow, he pointed out, Fortas was already on the Court. "What is the difference," he asked gesturing, "if he sits *here,* or sits *there?*"

By promoting Fortas to Chief Justice Johnson would, of course, give himself another vacancy to fill and the opportunity to put his personal stamp on the Court for years to come. The selection of the second nominee required a good deal more deliberation than the first. Apart from his other qualifications, the President wanted his candidate for Associate Justice to placate the likely critics of Fortas's promotion. "We went around the horn on a lot of alternative candidates," Califano said. The man they settled on was Homer Thornberry, a fifty-nine-year-old Federal judge and a longtime friend of the President. Thornberry had taken LBJ's old congressional seat when Johnson moved up to the Senate and he had been with Johnson through thick and thin: his heart attack in 1955, his campaign for the presidency in 1960 and his succession to the presidency on the day of John Kennedy's assassination. In 1963 Kennedy had made Thornberry a district judge and two years later Lyndon Johnson had promoted him to the Fifth Circuit Court of Appeals.

Though Thornberry was not famous for his distinction as a legal scholar, his background gave him certain practical advantages as a nominee. He had served in Congress for fourteen years and Johnson knew the Senate was generally disposed to look kindly upon appointments of Capitol Hill alumni. The Senate had already twice reviewed Thornberry's qualifications for the judiciary and twice approved them. Geography was another plus for Thornberry, the President believed. Tom Clark, another Texan, had retired from the High Court the year before when his son, Ramsey, became attorney general. Thornberry's appointment would once again give the Southwest representation on the Court. True, the Southwest was not quite the same as the Deep South, where hostility to the Warren Court was strongest. It was also true that some of Thornberry's decisions from the bench had a liberal slant to them. But his folksy manner and the "yew-alls" strewn through his conversation gave Thornberry the look and sound of Dixie. Hopefully, the senators from the old Confederacy would consider him and confirm him as one of their own.

To test this proposition, the President discreetly sent word of his plans to nominate the Fortas-Thornberry ticket to the two most powerful Southerners in the Senate, James Eastland of Mississippi and Richard Russell of Georgia. Eastland, an implacable enemy of civil-rights legislation and a stern critic of the Warren Court, ruled the Judiciary Committee, which would conduct hearings on the nominations. His response was favorable enough for Johnson to count on his support. Richard Russell's reaction sealed the President's decision. At seventy the courtly Georgian, who had served in the Senate since 1932, was a man respected by all his colleagues and revered by the South. As much as any Southerner, he resented the Supreme Court. But when the White House solicited his views, he indicated he would not oppose Fortas, particularly since Thornberry was part of the bargain. Thornberry and Russell had been duck hunting together, and the Senator remarked: "There's a man I can enthuse about."

Johnson was almost ready to publicly announce his nominations, but he had one more base to touch. On the evening of June 22 the President summoned to the White House the leader of the Senate Republicans, Everett Dirksen of Illinois. Dirksen, who was seventy-two and in his eighteenth year in the Senate, was equally renowned for his overblown rhetoric and his infinite capacity for changing his mind. His dissertations on the flag and motherhood were throwbacks to turn-of-the-century Fourth of July celebrations, and his proclamations in favor of the marigold, which he sought to make the national flower, verged on absurdity. No one could count how many times he had reversed himself in legislative battles, and it was said that at one time or another during his Washington career Dirksen had been on both sides over every public issue. Despite his buffoonery and his dedication to expediency, Dirksen had his moments of statesmanship. He had given vital support to the nuclear test ban treaty of 1963 and to civil-rights legislation in 1964 and 1965. Like Lyndon Johnson, he was a practiced hand at parliamentary maneuver, and the two had long worked together to their mutual advantage.

The President told Dirksen of Warren's intention to retire and of his own intention to nominate Fortas and Thornberry. There was bound to be some criticism of his making appointments to the Court in his last months as President, Johnson acknowledged. But, he pointed out, seven other Supreme Court Justices had been nominated by Presidents in their last year in the White House and had been duly confirmed by the Senate. He probably did not mention that nine other nominations, made under similar circumstances, had failed to win approval.

His choices, the President went on, were both men of ability and experience. Both were sitting judges who had previously passed muster in the Senate. Then Johnson brought up something that was to become the ugliest aspect of the controversy that lay ahead. It would be well for senators, Republican as well as Democrat, to bear in mind that Fortas stood to become the first Jewish Chief Justice in the nation's history. His none too subtle point was that it would be foolhardy for politicians of either party to risk antagonizing Jewish voters, not to mention Jewish financial contributors, in an election year.

By the time Dirksen left the White House that night, Johnson had his commitment to back the nominations. Later there would be much speculation about Dirksen's motives. It was recalled that Dirksen had been deeply disturbed by major Warren Court decisions on school prayer and voting reapportionment, so much so in fact that he had attempted to amend the Constitution to overturn these rulings. Yet now he was willing to support for Chief Justice a man likely to preserve the Court's position on these and other issues. Dirksen himself angrily denounced the suggestion that he might have received any special concessions from the White House in return for his support. But Dirksen was probably already indebted to Lyndon Johnson. Dirksen's Senate seat was being contested that election year and Johnson reportedly had persuaded Democratic leaders to select a relatively weak opponent for his old Republican friend.

Beyond that, it seemed more than coincidental that a week after Dirksen agreed to back Johnson's Court nominations, the Administration suddenly came to the rescue of Dirksen's pet agency, the Subversive Activities Control Board. The board had originally been set up in 1950 to investigate Communists and to compel them to register with the Justice Department, but Supreme Court decisions stripped the board of its registration powers. Dirksen then pushed through legislation which kept the SACB alive provided it was given more cases to investigate by June 30, 1968. That eventuality seemed unlikely, because the investigations would mean little except busy work for the board. Yet just before the legislative deadline, the Justice Department sent the board a group of cases that gave it a new lease on life and afforded Dirksen a personal triumph.

By the time Johnson and Dirksen had conferred on the nominations, word of Warren's intention to retire had already leaked to the press. Johnson had no reason to delay any longer the official confirmation of that news and the disclosure of his blueprint for the Court's future. On June 26 the White House released the text of Warren's letters to the President. At the same time the President submitted to the Senate his nominations of Abe Fortas to be Chief Justice in Warren's place and of Homer Thornberry to replace Fortas as Associate Justice.

Apart from the identities of the President's nominees themselves, what attracted most attention about the White House announcement was the wording of Johnson's reply to Warren's letter of retirement. In response to Warren's offer to retire at the President's pleasure, the President had written: "I will accept your decision to retire effective at such time as a successor is qualified."

Any doubts about what that meant were eliminated a few

days later when Earl Warren was asked at a press conference whether he could continue to serve if Fortas was not confirmed as his successor. "I neither expect nor hope that to be the fact," Warren said. But, "I am under oath to perform the duties of the office. And if the first of October rolls around and there is no successor, I suppose I would be obliged to act as Chief Justice." In simplest terms, then, the President's pleasure was to give the opponents of the Warren Court a choice between promoting Abe Fortas and keeping Earl Warren.

That proposition further angered the opposition to Lyndon Johnson's nominations that had begun to take shape even before he announced them. The leader of the opposition was Republican Senator Robert Griffin of Michigan. At first glance, he seemed an unlikely figure to challenge the power of the President and the will of the Senate leader of his own party. Mild-mannered and unprepossessing, Griffin, with little more than two years in office, was still a very junior senator. He was considered a moderate-to-liberal Republican and had never been one of the Court's strident critics. Early on, however, Griffin had displayed a willingness to gamble against long political odds. In 1956 he had won a seat in the House by taking on a supposedly unbeatable Democratic incumbent and beating him. A few years later he had helped engineer an uprising among House Republicans who deposed their aging leader, Charles Halleck, and replaced him with Griffin's Michigan colleague, Gerald Ford. In 1966 Griffin was appointed to the Senate to fill a vacancy caused by the death of Senator Pat McNamara. Few politicians thought he had much chance to stay on when Michigan Democrats put up their best vote getter, former Governor G. Mennen (Soapy) Williams, to run against him in the November election. But Griffin swept 75 of Michigan's 83 counties in a victory that ended Williams's political career. He was forty-four years old, resourceful and ambitious, and he saw in Johnson's attempt to replace Warren an issue of significance and a chance to make his mark in the Senate.

For Griffin the battle began on June 14, the day after Warren had written Johnson about his retirement. He noticed a brief report on the front page of the *Wall Street Journal* that Warren was considering leaving the Court before Johnson's term ended because he "hoped to have a voice in naming his successor." The story lacked any official confirmation and it made no mention of Warren's possible successor. Nevertheless, Griffin was disturbed. "I read that as a lawyer, as a student of the Constitution and as a Republican," he later said. "I thought what business does Warren have, having anything to say about his successor. It smacked of collusion." Griffin asked his staff to collect material for a speech he planned to make on the subject. A week later, a further report on Warren's plans made front pages around the country. The Chief Justice was said by "authoritative sources" to have already handed in his resignation. Though there was no comment from the White House, the story had the ring of authenticity to it.

Griffin hurriedly finished work on the speech he had been planning and rose that day on the floor of the Senate "to indicate emphatically that I shall not vote to confirm an appointment of the next Chief Justice by a 'lame duck' President." He did not know, Griffin asserted, whether Lyndon Johnson would appoint a Democrat or a Republican, a liberal or a conservative. "The point is that the decision should be made by the next President . . . after the people have an opportunity to speak in November."

When Griffin tried to rally opposition to the nominations at the regular weekly meeting of Senate Republicans, he immediately ran into opposition himself from Republican leader Dirksen. "There's nothing about lame ducks in the Constitution," Dirksen argued. He quoted Robert Taft, a revered figure in that group, to the effect that "the only considerations governing confirmation should be the nominee's character, qualifications and professional skills."

Despite Dirksen's irritating high-mindedness, Griffin and Senator George Murphy of California drafted a petition opposing an attempt to replace Warren before the November elections. This document was already being circulated in the

Senate cloakroom on June 26 when the White House announced the nominations of Fortas and Thornberry. Before the day was out Griffin and eighteen other Republicans had signed it. The petitioners expressed their "strongly held view" that nominations to the Court should be left to the next President. For this reason, and, they emphasized, "with absolutely no reflection on any individuals involved," they would oppose any Supreme Court nominations submitted to the Senate by President Johnson.

Griffin now had behind him half of the total Republican contingent of thirty-six senators. Two of them were from the East, John Williams of Delaware and Norris Cotton of New Hampshire. The rest were from states scattered through the West and the South. Ideologically they ran the gamut from moderates like Griffin himself, and Frank Carlson of Kansas, to such spokesmen for the party's right wing as George Murphy of California, John G. Tower of Texas and Strom Thurmond of South Carolina.

The emergence of this opposition bloc caught Lyndon Johnson off guard; it ran counter to his understanding of the flow of power in the Senate. Once Everett Dirksen had agreed to support the nominations, the President believed, few other Republicans would be willing to oppose them actively. The President's response to the unanticipated insurgency was along accustomed lines. He applied pressure. Griffin himself received a phone call from an official he described as "highly placed" in the Ford Motor Company who advised him not to persist in his fight. Others in his group heard similar messages from businessmen in their home states, men who were personal friends of Lyndon Johnson or whose companies depended heavily on government contracts.

Senators had grown used to imprecations of this sort during Lyndon Johnson's tenure in the White House and had learned to shrug them off politely. Now they encountered a different and more disturbing problem. Word spread on Capitol Hill that Senators opposing the nominations would risk retaliation from Jewish voters. Lyndon Johnson had made that very point to Everett Dirksen and some strongly suspected LBJ of inspiring the talk. In fact, soon after he announced the nominations, the President, in private chats with newsmen, had made clear his belief that there was more than a bit of prejudice behind the opposition to Fortas. These assertions could not be attributed to him, and the press treated them gingerly. Nevertheless, anxiety among dissident senators was fed by reports from home. Some Jewish constituents were expressing concern about opposition to Fortas, and Jewish leaders were pointedly rallying to Fortas's support.

In Griffin's own state of Michigan, the *Jewish News* of Detroit charged that the campaign against Fortas had opened "a Pandora's box of anti-Semitism." The paper acknowledged that Griffin's own opposition was not prompted by Fortas's religion. Nevertheless, it insisted, "his drive to keep Fortas from becoming the first Jew in American history to occupy the nation's third highest post has been gleefully welcomed by the lowest dregs of anti-Semitism."

Senate Republicans hastily called a private caucus to discuss what Everett Dirksen called this "delicate situation." Griffin immediately pointed out that before Fortas's nomination had been announced he had publicly stated he would not oppose Arthur Goldberg as Warren's replacement, since he considered Goldberg to be "on a leave of absence" from the Court. Whatever the logic of that reasoning, Griffin believed that it cleared him personally of the suspicion of anti-Semitism. As for the others, Senator Jacob Javits of New York, a Jew, a liberal and a supporter of Fortas, volunteered his services. If any senator's constituent believed that senator was motivated by anti-Semitism, Javits promised to phone the constituent personally to convince him otherwise. If necessary, Javits said, he would issue a public statement that anti-Semitism was not an issue in the controversy over the nomination, a pledge which he eventually kept.

The issue remained a vague but troublesome presence throughout the battle over the Court. Predictably, Fortas's nomination provoked the attacks of overtly anti-Semitic organizations, notably the American Nazi Party and the United Klans of America. It was also bitterly opposed by such right-wing extremists as the Liberty Lobby and the John Birch Society, but with groups in this spectrum it was difficult to tell where ideology left off and bigotry began. The ultra-right wing had been just as virulent in its attacks on Earl Warren, and the Supreme Court in general, as it was in condemning Fortas.

The complaints of prejudice from some of Fortas's supporters made Griffin and his allies uncomfortable, and eventually Griffin retaliated by accusing the White House of accusing him of anti-Semitism. In the end, though, there was no evidence that anti-Semitism changed anyone's mind or vote on either side. Its main impact was to add further suspicion and irrationality to a controversy that far too often strayed beyond the limits of reasoned discourse.

As part of its campaign to undermine the opposition, the White House, expressing an optimism it did not entirely feel, emitted statements that Griffin's cause was doomed. The President told visitors he could easily count sixty votes on his side; Griffin's allies, he said, were bound to defect. Everett Dirksen forecast that the names on Griffin's petition "would vanish into thin air."

Thruston Morton, one of the original nineteen signers of the petition, did drop out. He was forced to, when New York Governor Nelson Rockefeller, whom Morton was backing for the Republican presidential nomination, endorsed the Fortas and Thornberry nominations. But the others held firm. Griffin realized that Lyndon Johnson probably could, as he claimed, round up sixty votes for confirmation, but Griffin intended to prevent such a vote from ever taking place. He proposed to rely on the traditional weapon of outnumbered senators, the filibuster, and talk the nomination to death. The only way to stop a filibuster, barring physical exhaustion, was adoption of a motion to limit debate, called cloture, which required the support of two-thirds of the senators present and voting. Griffin knew that many senators, particularly those from the South, regarded unlimited debate as an inalienable right. He was confident that even some senators who supported the nomination would refuse to limit their colleagues' cherished right to speak.

The election year calendar favored Griffin's strategy. The Senate was driving for adjournment by the end of July in time for the national political conventions. The President could call Congress back for a post-convention session, but with a political campaign in full swing the lawmakers would be straining to break free. Meanwhile, before the Senate could even begin action, the nominations would have to come under the scrutiny of the Judiciary Committee, a procedure that held the possibility of considerable delay.

Two developments strengthened Griffin's confidence and resolution. The first was the reaction of Richard Nixon, who Griffin like most Republicans assumed would be the party's candidate for President. When the Fortas and Thornberry nominations were announced, Nixon criticized Lyndon Johnson for playing politics with the Court. It would have been better, Nixon said, for Johnson to defer to the President who would be elected in November. Nixon did not choose to discuss the qualifications of either nominee; he preferred to stay out of the controversy. But what he did say was quite enough for Griffin, who read his words as a green light.

A few days later Griffin received further encouragement from another influential source. Driving home to Michigan for the weekend, Griffin stopped on the way to call his Washington office. He was given a message to phone a number in Winder, Georgia. Even before he placed the call, Griffin knew whose number it must be. Of Winder's 6,000 citizens only one was likely to be calling Robert Griffin and that was Richard Russell. Not long before, Senator Russell had given Lyndon Johnson what the President regarded as a promise of support for the nominations. Both friend and foe counted Russell a man of honor and Johnson believed he would never go back on his word. But it sometimes happens in politics that two men differ on the meaning of a conversation. Moreover, besides being an honorable man, Richard Russell was an extremely practical one. Certain aspects of Johnson's nominations could not be ignored. It turned out that Russell's old duck-hunting friend, Homer Thornberry, despite his Texas upbringing, had ruled on civil-rights matters like a Yankee liberal judge. He had, for example, joined in the first Federal court decision that held a state poll tax unconstitutional. Another factor was the emergence of Griffin's opposition group. This opposition would be handicapped, as both Griffin and Russell realized, if it came from only one side of the aisle. It was a question not just of numerical strength but also of appearances. Griffin claimed to be opposing the nominations as a matter of principle, and principle is better defended with bipartisan support. Russell, by virtue of his personal prestige, could supplement the ranks of Griffin's allies with a dozen or more Southern Democrats.

Never one for tilting at windmills, Russell wanted to be certain that Griffin's Republicans would not waver under pressure from the White House and Dirksen. When Griffin phoned him in Winder, the old Southerner quickly came to the point.

"Are your eighteen votes firm?" he asked Griffin.

Indeed they were, Griffin assured him.

"All right," drawled Richard Russell. "I'm with you."

This was a pledge that for the time being Griffin would keep to himself. He could afford to remain silent. Now the odds were in his favor.

ADVICE AND DISSENT

THE UNITED STATES Constitution, for all of what Learned Hand called its "majestic generalities" on other points, makes clear that the power to appoint Supreme Court Justices is shared by the executive and legislative branches. The President alone has the authority to nominate, but the disposition of his choices depends on the "advice and consent" of the Senate. In the early years of the Republic the Senate did not hesitate to exercise its power. From 1795, when it rejected John Rutledge, nominated by George Washington to be Chief Justice, to 1894, when it turned back two successive nominations by Grover Cleveland, the Senate had withheld its consent from twenty presidential nominations to the High Court.

In more recent years, though, the Senate had almost let its authority lapse through disuse. Of forty-one Supreme Court nominees in the twentieth century only one, John J. Parker, selected by Herbert Hoover in 1930, had been rejected. Since Parker's defeat no nominee to the High Court had even been seriously challenged until Johnson submitted the Fortas and Thornberry nominations to the Senate.

Several factors gave Griffin and his allies the opportunity to reverse the trend of recent history. One was the widespread public antipathy toward the Warren Court. Another was the sorry state of Lyndon Johnson's prestige during his closing months in office. Finally, there was the surprising clumsiness of both Johnson and Fortas, which helped make it possible for the opposition to prolong the controversy, week after week, and, in the process, to discredit the nominations in the eyes of the public and the Senate.

After two weeks of preliminary sparring in the press and on the Senate floor the battle was joined head-on in the second floor hearing room of the New Senate Office Building, where the Judiciary Committee began its formal considerations. In the center of the horseshoe dais sat Chairman Eastland, who was stiffly neutral at the start, asked few questions and kept a cigar clamped in his mouth most of the time. The majority of the committee, like the majority of the Senate itself, was prepared to do the President's bidding. The Administration's supporters included Everett Dirksen and Philip Hart, Democrat of Michigan, who had been entrusted with the leadership of the forces backing the nomination. The chief spokesmen for the other side would be Sam Ervin of North Carolina and Strom Thurmond of South Carolina. Always outnumbered, they were never outtalked.

It was Ervin who launched the attack. He had been a state supreme court judge before coming to the Senate and was considered to be that body's foremost constitutional scholar and one of its shrewdest debaters. A hulking white-haired figure, he was given to rambling dissertations about legal concepts, to which he added stress by flapping his bushy eyebrows to register astonishment, indignation or amusement. Originally, the opposition to the nominations had relied solely on the contention that Lyndon Johnson was a "lame duck," but Ervin had seized upon the indefinite nature of Earl Warren's retirement as another target. Since Warren had not actually retired, and would not do so until his successor was confirmed, Ervin contended there really was no vacancy for Johnson to fill on the Supreme Court.

The first day of Judiciary Committee hearings, July 11, was

consumed debating Ervin's "no vacancy" argument. Summoned to defend the President's position, Attorney General Ramsey Clark ticked off a number of Supreme Court nominees who had been confirmed before the men they were to replace had actually left the bench. In each case, however, the departing Justice, unlike Warren, had fixed a definite date for leaving. It was true that some lower court judges had left their retirement date to the discretion of the President, as Warren had done, but to find a precedent on the Supreme Court, Clark had to go back to 1902, when Theodore Roosevelt and Justice Horace Gray agreed that Gray's retirement would become effective when his successor took office. As it turned out, though, Gray died before his successor, Oliver Wendell Holmes, was confirmed by the Senate.

Ervin did not find the precedents convincing. "It would have been very easy in this particular case for Chief Justice Warren to either resign or absolutely retire, would it not?" he asked Clark. "There was all the summer until October 1 to select a Chief Justice."

Clark argued that such a procedure "would have been absolutely contrary to good judicial administration." The Chief had acted wisely, he insisted, "to provide for continuity in office."

Ervin thought judicial administration had little to do with the matter. "It comes down to this," he said, "that the Senate must confirm Mr. Fortas as Chief Justice or retain Mr. Warren as Chief Justice. Is it not that simple?"

Ervin's "no vacancy" argument, like Griffin's "lame duck" argument, served mainly to use up time and to focus attention on the political maneuvering behind the nominations. The timing of Warren's retirement embarrassed even the Administration's supporters. The *New York Times* lamented the "calculated vagueness" of the arrangement. The *New Republic* said "the manner of the Chief Justice's retirement . . . does leave a great deal to be desired. Life tenure . . . is one thing. Life tenure with a right to influence confirmation of a successor is rather another."

[162]

On the second day of the hearings, Senator Griffin himself appeared as witness to exploit another opening Lyndon Johnson had given the opposition. Griffin had originally stressed that his opposition was based on the "lame duck" principle and had nothing to do with the particular nominees the President selected. Now he broadened his principles to complain that both Fortas and Thornberry were "cronies" of LBJ. "It is highly unusual for a President to subject himself to the charge of cronyism in connection with a nomination to the Supreme Court," Griffin declared. "And never before in history has any President been so bold as to subject himself to a charge of cronyism with respect to two such nominations at the same time." To name a crony to the Supreme Court, Griffin argued, threatened the doctrine of separation of powers, "the most fundamental concept embodied in our Constitution." The nation had a right to expect "that contacts between the Justices of the Court and the President will not breach the line which necessarily separates the branches of our government." Judging from reports in the press, Griffin said ominously, President Johnson and Justice Fortas had already violated that boundary. Fortas, by some accounts, had written speeches, drafted laws and proposed candidates for presidential appointment.

Senator Dirksen, who had made it his business to be on hand for Griffin's testimony, sought to undercut the cronyism charge. After all, Dirksen asked, what was a crony but a friend? Lyndon Johnson was not the first President to name a friend to the Supreme Court; Harry Truman had nominated several of his old comrades from Senate days. Dirksen also recalled that Abraham Lincoln had put his friend and campaign manager, David Davis, on the Court in 1862. "Mr. Chairman," Dirksen said, "I would hate to think that history is going to rise up to say that Lincoln was guilty of cronyism." Reaching back into his rhetorical resources Dirksen told his colleagues: "This is a frivolous, diaphanous—you know what that means, don't you—gossamer—you know what that means, don't you—argument that just does not hold water."

But the questions Griffin had raised caught the attention of the Senate and of the public. Nearly every citizen knew something, however vague, about the importance of separation of powers to the stability of the government. Moreover, the talk of behind-the-scenes decision-making at the White House had a whiff of drama and intrigue. It was the stuff headlines are made of, and it was the subject the committee pursued with vigor when the central figure in the controversy came before it on the third day of hearings.

Fortas's appearance before the committee in itself broke a precedent. No other candidate for Chief Justice had ever been invited to testify. Nor had any Justice already sitting on the Court ever testified, except for those who received recess appointments made by the President while the Senate was not in session. The Senate had found it so awkward to question sitting members of the Court about their views that in 1960 it passed a resolution urging Presidents to refrain from making recess appointments.

The same difficulty faced Fortas. His record as a Justice was an obvious target for questions that would be difficult to answer within the bounds of propriety. So was his relationship with the President. Under the circumstances, some men might have decided the prudent course was to decline to testify. But Fortas, not without reason, considered himself an expert at the art of argument. He had a swift wit and a cool head which he had used to good advantage in countless courtrooms, in congressional hearings and in the conferences of the Supreme Court. Rather than sidestep the opposition to his nomination, he preferred to deal with it directly.

Wearing a charcoal suit and a confident smile, Fortas took his seat in the hearing room and told the committee that he was "very happy" to be there and to answer "any and all questions" put to him. "There is nothing I love better," he said, "than a legal discussion or debate."

The argument that developed, however, differed from any Fortas had encountered before. He had been asked about his relationship with Lyndon Johnson at the hearings on his appointment to the Court in 1965, but the subject had not been nearly so sensitive then because their relationship had been between President and friend, not President and Supreme Court Justice. Fortas quickly made several basic points about his activities at the White House. Perhaps most important, he asserted that the President had never "directly or indirectly, approximately or remotely" discussed with him any matter that might come before the Court. The President had asked his advice only on "a few critical matters." He had never recommended anyone for public position or, in fact, initiated any proposals at all. Whatever he had done was out of patriotism; he was proud "to be of the slightest service to my President or to my country." Finally, he did not want to divulge any details that would be "an act of violence" to the presidency or the necessary confidentiality of that office.

The senators, understandably curious, prodded him for details. Fortas, either out of an access of candor or a desire to improve upon appearances, could not restrain himself from embellishing. The trouble was, each answer led to another question. Early on, Chairman Eastland asked him if he had, as had been reported, written the President's message ordering troops into Detroit during the 1967 riots.

"I did not write that message," Fortas said. "I did see it before it was delivered. But I did not write it."

"Did you approve it?"

"No, sir. The President does not ask my approval."

"Why was it shown to you," Eastland wondered, "if you had no authority in it?"

Fortas answered that the President, facing "that critical and desperate situation," had taken counsel with a number of people in whom he placed great trust. "And I was one of those people."

Next dour old John McClellan of Arkansas asked what specific matters of "critical importance" Fortas had been consulted on. Fortas referred to the Detroit riots and to "fantastically difficult decisions" about the war in Vietnam. "And that is about it, as I recall," he added. "I guess I have made full disclosure now."

It was a gratuitous remark. No one had asked him to make full disclosure. And his "guess" was to cause him embarrassment later that summer as further reports of his services to the President came to light.

At the moment, though, the committee was interested in a phone call Fortas had made in 1967 to Ralph Lazarus, a member of the Business Council, a group of influential corporate executives. Lazarus had publicly stated that the Vietnam War would cost $5 billion more than the President's budget indicated. Fortas, who had read Lazarus's statement in the press, challenged the estimate and declared, according to Lazarus, that the President was "quite upset."

Fortas would not tell the committee whether or not Lyndon Johnson had asked him to make the call. He did point out that Lazarus, the head of Federated Department Stores, was a long-time client and friend. But Senator McClellan was worried about the implications of the episode. Businessmen might come to feel, he suggested, that "they should keep their views to themselves if some member of the Supreme Court is going to call them up and take them to task about it." Did Fortas think this was a proper practice for a Supreme Court Justice?

"I hope I am not insensitive to these matters," Fortas said. "But I really don't see anything wrong, taking into account the fact of friendship and long association. I engage in parlor discussions as everybody else does about a variety of subjects."

In an effort to reassure the committee, Fortas dug back into history to find numerous examples of Justices who had advised Presidents, starting with the first Chief Justice, John Jay, and George Washington. He reminded the committee that his activities at the White House stemmed solely from his relationship with Lyndon Johnson, whose days in office were now numbered. "Whatever it may be, whatever opportunity I had to aid my country in these crises to which I have referred," he said, "that opportunity will be concluded on January twentieth of next year."

When he testified in 1965, he recalled, he had said that both his closeness to the President and his skill as a violinist were vastly exaggerated. "They are still exaggerated."

Sam Ervin, in a jocular mood, asked: "Do you put yourself in a class with Jack Benny as a violinist?"

"No, sir," said Fortas. "I am not as good as he is. He is really quite good."

The issue was not so easily laughed off. Fortas's role as presidential adviser troubled many of his friends in the press and the bar, and his tantalizing testimony on the subject served mainly to increase speculation and controversy.

The committee's other main line of inquiry, which focused on his judicial philosophy, also caused problems for the nominee. The limitations Fortas faced in responding to questions of this sort had been outlined by Senator Albert Gore from Fortas's home state of Tennessee, who had formally presented him to the committee. One restraint stemmed from another facet of the much discussed doctrine of separation of powers. "Just as a Senator or a Congressman may not be called upon by the courts to explain or justify his votes as a representative of the people," Gore said, ". . . so a Justice of the Supreme Court may not be required, by the Senate or a Senate committee, to explain or justify his votes on decisions by the Court or his judicial opinions." In addition, Gore pointed out, the nominee was obliged not to say anything that might intrude on the judicial process. As a Justice, Fortas must "avoid construing or explaining opinions of the Court lest he may appear to be adding to or subtracting from what has been decided, or may perchance be prejudging future cases."

But applying these limits to the questions the committee fired at him posed a dilemma for Fortas. In some respects he handled himself admirably. He was obviously well prepared. When Sam Ervin complained about the Supreme Court "habitually" overruling prior decisions, Fortas cited one of Judge Ervin's rulings on the North Carolina supreme court which had overturned a precedent of ten years' standing.

Fortas held his temper and kept his sense of humor. At one point Strom Thurmond stumbled and called him "Mr. Chief Justice."

"I thank you, Senator," Fortas said quickly.

"We all make mistakes," Thurmond snapped back.

"Well," Fortas replied, "yours is highly retrievable."

To some questions he managed short and snappy answers. "To what extent and under what circumstances," Senator Eastland asked, "do you believe that the Court should attempt to bring about social, economic or political change?"

"Zero," Fortas said, "absolutely zero."

When the senators brought up specific cases that the Court had decided, Fortas at first fell back on Senator Gore's thesis that the Constitution prohibited him from discussing these rulings with another branch of government. There was, however, an unavoidable irony in Fortas's invoking the doctrine of separation of powers which he had been accused of violating in his relations with President Johnson.

Fortas weakened his position further by departing from it occasionally when it suited his purpose. Ervin brought up an old charge made by the justices of the state supreme courts that the Warren Court was changing the meaning of the Constitution. Fortas referred him to a dissent he had written from a reapportionment decision applying the one-man, one-vote rule to county government. That dissent, Fortas said, expressed his feelings about the importance of the autonomy of state and local governments. "Perhaps I should not have said this—but I do not want to be associated with the object of the criticism of those state judges."

For his part, Ervin agreed not to question Fortas about his part in previous Court decisions, but he insisted that the decisions should be part of the record. So for the rest of that morning, on into the afternoon, and into the morning of the next day he cited fifteen decisions of the Supreme Court on labor-union picketing, control of subversives and criminal law, and offered his own lengthy interpretations.

Early in his recital Ervin suggested politely that Fortas might want to be excused. "No sir," said Fortas. "I shall not comment pursuant to the constitutional principle that I previously mentioned. And I shall remain if I may."

Even so, Fortas did not always keep silent. If the Warren Court had read the Constitution correctly in the *Miranda* decision, Ervin wondered "why one of the smart judges who sat on the Court during the preceding 176 years did not discover that?"

By way of explanation, Fortas referred him to *Powell v. Alabama*, a 1932 case in which the Scottsboro boys were defendants. That case, according to Fortas, was "the granddaddy" of *Miranda* and subsequent Warren Court rulings. "Now here I have done something I should not have done," he added quickly. "I am sorry, sir."

Then Strom Thurmond took over the questioning. More than any other man in the Senate, Thurmond symbolized the South's hostility to the Warren Court. He had first emerged as a national figure in 1948 when as leader of the Dixiecrat revolt against Harry Truman's civil-rights program he campaigned for President on the States Rights ticket. After that adventure, Thurmond returned to the Democratic fold, but in 1964 he bolted again, backed Barry Goldwater, converted to Republicanism, and became a leader of the GOP resurgence in the South. In the spring of 1968 he had cast his lot with Richard Nixon, laboring mightily to win Southern support for Nixon's nomination. A major general in the Army reserve with five World War II battle stars to his credit, at sixty-six Thurmond still stood ramrod straight and performed a daily round of pushups. As the Southern overseer of the Nixon forces he loomed larger than ever on the political scene.

As an interrogator, Thurmond was a good deal more belligerent than Ervin had been. He was not satisfied when Fortas begged off answering a question on constitutional grounds. "You have expressed your views to the President when he called you down there, and over the telephone, haven't you?" Thurmond complained. "Why shouldn't a Senator have the benefit of your views?"

"I have never, never been asked by the President," Fortas insisted. "Nor have I expressed my views on any pending or decided cases, never, Senator, never."

But Thurmond hammered away, demanding that Fortas explain the meaning of civil-rights and criminal law decisions, seemingly determined to goad him into answering. Suddenly he brought up a decision that reversed the conviction of a rapist named Andrew Mallory because police had delayed his arraignment too long. The case had been decided in 1957, eight years before Fortas joined the Court, but that made no difference to Thurmond. As he described the case, the senator worked himself into a rage. "Mallory—I want that name to ring in your ears," he shouted at Fortas. "Mallory," he shouted again. "Mallory, a man who raped a woman, admitted his guilt and the Supreme Court turned him loose on a technicality." Fortas glanced at Senator Eastland, but the chairman, slouched in his seat reading, did not look up, and Thurmond thundered on. "Is not that the type of decision calculated to encourage more people to commit rapes and serious crimes? Can you as a Justice of the Supreme Court condone such a decision as that? I ask you to answer that question."

For the first time in the hearings, Fortas was visibly shaken. He paused for a moment to compose himself before replying: "Senator, because of my respect for you and my respect for this body and because of my respect for the Constitution of the United States, and my position as an Associate Justice of the Supreme Court of the United States, I will adhere to the limitation that I believe the Constitution of the United States places upon me and will not reply to your question as you phrased it."

Thurmond would not give up. "Can you suggest any other way in which I can phrase that question?"

"That," Fortas said, "would be presumptuous."

But with Thurmond as with Ervin, Fortas did not always follow the example he had set for himself. Thurmond asked him about a 1967 decision on rules of criminal procedure in Texas courts. Fortas started to reply, then interrupted himself: ". . . I would like to withdraw that, because I must not discuss individual cases." Then he changed his mind again. He said that the case illustrated the impact of the Federal Constitution on state practices. He himself, he added, was opposed to the U.S. Supreme Court becoming a "super review tribunal for the states."

At last Thurmond ran out of cases and questions and Fortas's ordeal as a witness came to an end. It had lasted for twelve hours, spread over four days, consuming 145 pages in the record of the hearings. Fortas's composure in the face of Thurmond's bullyragging won him admiration and a measure of sympathy, but his refusal to answer most questions about the Court on "constitutional grounds" would have been more convincing if he had not responded to others when he saw a chance to score a point. His occasional colloquies with committee members took up time and left an impression of cleverness rather than candor.

Nearly thirty years earlier, when Felix Frankfurter testified at his confirmation hearings, he told the Judiciary Committee, "My attitude and outlook on relevant matters have been fully expressed over a period of years and are easily accessible. I should think it not only bad taste, but inconsistent with the duties of the office for which I have been nominated, for me to supplement my past record by present declarations." Unlike Fortas, Frankfurter had not been sitting on the Supreme Court when his nomination came before the committee. With three years of decisions behind him, Fortas had even more justification than Frankfurter to let his record speak for itself.

The conclusion of Fortas's own testimony did not end the inquiry into his record. The committee digressed briefly when it heard from Fortas's fellow-nominee, Homer Thornberry. A roundish, pink-faced man, Judge Thornberry was affable but adamant about refusing to discuss previous court decisions.

[171]

Prodded by Sam Ervin about his ruling that the poll tax was unconstitutional, Thornberry said: ". . . Nobody likes to be disagreeable, and certainly I am one of the least that does. But the opinion is the opinion of the court, and I have to stand on it, and I will." Strom Thurmond refused to ask any questions at all of this nominee, because, he argued, there was no vacancy on the Supreme Court for Thornberry to fill. It was clear that the committee would take no action on Thornberry until the Fortas nomination was settled.

Attention swiftly turned back to Fortas when a committee witness gave Fortas's foes a new target. The witness was James J. Clancy, an attorney for Citizens for Decent Literature, and the target was obscenity. Clancy complained that over the past two terms Fortas had joined in Court decisions overturning more than forty lower court obscenity convictions. As a result of these reversals, Clancy said, the nation's movie theaters and newsstands had been engulfed with pornography. "The smut industry takes its direction from the High Court's decisions," he charged, "advancing a giant step forward each time that the United States Supreme Court hands down a decision adverse to the people's interest."

Clancy's testimony touched off a wave of indignation. Thurmond, who had already charged Fortas with encouraging rapists, seized the opportunity to portray the Justice as an ally of pornographers. "How much longer are the parents, the Christian people, the wholesome people, the right-thinking people going to put up with this kind of thing?" he demanded to know. Brandishing a girlie magazine before the committee, Thurmond asked: "Should the Senate confirm a man for Chief Justice of the United States who has reversed the decisions in obscenity cases and allowed such material as this to be sold on the newsstands of this city and other cities of this nation?" Thurmond had a movie projector set up in the committee hearing room where some of the lurid films involved in the Court's decisions were put on display for the edification of the press and as many senators as Thurmond could persuade to come. Outrage quickly spread to the Senate floor. Returning from one screening, Senator Frank Lausche of Ohio denounced what he had witnessed as "a scandalization of the womanhood of the United States and of the world. If the nominee were my brother," Lausche declared, "I would not vote for him."

Such righteous rhetoric ignored the legal and moral complications that made obscenity probably the most difficult of all areas of constitutional law. Caught between concern for public morality and the First Amendment's protection of free expression, the Supreme Court had split into a number of different factions on the issue. Fortas himself was somewhere in the middle.

A majority of Justices, of which he was one, had given up as pointless and hopeless the task of trying to decide whether each book or movie that came before them was obscene. Instead they had suggested certain guidelines that met constitutional standards, as they conceived them, for controlling the distribution of pornography. They encouraged laws that prohibited "pandering" in advertising, protected people from being exposed to pornography against their wishes and set tighter controls on distribution of material to children. In the cases they decided, they sought to judge not the material itself, but rather the constitutionality of the laws under which the material had been suppressed. When the laws did not comply with constitutional safeguards, they reversed the convictions.

Fortas's supporters in the Senate were slow to make these points. The Court's complicated reasoning in this area did not lend itself readily to use as rebuttal evidence. Concluding that the obscenity issue could not help them, Fortas's backers tried to ignore it in hopes that it would be forgotten. It was not. Fortas's opponents, with the field to themselves, spent weeks attacking the nominee's permissiveness.

In any nomination fight the defense operates at a disadvantage. The opposition is free to range over the nominee's entire background to find ammunition; by the time one charge is answered two or three others have been leveled. In Fortas's case, his defense was further weakened by a lack of leadership and coordination.

Fortas had the support not only of the President of the United States but also of a substantial portion of what is often called the American establishment. The nation's most influential newspapers, including the *New York Times* and the *Washington Post,* were on his side. So were the leaders of the American Bar Association and the faculties of the ranking law schools. But there was no one to oversee and organize these forces. The White House, leery of direct involvement because of the charges of cronyism, turned quietly for help to Paul Porter, Fortas's devoted friend and former partner.

Porter gave nearly all his time to the effort. His law office became what one associate called a "command post" for the nomination struggle. Making use of a lifetime spent cultivating influential friends, Porter called around the country drumming up editorial support for the nomination. He was helped by a young associate at Arnold & Porter, Daniel Levitt, who had clerked for Fortas during the Justice's first two years on the Court. Levitt ghosted speeches for friendly senators and wrote a brief memorandum depicting Fortas as an apostle of judicial restraint, which Senator Hart placed in the record of the hearings without referring to its origins. Levitt also collaborated with a Justice Department staff member on a much longer memo which sought to rebut the criticism of Fortas on a case-by-case basis. When Hart entered this joint effort in the record he mentioned in passing that it had been prepared at his request by the Justice Department.

The memorandum, which reviewed Fortas's decisions in criminal law, subversive activities, civil disobedience, civil rights and labor relations, concluded:

> The judicial performance of a Justice cannot properly be assessed by selecting a scattering of cases decided over three years, in most of which the Justice did not write, and in disputing with him over the result in those cases . . . The proper measure by which to assess the performance of a Justice is to ask whether

his work as a whole reveals intelligent craftsmanship, insight and an understanding of the Constitution and government. On this score, Justice Fortas deserves extremely high marks.

This was not an unreasonable assertion, but it came from a questionable source. Senators were bound to resent being told how to conduct their deliberations by an agency of the executive branch of the government. There was also a question of propriety. The Justice Department, as the Federal government's lawyer, is the most frequent litigant to appear before the Supreme Court. Now it had been placed in the position of passing judgment on a member of the Court. It would have seemed far more discreet to have Fortas's opinions analyzed by Senate staff members. If their backgrounds were not adequate to the task, Hart might have turned to the law schools right in Washington, whose faculties included a number of men sympathetic to Fortas's views. Considering the dual participation of Arnold & Porter and the Justice Department in preparing the memo, Fortas's supporters got off lightly. It is not hard to imagine the cries of indignation from Ervin and Thurmond if they had learned that Fortas's former law firm had a behind-the-scenes role in supporting his nomination.

As it was, the Justice Department took the full responsibility—and the criticism.* Senator Ervin denounced the department for trying "to propagandize the committee" and demanded an explanation. Deputy Attorney General Warren Christopher was dispatched to testify, and Ervin and Thurmond spent a full day pecking away at him.

The net result of this brouhaha, apart from the Justice Department's embarrassment, was to kill more time. When Christopher finished testifying, on July 23, the hearings had taken up nine days, strung out over three weeks. The preliminaries to the Republican convention had already begun in Miami and Congress was preparing to adjourn. The nomina-

---

* In Richard Nixon's Administration the department's position would be just as awkward when it sought to defend *his* Supreme Court nominees against senatorial challenge. See Chapter Nine.

tion remained locked in the committee, which would do nothing further about it until Congress returned after Labor Day.

While his nomination hung fire, Fortas spoke out on his own behalf at a dinner of the American College of Trial Lawyers, which had just made him an honorary member. "I'm most grateful to you for confirming my nomination," he began, "that is, my nomination as an honorary member of this distinguished organization."

The Justice did not otherwise refer to his difficulties before the Senate. But the thrust of his speech was clearly designed to answer the charge that the Court's decisions had encouraged crime and violence. He affirmed his own belief in "the rule of law," which, he acknowledged, was threatened as never before. "Violence is intolerable," Fortas said; "lawlessness is impermissible whatever the cause." But to those who complained that the Court was overly concerned with procedural safeguards, Fortas asserted: "Constitutionalism is not a technicality. Constitutional rights are not technicalities. This," he added, in an unmistakable paraphrase of Strom Thurmond's tirade about the *Mallory* case, "is the phrase that should ring in the nation's ear."

But other phrases and events dominated the nation's attention that summer. A few days after Fortas's speech, Richard Nixon accepted the Republican nomination for the presidency in a speech that underlined the reasons for public hostility toward the Warren Court. Nixon spoke of "cities enveloped in smoke and flame," "sirens in the night," and unprecedented racial violence. He paid his respects to the judiciary, but added: "Let us also recognize that some of our courts have gone too far in weakening the peace forces, as against the criminal forces, in this country." Nixon's nomination strengthened the Republican opposition to Fortas in the Senate. Not only did Nixon prefer that the choice of the next Chief Justice be left to the next President, but also the attack on Fortas helped dramatize the criticism of the Warren Court, which was one of his major campaign themes.

The developments in the Republican camp were no surprise to Fortas and Lyndon Johnson. They could not have anticipated, however, the disaster at the Democratic Convention, which further damaged Fortas's chances. The violence in Chicago's streets climaxed a year filled with murder and riot, which inspired growing anxiety and fear in the nation. Many Americans watching television coverage of the demonstrators' battles with police outside the convention were convinced that the Warren Court's permissiveness, which Fortas seemed to exemplify, had encouraged the demonstrators and crippled the police.

The climate on Capitol Hill when Congress returned in early September was less favorable than ever toward Lyndon Johnson's nominations. Senator Eastland, on whose support the President had once counted, publicly announced his opposition. Moreover, Eastland said he did not know when his committee would resume its consideration of the nomination. When Mike Mansfield, the Senate Democratic leader, and Everett Dirksen, his Republican counterpart, reported to the President neither even pretended to be optimistic. The outlook, Mansfield frankly told newsmen, was "not encouraging." Dirksen, as always more poetic, said the prospects were "not roseate."

Lyndon Johnson, who had committed his crumbling prestige to the struggle, could not afford to give up. Next day he summoned Dirksen and Mansfield back to the White House and ordered them to get the nomination out of the Judiciary Committee and onto the Senate floor. The President called a press conference to upbraid the opposition as "a little group, a sectional group primarily, which disapproves of some opinions Supreme Court Justices have rendered." This faction, he declared, should not be permitted "by parliamentary tricks to filibuster and prevent the majority from expressing its viewpoint."

The President did what he could. His emissaries went forth to Capitol Hill bearing threats and promises. The Judiciary Committee agreed to resume hearings on the nominations and scheduled a vote. The White House still counted a substantial majority of the committee and sixty votes in the full Senate in favor of the nomination. If that support held firm and if a few others could be rounded up, then it might be possible to collect the two-thirds majority needed to pass a cloture motion halting a filibuster.

It was a slim hope at best. One final unexpected blow demolished it. Early in September a staff member at American University in Washington phoned Senator Griffin's office to suggest that Griffin look into the arrangements for a series of seminars Fortas had conducted at the university's law school that summer. Fortas's participation in the seminars was no secret. It had been publicly announced months before, but Griffin's tipster contended that Fortas had been paid an exorbitant sum which had been raised outside the university. Griffin passed the information on to Strom Thurmond who, as a member of the Judiciary Committee, summoned Dean B. J. Tennery of the law school to testify.

Before Tennery appeared, Paul Porter confided the essential details to Joe Califano at the White House. Fortas had been paid $15,000 for conducting the seminars. Porter himself had raised the money from five wealthy businessmen, three of whom were clients of Arnold & Porter. When Lyndon Johnson heard the news, Califano said later, "he was obviously troubled." He had reason to be.

In his explanation to the Judiciary Committee, Dean Tennery struggled to put the best face possible on the matter. The dean himself had conceived the seminars as an experiment in exposing law students to other academic disciplines, such as sociology, economics and psychology. Justice Fortas, Tennery learned, shared his interest in this interdisciplinary approach. Fortas's background as a teacher and his stature in the legal profession made him seem the ideal man to launch the project. When Fortas agreed to take on the assignment, there was no discussion of how much money he would be paid. And, Tennery said, Fortas did not know where the money came from.

At Tennery's request, Porter handled the financial arrangements. He had raised $5,000 each from Gustave Levy, chairman of the New York Stock Exchange; Troy Post, chairman of Greatamerica Corporation and Braniff Airways; Maurice Lazarus, vice chairman of Federated Department Stores; and John Loeb, a senior partner in the brokerage house of Carl M. Loeb. Paul D. Smith, vice president of Philip Morris, contributed $10,000. Half of the $30,000 went to Fortas for his services and the teaching materials he prepared. The rest was put aside to pay for subsequent seminars.

It was by no means rare for a Supreme Court Justice to teach in his spare time, Tennery told the committee. Justice Story had taught at Harvard; the first Justice Harlan and Justice Brewer taught at George Washington law school in the capital. Tennery was full of praise for Fortas's conduct of the seminars. He considered his own exposure to him "one of the more rewarding experiences" of his life. And for the seventeen students who had attended the nine sessions "it was probably the finest academic encounter they ever had." If $15,000 seemed like a good deal of money, Tennery argued: "We are in a competitive business in the sense of law schools. We compete for intellectual brains, not only studentwise, but facultywise." Besides, Tennery recalled that a popular folk singer who had recently played an engagement at the university had been paid about $10,000. "This may be a sad commentary on our society," he said. "But I submit that a Supreme Court Justice is of considerably more value in the long run."

No matter how the dean phrased it, the episode certainly was a sad commentary. Everyone knew that Supreme Court Justices sometimes gave lectures for money. But the $15,000 payment to Fortas, by comparison either to the standard lecture fee or to his own annual salary of $39,500, was out of proportion. More disturbing was the source of the money. When Senator Thurmond described the five donors as representing "a complex of business and financial holdings that scarcely could be extricated from anything touching upon the Court" it was difficult to quarrel with him. Fortas's supporters argued that the Justice had always exercised the greatest care in avoiding the possibility of favoritism by recusing himself from all cases in which his former law firm or clients were involved, however remotely. The fact remained, however, that he had permitted himself to become involved in a situation that inevitably would raise the suspicion of conflict of interest on a broad range of important issues.

What followed was almost anticlimactic. There were further charges about Fortas's activities at the White House. He was said to have helped draft legislation providing Secret Service protection to all presidential candidates. Two Administration officials called to testify on that point declined, pleading executive privilege. The committee also sought to verify a story that Fortas, together with Clark Clifford, had helped rewrite the President's 1966 State of the Union address. But Clifford asked to be excused from testifying "because of the complexities of the current world situation."

Fortas himself turned down, without explanation, an invitation to testify further. "I hope that during the interrogation of me by members of the committee," he wrote, "my respect for the Senate as well as my profound and unshakable devotion to the Court and the Constitution was evident."

As the committee prepared to vote on the nomination, Richard Nixon was heard from again. The Republican nominee went on record as being opposed to all filibusters, including the one planned against Fortas's nomination. But Senator Griffin did not seem to consider Nixon's statement as anything more than a *pro forma* objection. "At the outset Mr. Nixon said he'd stay out of this controversy," Griffin remarked, "and frankly I wish he would."

On September 17 the Judiciary Committee, as expected, finally approved the nomination, eleven votes to six, but the opposition of three Southern Democrats, Ervin, McClellan and Eastland, made certain that Griffin would have bipartisan support for his filibuster. On Wednesday, September 25, Senator Mansfield formally moved that the Senate consider the nominations. The majority leader called Fortas "eminently qualified," a man in the tradition of Brandeis and Cardozo. But even Mansfield did not attempt to disguise his distress over the American University seminars. That episode, he said, was "unfortunate because it breaches the extraordinary insulation which must exist between the Supreme Court and other branches of the government and private interests."

No sooner had Mansfield finished than Griffin opened the filibuster with a two-hour-and-forty-minute speech. The record of Fortas's testimony before the Judiciary Committee, Griffin charged, was "inadequate, inconsistent and contradictory." Other senators chimed in, each with a different point to make against the nomination.

Occasionally Phil Hart, slumped mournfully in his chair through most of the oratory, rose to complain that one of the speakers had strayed from the subject, but like most of Fortas's supporters he seemed too discouraged to press Griffin and his allies. The histrionics and grueling night sessions which had marked past filibusters were conspicuously absent. The Senate kept its usual hours and on Friday, after three days of debate, recessed for the weekend. By that time the forces supporting the nomination had been further weakened by the announcement of their erstwhile ally, Everett Dirksen, that he would not vote for cloture.

It was all over but the voting. That came on Tuesday, October 1, when Mansfield moved to limit debate. The count was forty-five in favor of cloture and forty-three against, fourteen votes short of the necessary two-thirds majority. Richard Russell voted against cloture, along with nearly all his Southern colleagues. Griffin's eighteen Republican votes had held just as firm as he promised Russell they would.

In somber tones Mike Mansfield briefly lectured his colleagues. "The Senate," he said, "has refused to face squarely the issue of the nomination of Mr. Justice Fortas." But with Congress pushing for adjournment in another week, no one had the heart to challenge the filibuster again.

The day after the cloture motion failed, Fortas wrote to Lyndon Johnson, asking that his name be withdrawn. "Continued efforts to secure confirmation . . . even if ultimately successful, would result in a continuation of the attacks upon the Court which have characterized the filibuster—attacks which have been sometimes extreme and entirely unrelated to responsible criticism." The President, "with deep regret," agreed. He still believed, he said, that Fortas was "the best qualified man for this high position. . . . The action of the Senate, a body I revere and to which I devoted a dozen years of my life, is historically and constitutionally tragic." A week later Lyndon Johnson announced he did not intend to make a second effort to nominate a replacement for Earl Warren. He called on the Chief to stay at his post "until emotion subsides" and "reason and fairness prevail." Warren agreed.

The reasons for Fortas's defeat were varied and cumulative. Success depended on the Senate deciding the issue quickly. The longer the struggle went on, the longer the odds grew against the nomination. Hindsight always offers advantages, but some problems facing the nomination were obvious enough to begin with so that certain mistakes might reasonably have been avoided. The indefinite timing of Warren's retirement, with the implication of forcing the Senate to choose between Warren and Fortas, served only to antagonize the opposition and to tarnish the nominations. The President could do nothing to conceal his long friendship with Fortas, but he could certainly have selected as the other nominee someone further removed from him personally and politically than Homer Thornberry. Fortas himself would have been better off had he said much less than he did before the Judiciary Committee. His testimony generated far more heat than light. Had different tactics been employed, Fortas's nomination might well have been confirmed before the disclosure of the $15,000 American University fee, which Joe Califano later called "the straw that broke the camel's back."

In the aftermath of his setback in the Senate, there was some speculation that Fortas might resign from the Court. Strom Thurmond, for one, had bluntly suggested that he do exactly that. But Fortas plainly had no such intention, not at the moment anyhow.

On the day after the President withdrew his name from Senate consideration, Fortas spoke at New York University at an observance of the one-hundredth anniversary of the Fourteenth Amendment. He shared the platform with his predecessor at the Court, Arthur Goldberg, who was moved to express "his profound regret at the wrongful action of the United States Senate." Goldberg added that his wife, Dorothy, had recalled some appropriate words of Benjamin Franklin's: "Do not in public life expect immediate approbation of one's services. One must persevere through insult and injury . . ."

When it was his turn at the lectern Fortas paused in the midst of a discourse on civil liberties, turned to Goldberg and with evident feeling said: "Tell Dorothy that so far as I am concerned I shall persevere." The audience of lawyers and students rose to its feet applauding.

A few weeks later, addressing a gathering of book publishers, Fortas once again sounded like his familiar ironic self. The Senate's attack on Supreme Court decisions, he remarked, had made the collected volumes of High Court rulings "the most denounced publication in history, except possibly the writings of Karl Marx." Moreover, Fortas told the assembled bookmen, "the people who denounce our literary products don't even buy them." But for all that, the harsh and persistent criticism was "only vaguely troublesome" to the Court, Fortas said. "We just go along, reading and writing as best we can, hoping that somewhere, somehow, we're doing something right."

The Supreme Court seemed much the same as it had been before the battle over Fortas's nomination. Earl Warren was still its Chief and would remain so until the newly elected President, Richard Nixon, replaced him in June of 1969. The liberals, Fortas among them, remained in command. Fortas personally could look forward to a calmer period in his life. With Lyndon Johnson preparing to leave the White House,

Fortas would finally be completely free to concentrate on his work at the Court, and he could expect that the gossip about his relationship with the President would soon diminish.

What remained to plague him, however, was the memory of the American University fee with all its implications. The uneasiness about Fortas's ethical standards and values which had ended his chance to be Chief Justice had also placed in jeopardy his future on the Court.

THE PATRON
OF PUBLIC SERVANTS

WHEN FORTAS'S arrangement with American University was first disclosed in September of 1968, his supporters in the Senate immediately wondered if there was anything else in his past that might cause him and them embarrassment. "He told us there was nothing," an aide to Senator Phil Hart later recalled. In fact there was something, which Fortas had either forgotten or chosen to overlook.

In June of 1965, some weeks before Fortas was appointed to the Court and three years before he was nominated to be its Chief, a new and affluent client came to his office and to his law firm. He was Louis Elwood Wolfson, industrialist, sportsman and philanthropist, a personage eminently pragmatic yet peculiarly romantic, a twentieth-century tycoon with the panache of a nineteenth-century freebooter. Nerve, ambition and shrewd business instincts had made Wolfson a multimillionaire when he was in his early forties and he worked and played on a grand scale. He raised his own thoroughbreds, bankrolled election campaigns and counted the big names of politics, sports and show business among his friends. Now fifty-three years old, he was turning grey, but remained a striking man, deeply tanned and ruggedly handsome. At the moment, as so often during his career, he was embroiled in controversy and litigation.

Like Fortas, Wolfson was born in the South of immigrant Jewish stock, and he had risen high and fast in the world. There the resemblance ended. No scholar and no aesthete, Wolfson was a rough-and-tumble type. As a teen-ager he had boxed professionally in his hometown, Jacksonville, Florida, under the ring name of "Kid Wolf." Later he played the line on the University of Georgia football team and briefly considered making his career as a football coach. Instead, he went into his father's junk business, expanded it by trading briskly in government surplus, and used it as a base for building an economic empire.

In 1949 Wolfson and his associates gained control of the Capital Transit Co., which ran Washington's buses and trolleys. Wolfson's group proceeded to deplete the treasury by raising dividends to stockholders, while infuriating the public by boosting fares and cutting service. Finally, in the midst of a crippling strike, the company was deprived of its franchise by act of Congress. In 1956 Wolfson sold out, taking with him a handsome profit but leaving behind bitter memories of his management style.

By this time Wolfson had become deeply involved in Merritt-Chapman & Scott, one of the nation's oldest marine salvage and construction firms. In 1898 Merritt's engineers had investigated the sinking of the battleship Maine in Havana Harbor, and nearly half a century later they were called in to raise the capsized French liner *Normandie.* Wolfson was less interested in past glories than in future growth and diversification. He gained control of the company and turned it into one of the first conglomerates, acquiring more than a dozen other firms in shipbuilding, steel making, money lending and other fields. Merritt's net worth jumped from $8 million just before Wolfson took over to $132 million in 1955.

On other fronts Wolfson's expansionism ran into opposition. When he sought to take over Montgomery Ward, the mail-order giant, in 1954, Sewell Avery, the company's elderly ruler, branded Wolfson a raider and resisted. After a widely publicized two-year battle, Wolfson gave up and withdrew.

For a while American Motors, which was beginning its rise in the auto industry under George Romney, seemed another likely target for takeover, but Romney discouraged Wolfson's ambitions and in 1958 he retreated once again. Wolfson, however, still owned 400,000 shares of American Motors stock whose disposition he turned over to a trusted associate, Elkin B. (Buddy) Gerbert. As Wolfson later told the story, Gerbert decided to sell the stock without Wolfson's knowledge; he not only sold all Wolfson's shares, but left him short in the stock. In other words the shares which had been sold were borrowed in the expectation of replacing them later when the market price dropped. Unfortunately for Gerbert and Wolfson, the price of the stock kept rising instead of falling. At this point another close Wolfson associate, Alex Rittmaster, publicly announced that Wolfson, in the belief that American Motors stock had reached its peak, had already sold about one-quarter of his holdings. This statement, which seemed likely to drive the price of the stock down, naturally aroused the suspicions of the Securities and Exchange Commission, the regulator of the stock market. An SEC investigation turned up the fact that far from still owning three-quarters of his American Motors stock, as Rittmaster's statement implied, Wolfson was actually short in the stock and stood to benefit from a price drop. The SEC accused Wolfson of trying to rig the market by putting out false and misleading information. Wolfson steadfastly denied knowing anything about either Gerbert's sales or Rittmaster's peculiar announcement. But when the SEC took him to court he consented, without admitting any wrongdoing, to a permanent injunction against issuing false statements or carrying out fraudulent operations in American Motors stock.

Soon after that imbroglio, the cornerstone of Wolfson's empire, Merritt-Chapman & Scott, ran into trouble. Under Wolfson's prodding the company had taken on vast construction projects, including a string of dams and power plants and sec-tions of the Mackinac and Throggs Neck bridges. As Wolfson conceded later, the company was growing too fast for its executives to supervise properly. Management bungling was compounded by various other problems: labor disputes, bad weather on construction sites and an ugly scandal. The corporation was convicted of bribing a public utilities official in connection with a dam project in the state of Washington. In 1960 Merritt-Chapman lost $52 million and Wolfson was forced to begin overhauling its management and cutting back its operations. Meanwhile, one of its subsidiaries, New York Shipbuilding, had gotten in over its head by taking on construction of the supercarrier *Kitty Hawk*. The deal not only cost the company money but led to a bitter wrangle. The Navy complained about the speed and quality of the work, while the company, for its part, complained about design changes ordered by the Navy after the job had been started.

It was this combination of difficulties that sent Wolfson to Fortas's law office in June of 1965. Like many of Fortas's clients, he had problems with the government. New York Shipbuilding still had a claim against the Navy Department, and Wolfson wanted legal help in settling it. At Merritt-Chapman & Scott, where Wolfson was board chairman and chief executive officer, there was another and potentially more serious problem. For more than six months trading in Merritt's stock had been under investigation by the SEC. Fortas promised that the law firm would look into both matters.

But Wolfson had more on his mind than his business problems. That year he would earn more than $500,000 from Merritt-Chapman, and by some estimates he was worth $100 million. He claimed he did not even keep track of such things. Money was not all that important to him, he said; it served mainly "as a medium of keeping score." It also enabled him to pursue a number of outside interests, among which was charity. Wolfson's friends pointed admiringly to his support of countless good causes, large and small. His long-time secretary, Monteen Tomberlin, once filled a twenty-six-page letter with examples of Wolfson's personal kindness. He gave sums of cash to old acquaintances who were down on their luck and to total strangers who seemed deserving. Each Christmas he provided every orphan in Florida's Duval County with a gift of candy and a brand new dollar bill; each June he donated a share of Merritt-Chapman stock to every graduate of his alma mater, the University of Georgia. On a more organized scale, he contributed also to fund-raising campaigns for schools, churches, and hospitals.

In philanthropy as in business Wolfson was ambitious. In 1955 he told *Look* magazine that what he wanted out of life was "ten more years to build an empire—then I might go into public service—juvenile delinquency maybe or fighting communism." That same year he had tried to enlist Frank Leahy's help in developing a program to reduce juvenile delinquency that would, Wolfson wrote, "do more for the future citizens of this country than anything else I know of." Leahy had been interested, but illness prevented him from following through.

In 1951 Wolfson, following the example set by many others in his economic stratum, had established his own charitable foundation. The privilege of income tax exemption enjoyed by such organizations not only encourages the support of worthy causes, but also offers their founders a range of economic advantages which, as one study has pointed out, are "limited only by the imagination of the rich man's attorney." Over the years the Wolfson Family Foundation had contributed to a variety of social welfare groups, religious institutions, scholarship funds and medical research programs, principally in Wolfson's home state of Florida. But Wolfson wanted his foundation to take on bigger and broader challenges, and for this, he decided, he needed Abe Fortas's expert advice.

Wolfson knew that Fortas's name had long been associated with various liberal causes and social reforms. His reputation, ability and connections in Washington would enhance the foundation and would do Wolfson himself no harm. At one of their early meetings Wolfson brought up the subject of the foundation and discussed his hopes and problems. Fortas, according to Wolfson, "showed a genuine and sincere interest in the work of the foundation, particularly in the area of juvenile delinquency."

Nothing more was said about the matter by either man until a few weeks later Wolfson read of Arthur Goldberg's resignation from the Supreme Court and the accompanying rumors that Fortas would be appointed in his place. Wolfson immediately wrote to Goldberg, whom he had known for years, congratulating him on his appointment as ambassador to the United Nations, and offering him financial aid. "I know that you will be making substantial personal sacrifices, from a standpoint of both finances and health, in undertaking these responsibilities," Wolfson said. ". . . The least a man in my position, and others similarly situated, can do is to assist financially or any other way, within the scope of our abilities." He did not want to embarrass Goldberg, but he hoped to meet with him to discuss his offer.

It was an extraordinary proposal. But Wolfson had made many similar offers in the past, and, by his account, a good number had been accepted. All his life, he later explained, he had made it a practice "to encourage qualified Americans to seek and accept positions in our government and, when possible, to assist them so they can do so with total dedication and without any strings attached." When he was asked how much he had bestowed as patron of the public service, Wolfson remarked: "A million dollars wouldn't even touch it."

The exact amount was difficult to calculate because arrangements varied, depending on the circumstances. Wolfson contributed to campaign funds, but he also made special dispensations. In the case of former Governor Fuller Warren, to whom it was said he had given as much as $300,000, Wolfson said: "I helped him as a friend over a period of years before he was elected Governor. . . . I got involved so deeply . . . I had to go ahead and make sure I stick with him until he gets elected."

Wolfson was always willing to be flexible. "Someone has to tell me what kind of financial assistance they need," he later explained. "And I have to see if they want to come in with our foundation . . . and do some consulting, making speeches around the country." Apart from Fuller Warren, Wolfson has declined to identify officials and candidates who accepted his help. But the names of some prominent men who turned him down indicate that his generosity was bipartisan and reached around the map of the country. In 1964 Wolfson sought to encourage former Oklahoma football coach Bud Wilkinson to run for the Senate on the Republican ticket by promising him a $30,000-a-year job in one of Wolfson's companies if the coach was defeated. Wilkinson ran and lost, but chose to go into broadcasting instead. Four years later Wolfson offered to make up any deficit in the Senate campaign of Democrat Abe Ribicoff. Ribicoff thanked him and said his campaign was adequately financed. In the intervening years Wolfson made other offers of aid to James Roosevelt, who was thinking of running for the Senate, and to former Florida Governor LeRoy Collins.

While some might look upon such beneficence with suspicion, Wolfson maintained that his own conscience was clear. No one, he insisted, "can or will ever say that I have asked for anything in return. The truth of the matter is that I have never been motivated by anything other than my sincere desire to see capable and conscientious men in office using their abilities in the best interests of our nation."

Arthur Goldberg, however, had his own compunctions and he politely refused Wolfson's offer of help. He appreciated "the spirit" of Wolfson's offer and "the kind sentiments." Nevertheless, the new ambassador wrote: "It has been my fixed rule . . . in my public career, to manage my personal affairs with my own resources."

Meanwhile, Wolfson had been in touch with Fortas, who at the time had not yet agreed to accept nomination to the Court. Wolfson told him that he realized Fortas's appointment to the bench would deprive Wolfson of his legal service. Nevertheless, he urged Fortas to take the position because "he could render a valuable service to our nation." It was true that giving up his law practice would mean a considerable financial sacrifice. But, Wolfson went on, Fortas should not let that stand in his way. There were legitimate ways to supplement his income as a Justice and he, Wolfson, was prepared to help him.

At the moment, Wolfson's encouragement had little effect. Fortas thanked him, but insisted that he could not accept the appointment.

The very next day Lyndon Johnson summoned Fortas to the White House and announced his nomination. Soon afterward, as Wolfson recalled, Fortas phoned and explained that he could not refuse the Court seat because of the President's insistence. Then, according to Wolfson, Fortas mentioned the Wolfson Family Foundation and "asked me to give some thought about the amount of time that would be required if he were to serve as a consultant."

Fortas himself wanted some time to think about the new situation that confronted him. "I did not seek the post of Justice of the Supreme Court of the United States," he later said. "This was not part of my life plan." Now his plan would need to be modified. He would have to give up the far-ranging activities of private practice for the more limited world of the Supreme Court. "I was afraid," he later said, "that I might go to seed on the Court. I couldn't bear the idea of not being fully occupied." Then, too, Fortas shared some of Thurman Arnold's impatience with the remoteness of the bench. Both men, according to one of their partners, "thought appellate judges were out of touch with reality."

The change in his financial circumstance was something else to ponder. Fortas's earnings would drop sharply from the $200,000-a-year range to a flat $39,500. To be sure, other money would be coming in. Fortas owned some stock and real estate and he would receive $50,000 a year for five years under terms of his settlement with Arnold & Porter. Carol Agger earned more than $100,000 a year at the firm, and this figure was bound to increase if only because the remaining partners' shares of the profits had been increased proportionately after Fortas left. By no standard could the Fortases be considered financially hard pressed. Still, it all added up to less than they had earned before, and Abe and Carol were accustomed to living well. The Fortases, one long-time friend later remarked, "had an uncurbed desire for a level of income and a standard of living which I personally couldn't understand."

Friends searched for explanations. One suggested that "Abe suffered from a strong attraction to money, a little like people who gamble or who have woman trouble." Others thought that Fortas felt pressured to compete with his wife's formidable earning power. Carol herself was decidedly unhappy about the change in their economic circumstances and notably uninhibited about voicing her feelings at the law firm and at Washington dinner parties. One acquaintance recalled her complaining frequently "about what a dirty trick LBJ had played by making Abe go on the Court."

There was no way for Fortas to close the entire gap between his past and future earnings. But a consultancy with the Wolfson Foundation would make up some of the difference.

As a Supreme Court Justice Fortas was legally free to do much as he pleased with his spare time. Congress had prohibited Federal judges from practicing law, but was otherwise silent on their off-bench activities. The American Bar Association's canons of judicial ethics, adopted in 1924, provided only hazy and unofficial advice on the subject. Judges were told that their personal behavior should be "beyond reproach" and admonished not to accept "inconsistent" obligations. But they were permitted to teach, write and lecture for money, provided these services did not interfere with their judicial performance.

Fortas certainly would not be the first member of the Supreme Court to serve a philanthropic organization. A number of his predecessors had been officers or trustees of educational institutions, hospitals, religious organizations and museums. His friend Justice Douglas had for several years been involved with a charitable foundation established by Albert Parvin, a Los Angeles businessman, to promote international understanding through fellowships, seminars and similar programs. Fortas may also have known, though it was not yet public knowledge, that Douglas was paid $12,000 a year to cover the costs of travel and other expenses. There was no restriction on how much a Justice could earn this way, nor any requirement that he publicly disclose his earnings.

It might have occurred to Fortas that certain characteristics of Louis Wolfson would make some consider him a questionable associate for a Supreme Court Justice. Wolfson had a reputation as a sharp operator. He had been in difficulty with the government in the past, and even now, as Fortas knew, he was under investigation by the Securities and Exchange Commission.

Fortas has never publicly discussed how he weighed these factors, if he considered them at all. But taking into consideration Fortas's experience and outlook, it is possible to surmise his thoughts. Big business was after all a dog-eat-dog world; men who rose to the top fast often trampled on convention and on other people. For all the furor Wolfson had aroused he had never been convicted of a criminal offense, nor even charged with one. If he was at loggerheads with the government, so, at one time or another, were many of Fortas's eminently respectable clients. Moreover, even if Wolfson's current difficulties with the SEC culminated in litigation, Justice Fortas would not sit on the case. Since Wolfson was a client of his former law firm, judicial propriety would ordinarily oblige Fortas to disqualify himself from any matter in which Wolfson was involved. Besides, Fortas was not going to work for Wolfson; he was going to consult for his foundation. Whatever one might think of Wolfson, no one could object to spending his money for a good cause. It was true that Wolfson's plans were hazy. But he had the money; Fortas would supply the ideas. Fortas must have known that Wolfson collected influential people as friends, and he might well have suspected that Wolfson was particularly interested in adding a presidential adviser to his collection. But that was Wolfson's business. Fortas would look out for himself.

In October of 1965, after Fortas had taken the oath as Justice, he invited Wolfson and his wife to a reception in Fortas's honor at the Court. Wolfson, by his account, was reluctant to attend; he told Fortas that he generally avoided functions of that sort. Fortas insisted; he and Carol would be disappointed if the Wolfsons did not attend. The Wolfsons came, and dined with the Fortases afterward. The next day, October 23, Wolfson visited Fortas's Georgetown home, where the two men had a "lengthy discussion" about the Wolfson Family Foundation.

During that talk, Wolfson mentioned the SEC's investigation of Merritt-Chapman & Scott. He had learned earlier that month from his lawyers, Wolfson said, that this was a more serious matter than he had first thought. Wolfson pointed out to Fortas, he said later, "that this investigation could be embarrassing to him if he were associated with the Wolfson Family Foundation." But Fortas reassured his friend. He told him, Wolfson recalled, that the SEC investigation appeared to involve "technical violations," and that he "did not think anything of a serious nature would develop."

With that problem out of the way, Fortas agreed to serve as a consultant to the foundation, concentrating, according to Wolfson, on juvenile delinquency. Wolfson asked him to draw up a contract.

Wolfson was not a man to quibble over money. Moreover, Fortas later explained, he and Wolfson had agreed that "the program in question was a long-range one, and that my association would be meaningful only if it were on a long-term basis." Accordingly, "instead of fixing variable compensation from time to time," Fortas set his fee at a flat $20,000, which would be paid to him each year for the rest of his life. He also added a provision that seemed likely to ease Carol Agger's sense of financial distress. Even after his death, Fortas stipulated, the foundation would continue to pay $20,000 a year to his wife.

On its face, this arrangement would seem to be a very large expenditure for an organization which the year before had disbursed $128,000 in grants and, during the period of Fortas's consultancy, would give away only $77,000. But perhaps

Fortas would find new outlets for the foundation's largesse. Wolfson himself saw no problem with the fee, or with the terms of the contract. "I was primarily interested and principally interested," he later explained, "in using this man's great knowledge in this field." In December the foundation's board of trustees reviewed the contract and approved it as Fortas had drafted it. In January of 1966 the foundation sent its new consultant his first check for $20,000.

MR. F. GOES TO FLORIDA

LOUIS WOLFSON would later complain that he had been the victim of a "political vendetta" and would liken the government's prosecution of him to the Dreyfus case. In truth, the SEC investigation that brought on his troubles began more through chance than calculation. Most of the initial impetus came from a junior staff member named Stuart Allen who had never even heard of Wolfson before. While Wolfson's exploits at Montgomery Ward and American Motors were making headlines, Allen was too absorbed in finishing high school and college to pay attention. He had joined the SEC in 1961, when he was twenty-four, as a financial analyst; the Wolfson case, which began in 1964, would turn into his first criminal investigation. "It's a wonder I didn't blow the whole thing," he said later. A stocky, serious young man, Allen proved to be a relentless investigator. Wolfson, who never met him, later complained that he had been "bloodhounding" the case. Wolfson's friend Buddy Gerbert, who did meet Allen, half jokingly called him "killer."

The Wolfson investigation was an offshoot of a general SEC effort in the early 1960's to tighten its regulation of the securities industry. Allen had been assigned to conduct a broad review of SEC policing techniques, one aspect of which focused on trading by corporations in their own stock. He came across records which indicated that Wolfson's company, Merritt-Chapman & Scott, had been making massive purchases of its own shares. Suspiciously, it seemed to Allen, many of these purchases had been made not in the open market but in private transactions at prices above the going market rate. Also he observed that the price of the stock, which had slumped badly after Merritt's disastrous year in 1960, had climbed rapidly during the spring and summer of 1964.

While Allen was quietly exploring this situation, another development dramatically called attention to Wolfson and to Merritt-Chapman. In November of 1964 the company announced a tender offer to buy 1.2 million shares of its stock from shareholders at an attractive price. Wolfson, who had been steadily buying the stock for his own account, disclosed that he planned to take advantage of the offer to sell about 345,000 of his shares. The SEC, suspecting that the tender offer was designed mainly for Wolfson's benefit, launched a formal investigation of the company, the tender offer and the private sales.

Wolfson promptly declared that he was not going to tender his shares after all. His tax consultants, he said, had advised against it. Wolfson and his associates, including Buddy Gerbert, and Marshal Staub, Merritt-Chapman's president, were summoned before the SEC and questioned about the company's purchases of its own stock from private parties. But their testimony shed no light on the transactions, and the SEC had little evidence to pursue this line of inquiry. In the SEC's New York office, which was doing much of the work on the case, interest faded. When the SEC lawyers principally involved in the inquiry left the agency for private employment, Stuart Allen recalled, "there was talk of dropping the whole thing."

Allen, however, was still interested. In the spring of 1965 he and a staff lawyer in the SEC's Washington headquarters resumed examination of Merritt's stock purchases. In the process of poking into Wolfson's financial affairs, Allen stumbled across indications of questionable dealings in another and much smaller company, Continental Enterprises, in which Wolfson also had a controlling interest. Allen's findings revived SEC interest in Wolfson's operations in general, and in the fall of 1965 the commission turned its attention back to the Merritt-Chapman case, assigned additional staff to the investigation and called more witnesses.

These activities account for Wolfson's concern about the SEC when he met with Fortas in October of 1965 to discuss the Justice's rôle in the Wolfson Family Foundation. Fortas's supposed remark that Wolfson had little to worry about probably reflected in part the attitude of Milton Freeman, whom Fortas had asked to handle the Wolfson case just before he joined the Court. A veteran of the SEC's legal staff during the New Deal years, Freeman had specialized in securities law with Arnold, Fortas & Porter for twenty years. After Fortas became a Justice, he and Freeman continued to see each other from time to time, Freeman recalled, and discussed "in general terms" some of Freeman's cases, including the Wolfson matter.

Freeman's first move had been to review the situation with the New York firm of Shea, Gallop, Climenko & Gould, which Wolfson had retained before coming to Fortas. "You never know what the SEC knows," Freeman explained later. "All you can do is to try to figure out what they are interested in from what they ask witnesses." From what he could tell, Freeman concluded that the investigators "didn't have very much and were in for a frustrating time." At any rate, Wolfson's lawyers believed that if the SEC turned up more damaging information, it would tell them so. "The idea of criminal prosecution," Freeman said, "never even occurred to us."

Though he had two prominent law firms working for him, Wolfson kept after Fortas about his troubles. He wrote to Fortas a number of times during the SEC investigation, some of his letters asking, in effect for Fortas's evaluation of his lawyers' advice. Fortas later acknowledged that Wolfson "on occasion" sent him "materials relating to his problems," though, he added, he had never "interceded" in Wolfson's legal affairs.

Fortas has never said how he responded to Wolfson's letters. It was his custom, though, even in matters of no great sensitivity, to deal mostly on the telephone rather than put anything on paper. "He didn't like to leave tracks," said one associate. "It would not be in Fortas's character to really give legal advice in that situation. He probably simply told Wolfson: 'Don't worry, Arnold & Porter will take good care of you.' "

For his part, Wolfson regarded Fortas's comments, as "the opinion of a friend," rather than legal advice. But this was a friend whose judgment evidently carried considerable weight. "I was comforted by his opinion," Wolfson wrote the author, "and, in that regard, did not feel it was necessary to aggressively push or ask friends to arrange necessary meetings with government authorities in order that I might present the facts concerning my position in these matters."

Wolfson seemed to have attached particular importance to Fortas's early assessment that the SEC investigation involved mainly "technical violations." This was a reasonable observation, as far as it went. The SEC's entire regulatory structure is of necessity highly technical. Much of it is mystifying to laymen and some of it open to varying interpretations by brokers, lawyers and government officials. Some violations are relatively minor and others appear to be the unwitting result of confusion. Accordingly, the SEC deals with many infractions by censure, injunction, suspension of trading privileges and other administrative and civil punishments. When it is confronted with a serious violation and evidence of deliberate intent, however, the SEC has the authority to recommend that the Justice Department undertake criminal prosecution. "Each case is different," said Manuel Cohen, who was then the SEC's chairman. "If a violation looked as if it were inadvertent, we might not recommend criminal prosecution. If it seemed willful, that would be something else." Eventually the SEC concluded that the Continental Enterprise case, which Stuart Allen had helped to uncover, was definitely "something else."

Continental's main business was real estate and movie theater operation, but in 1960 it acquired from Wolfson and his family the manufacturing and distributing rights to a new aerosol device called Propel-Pak, designed to dispense soft drinks. Continental organized an ambitious campaign to extol Propel-Pak's virtues. Spurred by the promotion for its new product, the company's stock soared from less than $2 a share to about $8 in about a year.

While the price was booming, Wolfson, who was strapped for cash at the time because of Merritt-Chapman's reverses, his relatives and his friend Buddy Gerbert were quietly unloading big chunks of the stock. In 1962 the enthusiasm about Continental's prospects faded, and the price of its stock slumped back to the $2 level. But by this time Wolfson and his associates had sold some 630,000 shares through various brokerage houses at a profit to Wolfson alone of $1.3 million.

In the eyes of the SEC this exercise in free enterprise posed a legal problem, of which Wolfson and Gerbert claimed ignorance. Because of their substantial holdings in Continental and their role in the company's management, both Wolfson and Gerbert were classified by the SEC as controlling stockholders. SEC regulations require that a controlling stockholder who sells more than a small percentage of the company's outstanding stock during a six-month period must provide the public with a registration statement just like the statement that accompanies an original issue of stock. The purpose of such a statement is to provide potential buyers of the stock with important information about the company, as, for example in this case, that its largest stockholders were selling much of their holdings. It was clear that Wolfson and Gerbert had far exceeded the legal limit of shares they could sell without filing a registration statement, and it was equally clear they had never filed any such statement.

The registration requirement for controlling stockholders was, at the time, a relatively obscure regulation. As Wolfson's lawyers would later point out, the government had never before initiated a criminal prosecution against a stockholder simply because he had sold shares he had invested in without registration. In this case, however, the SEC believed the failure to register was not an innocent error. Its investigators concluded that Wolfson and Gerbert, bent on making a killing in Continental stock, had deliberately sought to conceal their massive sales from the company's other stockholders and from the public. In March of 1966 the SEC referred the case to the Justice Department with a recommendation for criminal prosecution. Wolfson's lawyers were not notified. "There was nothing to talk to them about," said an SEC staff member. "It was just blatant."

With the Continental case in the hands of the Justice Department, the SEC pressed its inquiry into Merritt-Chapman, a far more complicated situation. The complexities stemmed from the company's huge loss in 1960, which in turn sent its stock plummeting to about $8 a share. This was less than half its book value, that is, the stock's worth measured in terms of the company's assets and liabilities. Around this time, Wolfson and his associates began looking into the possibilities of having the company purchase its own stock. By doing so, in addition to picking up a bargain, the company could reduce its capitalization and improve its overall financial situation. The company was unable to take advantage of the opportunity immediately because it had gone heavily into debt and its creditors had placed restrictions on its spending. In 1962, however, after paying off these restrictive loans, Merritt-Chapman began a three-year program during which it bought three million shares of its own stock. Of this total, more than 600,000 were purchased privately from a Boston financier named Joseph Kosow, who had previously formed several joint ventures with other investors to buy Merritt stock. In some cases the company paid Kosow and his partners more than the prevailing market price. When a few curious stockholders questioned these private transactions, company officials explained they had entered into them only when necessary to buy large blocks of stock.

But the SEC investigators had a different explanation. They

ultimately concluded that Kosow and his partners had bought Merritt stock, when the company was unable to do so, with the clear understanding that the company would later purchase the stock at a price that guaranteed the Kosow group a profit but still would be below book value. The company thus stood to benefit from getting its hands on sizeable quantities of its own stock, and so, the SEC reasoned, did Wolfson himself. The massive purchase of stock below book value would increase the value of shares retained by individual stockholders, of whom Wolfson was the largest. Also, the SEC, which calculated that Kosow's Merritt-Chapman ventures had yielded a profit of about $3 million, suspected that Wolfson might have shared in this windfall. This was a suspicion the government never could support with evidence, but it did spur the investigation of the case.

The company's annual reports made no mention of the commitments to Kosow which the SEC believed were behind the profitable stock sales he made to Merritt-Chapman. Such agreements would not be unlawful in themselves, but the SEC believed they had been concealed to avoid civil suits and complaints from stockholders and lending institutions. This subterfuge, if it in fact had been carried out, would be a violation of the securities laws.

When Wolfson and Kosow had testified before the SEC in 1964 they both denied that any repurchase agreement existed between them; Kosow insisted that he purchased the Merritt stock when he did simply because he considered it "a good buy." Evidence to the contrary was hard to come by. Persuaded that only a Federal grand jury could get the information to confirm its suspicions, the SEC took the same action on Merritt-Chapman that it had taken on the Continental case. On June 10, 1966, it turned the case over to the Justice Department with a recommendation for criminal prosecution.

Ordinarily SEC referrals to the Justice Department remain confidential until the department itself issues grand jury subpoenas. But special circumstances prompted the SEC to hasten to divulge its decision on Merritt-Chapman. The stock purchases which had brought on the SEC investigation had also led to civil suits against Wolfson by disgruntled stockholders. One such case was about to be settled, but the SEC believed, reasonably enough, that the forthcoming criminal investigation might turn up information that would bear on the stockholders' grievances. Therefore it publicly announced that the Justice Department was now looking into the Merritt-Chapman case, whereupon the proposed settlement of the civil suit was postponed.

Wolfson's lawyers immediately rushed to the Justice Department to complain that the handling of Wolfson's case was "an outrage" and to argue against criminal prosecution. The department was unmoved. Wolfson himself wrote an indignant letter to SEC Chairman Cohen. His lawyers had told him, he said, that the SEC would give him a chance to explain the results of the investigation before it acted.* Now his company's reputation and his own good name had been damaged by the SEC's public disclosures. He wanted the case to go back to the SEC "so that we may have the chance to explain the true facts and to answer any and all charges."

Cohen replied that if Wolfson wanted to explain anything, the SEC would be glad to hear from him. But, Cohen added: "Any fact or information that you supply to this commission would be made available to the United States Attorney for his consideration. Accordingly you may wish to present such facts directly to him."

That was close to the last thing Louis Wolfson wanted to do. Adding considerably to his distress at the moment was the identity of the United States Attorney who would be in charge of the prosecution, Robert M. Morgenthau of the southern district of New York. The Justice Department's decision to

---

* Cohen himself later said that he had no knowledge of a promise to give Wolfson a hearing before the SEC acted. "Such a move would be taken only in the rarest kinds of cases," he said. "Generally a person under investigation has plenty of opportunity to be heard before the commission acts." So far as he was concerned, Cohen said, "the Wolfson case was just another case."

assign the Wolfson cases to Morgenthau's office was in itself a subject of controversy. Wolfson's lawyers argued that the cases should have been sent to the middle district of Florida, where Wolfson would be near his home and office, and where, not incidentally, he would be on friendlier ground. The government insisted that the investigation should be conducted in New York because the brokerage houses that handled Wolfson's stock transactions were headquartered there. A more substantial reason, although the government did not officially acknowledge it, was the efficiency and experience of Morgenthau's staff in handling the sort of investigation that Wolfson faced.

Robert Morgenthau had built his reputation in large measure by waging war on white-collar crime—frauds, embezzlements and similar chicanery perpetrated by otherwise respectable persons. He brought indictments against such prominent citizens as Truman Bidwell, the chairman of the New York Stock Exchange, and James Landis, former chairman of the SEC and later dean of Harvard Law School. Some critics charged that Morgenthau went out of his way to indict headline names to promote his political ambitions. Morgenthau, the son of Franklin Roosevelt's Secretary of the Treasury, had taken leave from his prosecutor's post to run for governor of New York in 1962. Though he had been overwhelmingly defeated, it was believed he hoped to run for office again. But Morgenthau contended that his policies bolstered respect for the law and deterred corruption. "You try to enforce all the laws," he said, "against the rich and powerful as well as against the poor and the weak." With regard to Wolfson, Morgenthau had little doubt about his duty. "It was pretty clear that he had operated awfully close to the line for an awfully long time. Here was a fellow that somebody should have done something about a long time ago."

Morgenthau turned the investigation over to the chief of his securities fraud unit, Michael F. Armstrong. Aggressive and articulate, the thirty-three-year-old Armstrong had small patience with the theory that Wolfson was guilty of nothing more than technical transgressions. In biblical times, he would later tell a jury, the commandment "Thou shalt not steal" might have meant "that you don't hit your neighbor on the head with a rock and take his money from him. Maybe that is all it meant. But they didn't have companies with two million five hundred thousand shares of stock outstanding in the days of Moses and Hammurabi."

To start off, Armstrong had a mountain of data on stock purchases, sales and price fluctuations which Stuart Allen had dredged out of SEC records and brokerage house reports. Added to this were volumes of testimony taken from the principal suspects, their brokers and others at SEC hearings. But Armstrong knew that the best evidence about a conspiracy case generally comes from a member of the conspiracy. From the first, he probed for a weak link in Wolfson's inner circle. He found him in Alex Rittmaster.

Rittmaster, who was forty-nine, had been a broker, an accountant and then an investment counselor before he met Louis Wolfson in 1949. Ever since, he had been involved in Wolfson's far-ranging business activities and was considered to be his chief financial adviser. But their relationship had been strained at times. In 1958 Wolfson had professed to be furious at Rittmaster for putting out misleading information about Wolfson's American Motors stock which caused trouble with the SEC. "I don't know how he could have made such a statement," Wolfson grumbled later.

In 1964 Rittmaster had been convicted of conspiracy to bribe a New York City official to obtain a parking meter contract. He got off with a light penalty, a $500 fine. But he realized that in the event of a second conviction his sentence would probably be much more severe. He also realized that he had perjured himself before the SEC when he had been called to testify in the early stages of the Merritt-Chapman investigation. As the investigation continued, Rittmaster's anxiety grew, and in February 1966 he had taken his worries directly to Wolfson in Florida. As Rittmaster later recalled, Wolfson talked confidently of friends in high places. If push came to shove, Wolfson promised, he would "go to the top man," whom he did not otherwise identify. The worst that could happen, Wolfson promised, would be "a slap on the wrist." The case would never get out of Washington.

By midsummer Rittmaster's faith in Wolfson had faltered. The case had moved from Washington into the hands of Robert Morgenthau and a Federal grand jury. Clearly something more severe than wrist-slapping was in prospect. Haunted by his past, distraught about his future, Rittmaster agreed to cooperate with the government.

Rittmaster, and his attorney, Norman Ostrow, began a series of almost daily meetings with Michael Armstrong and Stuart Allen, who had been temporarily assigned to Morgenthau's office. Under Armstrong's insistent prodding, Rittmaster divulged a flood of details about the operations of Wolfson and his associates, which were to lay the foundation for the prosecution of the Merritt-Chapman case. He also provided one piece of totally unexpected information whose ramifications extended far beyond the Wolfson investigation.

Rittmaster's story was based on two long distance phone conversations with Buddy Gerbert in Florida not long after the Merritt-Chapman case had been turned over to the Justice Department. Rittmaster had not yet decided to help the prosecution, but he must have sounded on the brink, and Gerbert frantically tried to strengthen his resistance. He told him, for one thing, that Wolfson was striving to get the case sent back to the SEC. And he indicated, according to Rittmaster, that Wolfson had a very formidable friend, namely Supreme Court Justice Abe Fortas.

Gerbert, who was fearful that the phone call might be tapped, took the precaution of referring to Fortas as "Mr. F." Rittmaster, who remembered that in February Wolfson had mentioned Fortas's connection with the foundation, had little difficulty in comprehending whom Gerbert was talking about. "Mr. F.," by Gerbert's account, was "furious" that the SEC had reneged on its supposed promise to give Wolfson a hearing before taking action. "Mr. F." had been on the phone with Lou about this, Gerbert said. More than that, Gerbert told Rittmaster, in June, when Wolfson's affairs were at a crisis point, "Mr. F." had come to Florida to discuss the investigation with Wolfson.

Armstrong, who had been hanging on Rittmaster's every word, found this exceedingly hard to believe. "Bullshit," he said.

Rittmaster acknowledged that he himself had been dubious at first. He had told Gerbert that the story of Fortas's visit sounded like "a crock" to him.

"Don't tell me it's a crock," Gerbert shot back. "I picked him up at the airport myself."

Gerbert added that Wolfson and Fortas appeared to be pretty thick. Not only was Fortas involved with Wolfson's foundation, but he had also invited Wolfson to a cocktail party in Washington—an apparent reference to the reception at the Supreme Court the preceding October.

Gerbert seemed to be implying that Fortas would somehow intervene in Wolfson's difficulties. Rittmaster had not been persuaded this would happen, and neither was Armstrong. The prosecutor was well aware, however, that Fortas was only one of Wolfson's many influential friends. Furthermore, he suspected that some witnesses who had refused to testify before the grand jury on Fifth Amendment grounds believed that Wolfson had enough influence to get the case returned to Washington. Armstrong decided to meet the influence problem head-on. In September, not long after Rittmaster's disclosure about Fortas, when Merritt-Chapman President Marshal Staub was summoned before the grand jury, Armstrong braced him: "Have you had any discussions to the effect that the investigation was going to come to a halt as a result of influence in Washington?" Staub, citing the Fifth Amendment, declined to answer on the grounds that he might incriminate himself. But Armstrong went on: ". . . If you have heard any talk that influential people in Washington are going to be able to reason with government officials and persuade them that this investigation is not advisable, and if you

are refusing to testify before this grand jury because you are
under that misapprehension . . . then you are indeed laboring
under a misapprehension."

It was Armstrong's way of putting the potential defendants
on notice that Morgenthau's office meant business. Whatever
strings Wolfson might be trying to pull, Morgenthau and his
staff had no reason to believe that his efforts were having any
effect. "We dealt with Justice Department people in Washington every day, on a first-name basis," said Paul Grand, who
later tried the Merritt-Chapman case after Armstrong left
Morgenthau's office for private practice. "If they felt any pressure they never said anything to us about it." Besides, such
was Morgenthau's reputation that his staff felt immune to
outside influence. "Nobody alive," said Grand, "not Fortas,
not Lyndon Johnson, could fix a case in Morgenthau's office."

Morgenthau himself did not consider the possibility of Fortas's intervention on Wolfson's behalf a serious problem. "We
knew Wolfson had powerful connections anyway," he said
later. "But when we are told that somebody is trying to use
influence on us in this office we have a standard reaction. We
always make sure that case is expedited."

Despite the rumors of influence, in September 1966 the
grand jury indicted Wolfson and Gerbert in the Continental
Enterprises case. The next month the investigation of Merritt-Chapman produced other indictments against both men,
as well as against Rittmaster, Joseph Kosow and Marshal
Staub.

Still, the prosecution worried that Fortas's friendship with
Wolfson might yet cause problems. Armstrong correctly anticipated that Wolfson's main defense in the Continental Enterprises case would be confusion and ignorance of the SEC's
registration provision. It seemed possible to him that Fortas
might be called on by Wolfson as a witness to support that
alibi by testifying that Wolfson had indeed been mixed up
about the crucial SEC regulations.

Though this was sheer speculation on his part, Armstrong
meant to be ready. To avoid alerting the defense, he tried to

camouflage his preparations. First, Armstrong wanted to check Rittmaster's story about Fortas's visit to Florida. In December of 1966 he dispatched the versatile Stuart Allen, ostensibly to interview Florida's governor elect, Claude Kirk, who had been an official of one of the brokerage houses involved in Wolfson's dealings. After giving Allen a brief lecture on states' rights, Kirk, who was not personally implicated in the case, answered his questions. Then Allen went on to the main purpose of the trip. After three days of searching records in the Miami office of Eastern Airlines he found what he was looking for. It was a copy of a ticket which showed that on June 14, 1966, Fortas had flown to Jacksonville. He had returned to Washington on June 16.

The trip, as Fortas later explained it, was to attend a meeting of the trustees of the Wolfson Family Foundation. Afterwards, he visited Wolfson's horse farm in Ocala and stayed there overnight. At no time during his stay in Florida, he said, had he participated "in any of Mr. Wolfson's business or legal affairs."

Nevertheless, the fact remained that Fortas had arrived in Jacksonville only a few days after the Merritt-Chapman case had been referred to the Justice Department. Though the SEC's action had not yet been publicly disclosed, the government suspected that Wolfson's lawyers had already learned that their client faced serious difficulty. Justice Fortas's arrival on the scene at this crucial moment in Wolfson's affairs might be awkward for him to explain publicly. At any rate, if Fortas did ultimately testify for Wolfson, Armstrong planned to question him about his trip to Florida, to the witness's presumed surprise and embarrassment.

Meanwhile, he assembled a cross-examination folder for the defense's potential star witness to whom he gave the name of Edward Bramfield. Paul Grand kept the folder on file during the Merritt-Chapman trial, though he changed the code name to Charles Huffnagel. As it turned out, the precautions were unnecessary. Fortas never testified.

Fortas's trip to Florida also caused concern among the

members of the Justice's staff at the Supreme Court. The day
before he left, the Court had handed down one of the most
controversial rulings in recent years, the *Miranda* decision.
No further sessions of the Court were planned until the next
week, when the Justices would recess for the summer. Fortas's
clerks and secretary might not have thought much about his
whereabouts except that during his absence Lyndon Johnson
tried to reach him. Late at night the White House operator
finally called the home of Daniel Levitt, one of Fortas's law
clerks, who explained that the Justice was visiting Louis
Wolfson in Florida.

The next day Levitt mentioned the phone call to Fortas's
secretary, Gloria Dalton, who told him that months before
Fortas had received a substantial check from Wolfson's foundation. Levitt knew that Wolfson was having difficulties with
the SEC and that he had asked Fortas's advice about his problems. If this combination of circumstances should come to
light, Levitt realized, it could prove damaging to Fortas and
to the Court. In fact, Levitt worried that Fortas's arrangement
with Wolfson might be construed as a violation of the Federal statute prohibiting judges from practicing law.

Levitt liked and admired Fortas. But he knew him well
enough not to approach him directly on this matter. Instead,
he asked Mrs. Dalton to tell Fortas that Levitt thought the
Wolfson relationship could lead to trouble, and, as an example, he cited the prohibition against the practice of law.

Fortas's curt response was relayed to Levitt by Mrs. Dalton:
"He said you should mind your own business." But a few days
later, on June 21, Fortas sent Wolfson his resignation from
the foundation. The only reason he gave Wolfson was the
unexpectedly heavy burden of his work at the Court. Fortas
never mentioned his resignation directly to Levitt. Much
later, though, when he was engulfed by scandal, Fortas confided to a former law partner that his predicament would be
even worse if Levitt's warning had not helped persuade him
to quit the foundation when he did.

Though Fortas resigned from the foundation in June of

1966, he did not return the $20,000 fee until December, six months later. Why, after waiting all that time, did he finally decide to send the money back? Fortas later explained he had concluded "because of the developments that had taken place" his services to the foundation, which he did not specify, "should be treated as a contribution."

Presumably the developments to which he referred were the indictments handed down against Wolfson in the Continental and Merritt-Chapman cases. Fortas may also have been disturbed about the unfavorable publicity Justice Douglas received that fall when it was disclosed that he was receiving $12,000 a year from the Parvin Foundation. Ronald Ostrow, who broke the story about Douglas's fee in the *Los Angeles Times*, also pointed out that the Parvin Foundation derived much of its income from a mortgage on a Las Vegas hotel and gambling casino. Whatever Fortas's reasons, his return of the $20,000 before the end of the year made it unnecessary for him to pay income taxes on the money, a circumstance that would later cause considerable confusion and anxiety in the Internal Revenue Service.

In January of 1967, according to Wolfson, he and Fortas met at the Deauville Hotel in Miami Beach at Fortas's suggestion. It must have been a dreary reunion. Wolfson complained about his treatment by the government, particularly by the SEC. Fortas heard him out sympathetically but "made no offer of assistance." This was the last meeting between the two men that either of them has acknowledged.

Wolfson's fate was now in the hands of judge and jury. The Continental Enterprises trial, in September of 1967, was made memorable chiefly by the flock of notables Wolfson called as character witnesses, including Ed Sullivan, Joe DiMaggio, Sid Luckman, Dore Schary and former Florida Governor Fuller Warren. Wolfson also took the stand in his own defense. Though he had made millions in investments, Wolfson insisted that he was largely ignorant of the Securities Act he was accused of violating. As for stock registration statements, Wolfson said he did not even know what they were, at least "not exactly." When Prosecutor Armstrong pressed him during cross-examination, Wolfson explained that he left such matters to subordinates. "I'm not a detail man," he said.

Nevertheless, the jury found both him and Gerbert guilty of conspiracy and of selling unregistered securities. In November Judge Edmund L. Palmieri sentenced Wolfson to a year in prison and fined him $100,000. Gerbert was given six months and a $50,000 fine.

The Merritt-Chapman case came up for trial in June 1968, with Palmieri presiding again. On the first day, Rittmaster pleaded guilty to conspiracy. He became the government's chief witness against Wolfson and the others and ultimately was sentenced to four months in prison. Besides Rittmaster, the government also produced documents which it contended proved that Merritt-Chapman was committed to purchase the shares Kosow had bought at a guaranteed profit, evidence which the defense hotly disputed. Late in the trial, Judge Palmieri dismissed the part of the indictment that accused the defendants of conspiring to defraud stockholders, but the other charges remained. In August the jury found all four defendants guilty of conspiracy to violate the securities laws. Wolfson and Gerbert were also convicted of perjuring themselves before the SEC and, together with Marshal Staub, of filing misleading annual reports.

Wolfson had fallen upon hard times. Merritt-Chapman & Scott had begun the process of liquidation. In court penalties, lawyers' fees and loss of income, his legal battles with the government would cost him an estimated $10 million. He had suffered a heart attack in 1966 and his wife was dying of cancer. In December 1968, on the day of his sentencing in the Merritt case, he addressed the Court in bitter terms. He complained of being tried twice before the same judge and of being convicted the second time on the testimony of Rittmaster, "whose past," Wolfson said, "is replete with lies and whose record is blemished by criminal convictions." He had been a victim of "bias and discrimination," Wolfson charged. Others had been guilty of SEC violations but had not been indicted, which led Wolfson to conclude "that there is one set of rules for me and one set of rules for the others." Wolfson declared that he had always had confidence in the judicial system. But, he added, "It would be wrong for me not to tell you that I stand here today wondering if that confidence has been misplaced because of what has happened to me."

Judge Palmieri sentenced him to eighteen months in prison, to follow his sentence in the Continental case. His lawyers, who were already contesting the Continental conviction, prepared another appeal.*

During Wolfson's long struggle in the courts, Fortas's name had never been publicly linked to his. The stock transactions for which Wolfson was convicted had all taken place well before he came to Fortas's office in June of 1965. Fortas had severed his last link with the Wolfson Foundation in December of 1966, months before Wolfson first went on trial. For a while it must have seemed to Fortas that his relationship with Wolfson was safely buried in the past. But Fortas's connection with Wolfson's foundation had not gone unrecorded, and in the fall of 1968 fragments of the story began to surface.

---

* The Continental conviction was ultimately sustained (see p. 224). But in November 1970 the U.S. Court of Appeals reversed the convictions of Wolfson, Gerbert, Staub and Kosow in the Merritt-Chapman case. The appeals court pointed out that before the trial judge dismissed the fraud charge against the defendants, the government had spent four weeks trying to prove that charge. It was unreasonable to expect, the court said, that this evidence could be erased from the jurors' minds. Though Rittmaster, its chief witness, died in 1969, the government decided to try the case again.

THE INVESTIGATORS

THE SUMMER and fall of 1968 had been long and punishing seasons for Ramsey Clark. First his department had been assailed in the Senate for its efforts to help confirm Fortas as Chief Justice; then, during the presidential campaign, Clark himself had been singled out for attack. Indeed, one of Richard Nixon's earliest and most gratuitous campaign promises was that he would begin the restoration of law and order by appointing a new attorney general. When the election results assured that Nixon would be able to keep that pledge, Clark could at least look forward to an end to his personal travail. Just as he and his staff began preparations for the transfer of power, however, the attorney general received news that threatened to cast a pall over his closing weeks in office.

The bearer of troublesome tidings was Robert Morgenthau, who had just successfully concluded the prosecution of Louis Wolfson. Morgenthau called Clark to warn him of an impending story in *Life* magazine concerning Wolfson and Justice Fortas. Its gist, as Clark understood it, would be "that Wolfson had a foundation, the foundation had paid Fortas some money, and Fortas had not paid his income tax on it."

This alarming information, which as it turned out was only two-thirds correct, was the product of a still incomplete investigation conducted by the Internal Revenue Service into the Wolfson Family Foundation. Under prodding from Congress, which was growing increasingly skeptical about the activities of tax-exempt foundations, the IRS had been taking a closer look at the financial operations of a good many such organizations. In the case of the Wolfson Foundation, the criminal charges against its founder, chairman and namesake made an IRS inspection of its records almost inevitable.

Like the mills of God, the wheels of the bureaucracy grind exceedingly slow, but exceedingly small. The Wolfson Foundation's tax return for 1966, the year in which it had paid Fortas $20,000, was due in February of 1967. Sometime later in the year, the IRS auditors began their tedious task.* By the fall of 1968 the auditors had discovered the foundation's check to Fortas, which had been sent in January 1966. Since the foundation's fiscal year ended on September 30, the 1966 return did not show that Fortas had returned the money the following December. Ignorant of that vital fact, the auditors sought to confirm the payment by checking Fortas's personal income-tax return. To their consternation they found that he had not reported receiving a single cent from the Wolfson Foundation.

Now the IRS was confronted with a set of facts which, on their face, suggested that Fortas might be guilty of an income-tax violation. Some further explanation was possible, of course, but getting it required interrogating a Justice of the Supreme Court, who also happened to be the President's intimate friend. Discretion dictated that the utmost tact be used, and the IRS officials in charge of the case paused to ponder the best approach.

While they deliberated, a hint of their dilemma reached the ear of William Lambert of *Life*. To begin with, Lambert heard only that IRS had learned Fortas was involved in "a

---

* The foundation ultimately passed inspection for 1966. But in 1971 the IRS reported that it had suspended the foundation's tax-exempt privileges for at least one year, for undisclosed reasons.

money deal." With this scrap of information as a wedge, he pried from friends in the government the further details that the money had come from Louis Wolfson and that Fortas had not reported it on his income-tax return. The mention of Wolfson's name sent Lambert hurrying to New York to see Robert Morgenthau, in whose office Wolfson's activities had recently been the subject of intense scrutiny.

As it turned out, Morgenthau learned as much from Lambert as Lambert learned from him. From his own staff's investigation, Morgenthau knew, of course, that Fortas had some connection with Wolfson and with the Wolfson Foundation. Earlier in the year, when Fortas's nomination was pending in the Senate, Morgenthau had made it his business to tell Fred Vinson, Jr., the chief of the Justice Department's criminal division in Washington, of Fortas's visit to Wolfson in Florida back in 1966. This was a piece of information which, had they learned of it, Fortas's critics would certainly have seized upon and used against him. The Justice Department, forewarned of a potential problem, kept the matter secret throughout the long battle over the Chief Justiceship.

Neither Morgenthau nor any of the department's Washington officials had any inkling at the time of the nomination that Fortas had received money from the Wolfson Foundation. When Morgenthau learned from Lambert of the fee, of the IRS investigation and of *Life's* interest in the subject, he decided he had better sound the alarm again in Washington. This time he chose to speak directly to Ramsey Clark.

Morgenthau reached Clark at his home in Lake Barcroft, Virginia, on Saturday morning, November 9. On the preceding Tuesday, Richard Nixon had been elected President. As he talked to Morgenthau on his bedroom phone Clark mused briefly on what effect the allegations against Fortas might have had if they had been disclosed before the election. Fortunately, this was one complication the attorney general did not now have to consider. The prospect that a Supreme Court Justice might be publicly accused of violating the income-tax laws was staggering enough in itself.

Clark took the problem with him that morning to his office, where he conferred with his deputy, Warren Christopher, and with Fred Vinson. The main theme of their discussion, one of the participants later recalled, was the reputation of the Court. This was a matter with which Clark and Vinson had particular reason to feel personal concern. The attorney general's father, Justice Tom Clark, had retired from the Supreme Court only two years before, and Fred Vinson's father had sat alongside him as Chief Justice until his death in 1953. As a result of the presidential campaign and the fight over Fortas's nomination, Clark felt that "the Court had already suffered a tremendous amount of damage." Now it was further threatened by the story about Fortas's supposed tax problems, whose publication Clark believed, from his conversation with Morgenthau, to be imminent. Under the circumstances, the attorney general decided the proper course to follow was for him, Clark, to inform Fortas forthwith. If Fortas had a satisfactory explanation the Court could be spared unnecessary injury. If there was no satisfactory answer, then the injury might be minimized by prompt action. Clark did not relish his self-appointed task, but he considered that the urgency of the matter left him little choice.

Early that afternoon, only a few hours after he had talked to Morgenthau, Clark arrived at Fortas's home in Georgetown. Fortas listened attentively while Clark repeated the story Morgenthau had told him. Then, after checking by phone with his secretary, who had custody of his tax returns, Fortas said that he had indeed been given money for some work he planned to do for the foundation; it had something to do with integrated housing. But, Fortas added, he had decided against going ahead with the project. Since he had returned the money during that same year there was no need to pay taxes on it.

Clark was immensely relieved. As far as he could see, he told Fortas, there was no need for any further government action. He did suggest, though, that Fortas might try to communicate to *Life* any information that might avoid injury to his reputation and the Court's. When Clark returned to the Justice Department he saw to it that word of Fortas's explanation was quickly passed to the Internal Revenue Service. With that, the attorney general considered the incident officially closed. He did not discuss it with Lyndon Johnson. "I never talked to the President about matters like that," Clark said.

Since, a few months later, much the same information would spur the Justice Department under a new Administration into intense activity, Ramsey Clark's attitude is worth examining. Obviously, Lyndon Johnson's presence in the White House would weigh heavily on any attorney general who considered examining Justice Fortas's affairs. Moreover, Clark himself had considerable admiration for Fortas. A week after his tense visit to the Justice's home, Clark paid glowing tribute to Fortas at a dinner at Yale in his honor. "I have been a lucky person," the attorney general told the assembled guests. "I consider among my greater good fortunes having come to know and love Abe Fortas as a human being, as sensitive, incisive and keen a legal intellect as I have encountered, as a man of wisdom and compassion."

Allowing even for the effusiveness customary to testimonials, there is little reason to doubt Clark's sentiments. Although he and Fortas had sharply different personalities, both shared most of the same liberal views and many of the same conservative enemies. While Fortas was under fire in the Senate, Clark was being assaulted at Republican campaign rallies around the country.

With all that, had the allegations against Fortas been more specific and substantial, conscience and practical considerations would have made it difficult for the attorney general to ignore them. If Fortas had not been able to explain the income-tax problem, Clark said, "We would enforce the law. If it had proven to be a violation, I would have prosecuted." But Fortas was not guilty of an income-tax violation, or, Clark believed, of any other violation of the law. However questionable the propriety of the Justice's relations with Wolfson might be, Clark did not consider that propriety was an appropriate question for the Justice Department to pursue. "You can't use the Department of Justice to go out and develop unattractive facts about judges or other people just for the sake of public information," he said later.

Clark did not recall being told by Morgenthau of the talk about Fortas's aiding Wolfson in his troubles or of the concern that Fortas might testify at Wolfson's trial. If he had known about these things, he said, "the most that I would have done would have been to ask Bob to make sure to look at it very carefully to see if there was anything we ought to do." But, he pointed out, when Morgenthau called him Wolfson had already been tried and convicted twice. "Your fears as to what might happen before trial," he said, "would no longer be the basis for very long consideration." Besides, Clark had no indication that anyone had tried to exert pressure, either on Morgenthau's office or on the Justice Department in Washington. The department would have "a high obligation" to pursue any evidence of obstruction of justice. "But if you're Justice, and you haven't been obstructed," Clark said, "you don't look into it very much."

In sum, Fortas's relations with the Wolfson Foundation reminded Clark of the disclosures about the American University seminars. Based on what Morgenthau had told him, he said, the Wolfson episode "didn't appear to me to be more than another little story about something that didn't seem to be a very happy event."

For several weeks after his visit to Fortas's home Clark scanned each new issue of *Life* for the story Morgenthau had warned him about. When time passed and the story did not appear, Clark dismissed the subject from his mind.

Actually, Lambert was nowhere near as ready to publish the story as Clark had thought him to be. But he had not forgotten it. A sober, determined man in his late forties, Lambert already had made an impressive reputation as a journalistic watchdog. In the 1950's he had teamed with another reporter on the Portland *Oregonian* on a series of stories which helped send Teamster Union President Dave Beck to prison, and won nearly every high honor in journalism. Lambert took his work seriously. As a Nieman Fellow at Harvard he had spent a year poring over law books on the rules of evidence and the right to privacy. His most important resources, though, were the relationships he had formed over the years with staff members in the IRS, the SEC, the FBI and other official storehouses of information. From time to time, out of malice, honest indignation or simple friendship, they passed on to him a smattering of facts and rumors. It remained his job to discard the gossip, sift out the truth and measure its significance. With all its attendant pressures, Lambert considered his work "an agonizing business." Mindful of the perils of self-righteousness and sensationalism, he nevertheless believed that a reporter should have "a low threshold of indignation." What he had learned so far about Fortas and Wolfson had been enough to stir both his indignation and his curiosity.

Lambert had met Abe Fortas only once, in 1964, but that had been a memorable experience. The encounter came about because he was working on a story about Lyndon Johnson's finances.* The President, worried about the impact of such a story in an election year, personally urged Henry Luce to send his men to Washington for a firsthand accounting. Lambert and several colleagues were subsequently dispatched to the White House, expecting to meet with the President or his accountant. Instead they were directed to the offices of Arnold, Fortas & Porter, where Fortas greeted them hospitably and poured drinks all around. "I've been the President's attorney for thirty years," Fortas said. Tapping a briefcase on his desk, he added: "All the material is right here."

But instead of opening the briefcase he demanded to see a complete draft of the *Life* story on Johnson. His guests refused

---

* See p. 100.

and, after some further argument, prepared to leave. At this point, Fortas decided there was nothing for it but to take them to the President.

It was late in the evening by the time they arrived, and Johnson urged the First Lady to "rustle up some food." While they all dined on leftover collard greens, chicken and ribs, Johnson scanned a summary of *Life's* estimate of his holdings. "Preposterous," he cried. "What kind of marijuana have you been smoking?" Then Johnson revealed that he had ordered up his own audit of his finances, which he insisted was far more accurate than *Life's*. "I don't think you should discuss that," said Fortas, who sat at the President's right hand. But Johnson was all for full disclosure, an attitude he vividly expressed with an earthy analogy between the dimensions of his wealth and the size of his manhood.

The *Life* contingent promised not only to read the President's audit, but to print it, whereupon LBJ, over Fortas's continued protests, turned it over to them. Then, after polishing off an enormous bowl of tapioca, Johnson took the journalists and his lawyer on a tour of the White House that concluded at 2:30 A.M.

What Lambert recalled of the evening, four years later, besides the President's performance, was Fortas's stubborn hostility. Lambert knew Fortas by reputation as a brilliant lawyer, but he considered his tactics that evening to be "just pettifoggery." If Fortas had been difficult to deal with about Lyndon Johnson's financial arrangements, Lambert assumed he would certainly be no less difficult when it came to unraveling his own affairs.

Indeed, Lambert was having trouble getting anyone to talk. Never before had he encountered such sensitivity. "Everybody I talked to was frightened to death," he said. "People were diving under desks." Lambert managed to find out that the IRS did not think it had a tax case against Fortas, but, unaware of Ramsey Clark's visit to Fortas, he still did not know why.

The answer came from an unexpected source, Fortas's

friend and former law partner Paul Porter. Evidently acting on Ramsey Clark's suggestion that he get in touch with *Life,* Fortas had asked Porter to serve as his agent. Porter, who was still brooding over the damage done to Fortas by the American University seminars, which he had helped arrange, was eager to make amends by helping the Justice out of his latest difficulty. When Lambert came to see him in early December, Porter exuded his celebrated charm. He showed Lambert around the office, pointed out the momentoes on his wall, and talked freely about Fortas's reluctance to join the Court, which was due chiefly, he said, to Carol Agger's opposition. Then he brought up Louis Wolfson. Wolfson and Fortas, as Porter explained it, were both greatly interested in Jewish charities; it was only natural therefore that Fortas would agree to help Wolfson's foundation carry on its good works. Fortas had taken a check for "fifteen or twenty thousand dollars" from the foundation, Porter said. But then finding himself with "a whole sack full of Court petitions" and little time for anything else, Fortas was forced to give up his connection with the foundation. He had sent the money back the same year it was given to him, so it was not taxable income. Having cleared up that point, Porter ushered Lambert out with a smile and a handshake, apparently convinced that the Wolfson problem was ended.

But Lambert was just getting started. Fortas's return of the foundation's money, in the wake of Wolfson's indictments, made the episode seem, as Alice remarked down the rabbit hole, "curiouser and curiouser." Armed with what Porter had told him. Lambert pressed his sources in the government for more details. As the weeks passed, in between working on other assignments, he gradually put most of the story together. He learned the dates of Wolfson's original check to Fortas and of Fortas's check returning the fee, which the IRS had since obtained. Moreover, he heard reports that Fortas's name had been used to placate the fears of Wolfson's associates when the Justice Department was closing in on them. Lambert did not know of Fortas's lifetime contract with the foundation. But what he did know was enough to convince him that Fortas's conduct was most unbecoming a Supreme Court Justice.

However, the story was still unfolding. Wolfson had asked the Supreme Court to review his conviction in the Continental Enterprises case on the grounds that the securities regulations he had been found guilty of violating were unconstitutionally vague. Lambert wanted to see what the Court would do and what role, if any, Fortas would play in its deliberations. On April 1, 1969, the Court refused to consider Wolfson's appeal. The official Court order noted that Justice Fortas had not participated in consideration of the case. There was no explanation, but there rarely is when a Justice recuses himself. No one was surprised, since Fortas had made it a point not to sit on matters involving clients of his former law firm.

Now Lambert set two final tasks for himself. One was to see Fortas; the other was to see Wolfson before he went to prison. He was to fail in both efforts, but not for lack of trying.

Lambert called Paul Porter, reminded him of their December conversation about Wolfson and told him he wanted to discuss the subject further with Fortas. Porter talked to Carol Agger, then advised Lambert that Fortas was too busy with the Court's work to be burdened by a "confrontation." Whatever Lambert wrote about Fortas, Porter said, "he can answer it after it's in print." On April 20 Lambert sent a registered letter to Fortas himself, asking for a meeting to discuss "any information in my possession that might indicate an impropriety on your part."

Fortas's answer came by return mail. "Since there has been no impropriety or anything approaching it in my conduct," he wrote, "no purpose would be served by any such meeting." His contacts with Wolfson since he had joined the Court consisted only of "conversations" about the work of Wolfson's foundation and "a brief visit to Mr. Wolfson's famous horse farm in June 1966." At that time, Fortas said, he had attended a meeting of the foundation's officials, at which, as near as he could remember, Wolfson was not even present.

Next, Lambert tried to arrange a meeting with Wolfson through one of his attorneys, William Bittman, whom he had first met when Bittman was a crack prosecutor with the Justice Department. On April 22, three days before Wolfson was due to enter prison, Lambert dined with Bittman at Chez Francois, a popular Washington restaurant, outlined the story he was planning to write and declared himself ready to fly anywhere immediately to see Wolfson. Lambert added a caveat. He was concerned that Wolfson might say things out of spite to damage Fortas.

"If your story is true," Bittman said cryptically, "my client will be able to document it."

But two days later Bittman called Lambert to tell him there would be no interview with Wolfson. "My client could help you," he said. "But you would be of no help to him."

Lambert had nothing left to do but write the story. He began work on April 25; publication was scheduled for May 5. Lambert was well aware that the story might wreck the career of Fortas, whom he personally considered "one of the most able men on the Court," and might hurt the reputation of the entire Court. He felt however, that these consequences were overshadowed by what he considered "the obvious impropriety of what Fortas had done." Moreover, Lambert believed that what he had learned about Fortas and Wolfson was almost certain to become public knowledge anyhow, for the subject of his journalistic exposé had now become a matter of enthusiastic official interest at the Department of Justice.

In dredging out his information over a period which spanned two Administrations, Lambert had been careful to limit his contacts to career officials and to avoid political appointees. "I didn't want the story tainted by too much Government involvement," he said later. "And I didn't want anybody to tip it off." But one of the career lawyers in the Justice Department in whom he confided considered the matter too important to keep to himself. Early in April he passed the word to Will R. Wilson, who had replaced Fred Vinson as head of the criminal division. Since Ramsey Clark had left no record of the Fortas-Wolfson connection behind him when he left office the previous January, this was Wilson's first information on the subject. He immediately sent for Lambert to find out more. On April 10, Lambert met with him, hoping to convince Wilson to agree to protect his scoop.

Probably nowhere in the land could Lambert have found a more attentive audience. Will Wilson, at fifty-six, was weathered and gnarled as if he had spent years riding the range in his native Texas. Back home he was famous for his zeal as a prosecutor, a reputation he had earned as a racket-busting state attorney general. He was also said to be deeply resentful of Lyndon Johnson, who had helped to frustrate his political ambitions within the Democratic Party. Stymied among the Democrats, Wilson switched to the Republican camp and barnstormed the state in 1968 on behalf of the Nixon ticket. He was rewarded with the leadership of the criminal division, which was expected to bear the brunt of the new Administration's much heralded onslaught against crime.

In his first weeks on the job Wilson had kept his division busy mounting plans for major offensives against narcotics, gambling and obscenity. When Lambert came to see him, Wilson said later, "We were covered up with work. We weren't looking for anything else." Lambert's story, however, was swiftly given priority. The idea of any judge accepting a substantial fee for off-bench services was enough in itself to arouse Wilson's prosecutorial instincts. "Anytime you find a payment like that to a judge you immediately want to find out more about it," he said. The realization that this particular judge was so closely linked to Lyndon Johnson, whom Wilson held in low regard, darkened his suspicions. Wilson's first thought was to hale Fortas before a grand jury, an idea that sent Lambert quaking from his office fearful that his exclusive story would soon be spread all over Washington.

Wilson's conduct, however, would be moderated by the restraining guidance of the attorney general. John Mitchell was "shocked and surprised," Wilson recalled, when Wilson told him what he had learned from Lambert. Mitchell quickly notified the President and kept him "fully informed" throughout the investigation. Mitchell, who as Wilson noted "generally favored the indirect approach," believed that indirection was particularly important in this case. "He made it plain that we should be very discreet," Wilson said. "He didn't want it to appear as an attack on the Court."

Because of Mitchell's attitude and Wilson's own promise to Lambert that he would try to keep the matter confidential, Wilson abandoned the idea of a grand jury or any other action that might attract public attention. Still, a good deal could be learned quietly, within the government itself. As soon as Lambert left his office, Wilson swung into action. He summoned SEC and IRS staff members, who confirmed Lambert's story. He pulled out the Justice Department's case history on Louis Wolfson, studied it and locked it in his office safe. He sent to the SEC for the records of Wolfson's stock dealings and to the IRS for Wolfson's and Fortas's tax returns. His men scavenged through Robert Morgenthau's files, unearthing Rittmaster's account of Wolfson's promises to stave off prosecution and of Fortas's visit to Florida. To Morgenthau it seemed that Wilson was "wallowing in the stuff."

Eager for more, Wilson sent a memorandum on the case to J. Edgar Hoover and paid a call on the FBI director, whose cooperation was never to be taken for granted. The FBI had nothing to add at the moment, but Wilson would get the bureau's help when the time came to expand his probe.

As the material flowed across his desk, Wilson began to reach some harsh conclusions. "My appraisal was that Fortas was doing on the bench what he'd been doing before," he later said. "He should not have done it. He never should have been on the Court in the first place, and he never would have, except for his friendship with Lyndon Johnson."

The salient fact was that Fortas had taken money from a foundation headed by a man who later became, as Wilson put it, "involved in the criminal process," and then had returned the money. The reasons for this transaction were still obscure. But in Wilson's mind the circumstances raised the possibility that Fortas was guilty either of practicing law on Wolfson's behalf or, even worse, trying to influence the outcome of the government's prosecution.

Further fuel for Wilson's suspicions was soon provided by Louis Wolfson himself. Though William Lambert could not reach him, Wolfson did give an interview to Stanley Penn of the *Wall Street Journal* a few days before he went off to prison. He bragged that a presidential pardon, which would have kept him out of prison, had been his for the asking the previous December. He had been given this assurance, Wolfson said, "from somebody who is as close as anybody could be" to Lyndon Johnson. But, Wolfson said, he refused to take advantage of this offer because he did not want any special favors.*

Obviously, that sort of statement needed to be viewed with a large measure of skepticism. Still, there was no question that Wolfson was in a position to shed some light on the case, and Will Wilson wanted a chance at him. To approach him directly might compromise the secrecy that still veiled the Justice Department's inquiries. Wilson decided to put off the questioning of Wolfson until after the Wolfson-Fortas affair was a matter of public knowledge, but he did not want to wait any longer than he had to. Soon after Wolfson was locked into his cell, on April 25, Wilson phoned his lawyer, William Bittman. From his earlier conversation with Lambert, Bittman already had a fairly good idea of what the Justice Department was up to. He agreed to come to Wilson's office on May 5, the publication date of Lambert's story.

Though Wilson's probing into Fortas's affairs had so far been secret and informal, it was already beginning to touch

---

* If that story was true, Wolfson must have changed his attitude dramatically after December of 1968. Even as he talked to the *Wall Street Journal*, he was frantically writing letters to friends on Capitol Hill asking them to intervene with President Nixon. (See Chapter One.)

on one of the most sensitive of constitutional questions: Who shall judge the judges? The drafters of the Constitution decreed that Federal judges would serve for life. Yet they tacked on the qualifying words "during good behavior," and that enigmatic phrase has beclouded every effort to discipline judges or regulate their conduct.

Clearly, the Founding Fathers meant to endow the judiciary with a shield of security to protect them against encroachments by the Congress or the President. Alexander Hamilton argued that the judges, lacking authority over either sword or purse, were in a state of "natural feebleness" that required the assurance of lifetime tenure. "Nothing will contribute so much as this," he wrote, "to that independent spirit in the judges which must be essential to the faithful performance of so arduous a duty."

Still, the words "during good behavior," imbedded in the Constitution, lingered as a hedge on the promise of lifetime tenure. But what was the standard of good behavior, and what was the remedy when judges fell below it? The chief clue the Founders left behind them was in Article II, Section Four, which provides that ". . . all civil officers of the United States shall be removed from office on impeachment for and conviction of treason, bribery or other high crimes and misdemeanors."

History has demonstrated that impeachment is easier to threaten than to invoke. The process is ponderous, excruciatingly slow and disruptive of the normal business of the government. The entire House of Representatives must bring the charges and the full Senate must sit as judge and jury. Only nine Federal judges, including Justice Chase of the Supreme Court, have ever been impeached. The briefest of these proceedings, against Judge Robert Archbald in 1912, took three months to get through the House and six months more in the Senate. The longest dragged on for more than four years, and the most recent, begun in 1933, lasted for nearly three years. No wonder then that the chief effect of the impeachment clause has been to pressure judges under attack to resign, thus sparing themselves the indignity of a formal verdict on their behavior.*

Attorney General Mitchell and his aides were of course familiar with the broad constitutional dictates on impeachment. What was not entirely clear, to them or to anyone else, for that matter, was what role the Justice Department could properly play in dealing with judicial misconduct. The power of impeachment, with all its shortcomings, is reserved by the Constitution to the Congress. Whether the judiciary had some form of immunity to ordinary criminal prosecution remained in the spring of 1969 an unsettled question. For a number of reasons the Justice Department had never directly tested its authority by bringing an indictment against a sitting judge. In some cases it would have been difficult to get testimony against a defendant still vested with judicial authority. In others political allegiances complicated the situation. Besides, the Justice Department has always been hesitant to seem to threaten the independence of the judiciary.

Now the department was investigating not just an ordinary Federal judge but a member of the Supreme Court. To the best of anyone's knowledge it had never conducted such an inquiry before, and the attorney general wanted to clarify the legal ground rules. As Mitchell said later: "We were struggling to find an answer to what we should or shouldn't do."

He turned for help to Assistant Attorney General William Rehnquist, who as chief of the office of legal counsel was, in a sense, the attorney general's lawyer. Rehnquist had been first in his class at Stanford Law School and later clerked for Supreme Court Justice Robert Jackson. He brought to his post a combination of unyielding conservatism and intellectual adroitness, qualities that assured him an influential voice in the councils of the Justice Department and would eventually

---

* All told, more than fifty Federal judges have been the subject of congressional inquiry, according to Joseph Borkin, author of *The Corrupt Judge*. Of the nine impeached, four were convicted. Seventeen others resigned while they were under investigation and an uncounted number quit because of the threat of such an investigation.

earn him the recognition of the President and appointment to the Supreme Court. As it happened the constitutional issues raised by the Fortas case were fresh in Rehnquist's mind. His staff had been researching much the same ground in connection with new legislation that sought to establish a simpler method than impeachment for removing judges whose conduct was something less than "good behavior."

Rehnquist himself took no part in the direct investigation of the Fortas affair. That was left to the criminal division. Instead, he was asked as he put it "to assume that the most damaging set of inferences about the case were true," and to determine what action the Justice Department could take.

The worst inference that could be drawn was that Fortas had attempted to intervene in the government's prosecution of Wolfson's stock-market activities. Rehnquist and his aides plunged into the statute books, looking for a relevant law. They quickly dismissed the prohibition against the practice of law, which had so concerned Fortas's own law clerk that he had called it to the Justice's attention. Apart from its failure to define the practice of law, the statute imposes no penalty. It appears to have been enacted mainly for application in impeachment proceedings and thus would be of more use to the Congress than to the Justice Department.

They turned instead to Chapter Eleven of the United States Criminal Code, which deals with bribery, graft and conflicts of interest. One section covers payments to judges to influence their official acts. But since there was no indication that whatever Fortas was involved in directly affected his duties as a Justice, this also seemed pointless to pursue.

Of more direct bearing was another section of the law prohibiting Federal officials, including "officers of the judicial branch," from being rewarded "for services rendered on behalf of another person before a Government department or agency in relation to any particular matter in which the United States is a party." This seemed to cover the Fortas-Wolfson relationship, as Rehnquist understood it. Fortas was certainly an officer of the judicial branch. He had taken money from Wolfson, or at least from his foundation, while Wolfson had been under government investigation. Just what services Fortas had been expected to render in return remained to be established, but this was not Rehnquist's responsibility.

Having found an applicable statute, Rehnquist next sought to determine whether the Justice Department could prosecute Fortas for violating that law while he remained on the Court. He found several precedents which, if they did not fit the present case exactly, at least seemed relevant. In the 1930's, Chief Judge of the Second Circuit Court of Appeals Martin Manton, who had suffered severe financial reverses in the Depression, attempted to recoup by selling his decisions to the highest bidder. He was investigated, first by Tom Dewey, then New York district attorney, and, after his resignation, by Federal authorities who ultimately convicted him of conspiring to obstruct justice. Around the same time the Justice Department was probing the conduct of Federal District Judge Albert W. Johnson of Pennsylvania. After Johnson resigned to avoid impeachment, he too was indicted for obstructing justice. If sitting judges could be investigated, Rehnquist thought, it was reasonable to infer that they could be indicted.

An earlier precedent suggested another option. In 1912, at the behest of President William Howard Taft, the Justice Department had looked into the conduct of Judge Robert Archbald of the U.S. Commerce Court, who was accused of, among other things, accepting loans and gifts from litigants who appeared before him in court. In this case the department turned its evidence over to Congress, which impeached and convicted Archbald.

Going further back, Rehnquist found that in 1790 the First Congress, which included among its members James Madison and other drafters of the Constitution, had passed a law making it possible to prosecute Federal judges for bribery. A few years later, in 1796, Charles Lee, third attorney general of the United States, held that a judge could be called to account for unlawful behavior by criminal indictment as well

[232]

as by impeachment. Rehnquist believed that Attorney General Lee's conclusion was well grounded enough for Attorney General Mitchell to follow some 170 years later. On May 1 he sent Mitchell a memorandum advising him that if the department had the evidence, it could prosecute Justice Fortas.

Now that the constitutional questions had been faced, the department focused its attention on a more immediate matter, the article Lambert was writing for *Life*. Mitchell's press officer, Jack C. Landau, had been keeping the attorney general posted on Lambert's progress. Landau knew when the story was to be published, and a few days before, on Thursday, May 1, he called Lambert in New York to ask for an advance copy. "We were quite sure there was going to be a huge furor," he said later, "and we wanted to see what was going to be in print as soon as possible." Not only did the attorney general want the story, Landau told Lambert, but so did the White House. Lambert already knew of the White House's interest, since Ronald Ziegler, the President's press secretary, had been making inquiries at *Life*'s Washington bureau. Lambert found this attention more worrisome than flattering. In nearly every Administration the White House staff has been notorious for passing out news tips to friendly journalists and Lambert did not want to read his story under someone else's byline.

Lambert promised Landau that he would send him proofs of the story on the next day, Friday, when they arrived in New York from *Life's* printers in Chicago. "But," he added, "I don't want copies floating all around Washington. I want Mitchell to keep control of it." Landau agreed that only two copies of the proofs would leave the Justice Department—one to a high official of the SEC, which had begun the investigation of Louis Wolfson, and the other to the White House. At Lambert's insistence, the White House copy would be entrusted to no one less than John Ehrlichman, counsel to the President.

The next morning Landau was on the phone to Lambert again. Had the proofs arrived yet?

No, Lambert told him, they were not due until later in the day. He would let Landau know.

While he waited to hear from Lambert, Landau made arrangements for a Federal marshal to make the pickup in New York and the delivery in Washington. As soon as Lambert called in midafternoon to announce the arrival of the proofs, the marshal was sent on his errand. The day of public disclosure was swiftly approaching. Though the next issue of *Life* would not appear on the newsstands until Monday, the magazine was planning to distribute advance copies to members of the Washington press corps on Sunday afternoon.

By now Landau was in a swirl of anxiety and mixed emotions. "Everybody's adrenalin was running high," he said later. Landau himself was particularly agitated. He was worried about the Constitution, the Court and the need for secrecy.

Though Landau had a law degree, he had been a newsman when John Mitchell hired him, and in the turmoil Friday afternoon he reacted like one. He reached for the phone and called the dozen or so reporters who regularly cover the Justice Department and the Supreme Court to alert them that a story of major importance would break that Sunday afternoon. His reasoning was that a story of this significance required the reporters most familiar with the Court to cover it; unless they were forewarned, some might be out of reach during the weekend. The idea may have had merit, but it also, in effect, put the Justice Department in the dubious position of promoting *Life's* exposé. The story was bound to compel attention anyway, but Landau's early warning underlined its importance and endowed it with an aura of government support and credibility.

The next person to call attention to Lambert's story was, curiously enough, Justice Fortas. He had been put on notice by Lambert two weeks before that the story would soon be published. By the Saturday afternoon before publication his chambers and the Supreme Court press office were getting phone calls from newsmen who had gained a hint of the story's contents either from Landau or from some other government source or from each other. Supreme Court Justices rarely if ever choose to reply to comments in the press. In 1966 when Justice Douglas's financial arrangement with the Parvin Foundation was disclosed, his only response was a letter to Chief Justice Warren that was not made public for nearly three years. Fortas, always the activist, chose to deal with his problem directly. Late Saturday, Banning Whittington, the Supreme Court press officer, disclosed to newsmen that Fortas would issue a statement on *Life*'s story from the Court the next afternoon, as soon as he had read it.

Sunday afternoon found a crowd of newsmen gathered in the Supreme Court's basement press room, studying their copies of *Life* while they awaited word from Fortas. Lambert's story was spread over six pages of the magazine under the headline: "Fortas of the Supreme Court: A Question of Ethics." The heart of the article was a chronicle of Wolfson's legal troubles and his relations with Fortas. It began with the payment of the $20,000 from the foundation in January of 1966, recounted the Justice Department's actions against Wolfson, Fortas's visit to Florida, and Gerbert's assurances to Rittmaster of Fortas's support, and concluded with Fortas's return of the $20,000 in December of 1966. No evidence was presented to indicate that Fortas had actually intervened on Wolfson's behalf, but the article cited two canons of judicial ethics: "A judge's official conduct should be free from impropriety and the appearance of impropriety" and "a judge should not accept inconsistent duties . . . which will in any way interfere or appear to interfere . . . with his devotion to . . . his official functions."

Upstairs in his chambers, Fortas worked on his statement. One of his law clerks had been summoned to assist him, but the Justice kept his thoughts to himself. "He was obviously not in one of his happy moods," the clerk said later. "But you wouldn't have known to look at him that he was under any particular strain." Fortas certainly realized that the *Life* story did not mention that the $20,000 fee was intended as the first in a series of annual payments on a lifetime-and-after contract. Neither Lambert nor the Justice Department was yet aware of that generous proviso. Fortas probably would have been better off had that information come from him rather than from an unfriendly source, but he decided to keep it to himself.

The statement he released through the Court's press officer was uninformative and unconvincing. In this moment of crisis, Fortas's spirited prose style and his astuteness both seemed to desert him. Of all the thousands of words printed and uttered about the case that followed, none were so damaging to Fortas as the three hundred that issued from his own hand on Sunday afternoon.

"I have not accepted any fee or emolument from Mr. Wolfson or the Wolfson Family Foundation or any related person or group," Fortas began. Then to all intents and purposes he contradicted himself. "In the hope" that he could find time to undertake studies and writings, Fortas wrote, "the Wolfson Family Foundation tendered a fee to me. Concluding that I could not undertake the assignment, I returned the fee with my thanks." He did not mention that nearly twelve months elapsed between the "tender" and the return. He had no reason to believe, Fortas said, that the "tender of the fee" was a quid pro quo for his intervention on Wolfson's behalf. Moreover, he stressed, he had never spoken to any official about Wolfson's criminal case or his SEC problems. Nor had he ever given Wolfson or his associates any legal advice or services.

No one had evidence to the contrary, but the tortured reference to the "tendered fee" seemed downright disingenuous. Newsmen badgered the press officer for an explanation, but the harried Whittington would say nothing to add to Fortas's statement.*

The Justice Department was more forthcoming. The department ordinarily avoids any announcement of an investigation in progress until it becomes a matter of public record.

---

* For full text of statement see Appendix A.

The reasons for this policy are well founded: to protect the subjects of the investigation, who may turn out to be completely innocent, and to preserve the confidentiality of the department's own operations. Newsmen seeking information on such matters had become accustomed to hearing nothing more than "no comment." On that Sunday afternoon reporters who called the Justice Department for reaction to the *Life* story were given something to chew on. The statement, personally authorized by the attorney general, was only one sentence long, but its significance was unmistakable. "The department is aware of the matter," the press was told, "and has it under consideration."

"GOD SAVE THIS
HONORABLE COURT"

JUDGING from outward appearances, nothing had happened to mar the stately splendor of the United States Supreme Court. As the Justices filed into the courtroom on the morning of May 5, the burnished mahogany gleamed as lustrously as ever, the Ionic columns still supported the ornate ceiling and the Court marshal sounded the traditional oyez, culminating with the words: "God save the United States and this honorable Court." Anyone who had read the morning papers would conclude that at the moment one of the Justices was in special need of divine support. Whatever help heaven might provide would certainly be welcome, because Abe Fortas could count on few earthly forces to take his part.

Justice Douglas, Fortas's closest friend on the Court, the only colleague in whom he would feel free to confide his current problems, was absent from the bench, and indeed from the country. Douglas was off on a speaking trip to Brazil and would not return until the following week.

The members of the liberal establishment, who had fought vainly to elevate Fortas to Chief Justice the preceding summer, were confounded by the revelations of his association with Louis Wolfson. Many had been uneasy about Fortas since the disclosure of his fee for the American University seminars. The latest allegations, which had been given front-page play by newspapers around the country, and Fortas's response to these charges left most of them in an embarrassed silence. By the time the Court had concluded its routine session that Monday morning, some of Fortas's former allies were already wondering whether, when the Justices returned to the bench in two weeks, Fortas would still be among them.

The liberals who did speak out offered Fortas little comfort. The first rumblings from Capitol Hill on the Wolfson affair came from the newly chosen whip of the Senate Democrats and the heir to his family's political legacy, Edward M. Kennedy of Massachusetts. In less than three months Senator Kennedy would take a wrong turn on a road on Martha's Vineyard, a young woman would drown and he would have his own embarrassing explanations to make. At the moment, however, as he met with newsmen on the Senate floor many considered his nomination for the presidency three years hence all but automatic, and his words carried considerable weight. The published allegations about Fortas were, he said, "extremely important charges," which "reach the integrity of the Justice as well as the Court." The Senator noted that the Justice Department was investigating and suggested that the Judiciary Committee, of which he was a member, "would make itself available to Mr. Justice Fortas should he wish to present his case." He expressed the hope "that the enemies of the Court in the past would not be able to take advantage of this."

Fortas's foes, of course, were unwilling to be classified as the Court's enemies. They preferred to consider themselves as its conscientious friends who were nevertheless critical of the Warren Court's policies or of Fortas's personal conduct or of both. Fortas's most conspicuous critic was Robert Griffin of Michigan. The latest disclosures made it seem likely that even many who had attacked Griffin's motives for opposing Fortas's nomination for Chief Justice would now have to concede, however grudgingly, that he had performed a service to the Court and to the country. But that point, Griffin realized, was best made by others.

"We must be careful not to gloat," Griffin told one of his aides. Accordingly, his first public statement on the Wolfson affair was relatively restrained. He said simply that the allegations raised "most serious questions which need to be resolved if public confidence in the Court is to be restored."

But some of his colleagues could not wait to express their indignation. The Senate had been in session only thirty minutes when Jack Miller of Iowa rose to declare that, "taken together," Fortas's fees from American University and the Wolfson Foundation "strongly suggest that Mr. Justice Fortas should resign. They place a cloud over the Court which is already in disrepute among a majority of the people in this country."

Next, John Williams of Delaware, who considered himself a guardian of both public funds and public morality, broadened the attack to cover the $12,000 annual retainer Justice Douglas received from the Parvin Foundation. The Douglas and Fortas cases were two of a kind, Williams maintained. Both the Wolfson and Parvin Foundations had a disreputable character, he charged, Wolfson being a convicted criminal and Parvin being associated with Las Vegas gambling interests.* The Justices of the Court, Williams argued, are given lifetime tenure and substantial salaries so they will have no need to accept fees from outside activities. "The mere fact that Justice Fortas takes the same position that did Justice Douglas—namely that they still see nothing wrong with what they did—causes one to assume that they will do it again, only hoping that the next time they will not get caught."

---

* There were other links, coincidental or not. Albert Parvin himself was allegedly one of the investors enlisted by Joseph Kosow to purchase the Merritt-Chapman stock later bought by the company, and he was named by the Justice Department as an unindicted co-conspirator in the case. Also, Carol Agger was for a time retained by the Parvin Foundation as its tax attorney.

Williams's revival of the three-year-old charges against Justice Douglas, which had been all but forgotten, would have considerable significance in the months ahead, but for the time being the anger in the Senate was focused on the most immediate and vulnerable target. Strom Thurmond, who had suggested that Fortas quit the Court months before, predictably brought that idea up again. "I hope he will search his conscience," said Thurmond, "to determine if the faith of the people in the integrity of the Supreme Court would be better served by his resignation."

Over on the House side, Representative H. R. Gross of Iowa saw no reason to waste time with the subtleties of Fortas's conscience. A lonely and sometimes cranky crusader, Gross sensed that he could now ride a broad crest of indignation. It was "imperative," he said, that Justice Fortas resign. "His failure to do so should lead to the institution of impeachment proceedings."

Gross's mention of a weapon that had not been used against a Supreme Court Justice since the infancy of the Republic sent Gerald Ford of Michigan, leader of the House Republicans, scurrying to his manual of House rules to study the section on impeachment.* The following morning, Tuesday, the Republican leaders were scheduled to meet with the President, and Ford surmised that the subject was likely to come up.

Ford's assumption was quite correct. Richard Nixon, who had watched the early developments in the Fortas affair from the sidelines, decided that matters had reached a point where he should take a hand. The President had no detailed blueprint for action; the situation was too complicated and too unpredictable for that. Nixon himself could not keep up with every detail. This responsibility was delegated to the attorney general, who made decisions as he went along, reacting to new information, to public opinion and to Fortas's own

---

* Information which Ford was finally to put to use in April of 1970 when he led an attempt to impeach Justice Douglas.

reactions. But throughout the controversy the attorney general and the President were guided by two chief objectives. One, unstated publicly but implicit in nearly every tactic of the Administration, was to force Fortas off the Court. The other was to avoid as much as possible the appearance that the Republican Party, and particularly the Republican President, was exerting a partisan influence on events.

The reaction of the opposition party aided the Administration in this regard. No Democratic voice was ever raised in Congress to support Fortas, and as time went on many Democrats joined the ranks of his critics. Already, as the GOP leaders gathered at the White House, the nation's two most powerful liberal newspapers had expressed their disapproval of Fortas's actions and their dissatisfaction with his explanation. "The dignity of the Supreme Court requires the most exhaustive disclosure of every aspect of the Wolfson matter," said the *New York Times.* The *Washington Post* was stronger: "Unless Justice Fortas can provide a more compelling explanation, he can best serve himself, the Court on which he sits and his country by stepping down."

Still, the President was troubled by something else he had read in the papers, a story in Tuesday morning's *Times,* under the headline: "Some in GOP Ask Fortas to Resign." Both the headline and the story were accurate, which was exactly what bothered Nixon. It would take only a few more such stories to ruin the nonpartisan appearance he was trying to foster.

Justice Fortas's problems were not on the agenda for the meeting that brought together the ranking Republicans in both houses: the leaders, the whips and officers of the party conference and policy committees. Nevertheless, the President himself immediately raised the issue. "I suppose," he remarked, "that some of you want to take a little time on the Fortas matter." Since Richard Nixon was not given to idle remarks, several heads immediately nodded assent. The legislators also took note that the President had brought as a guest to their meeting the attorney general, whose department was known to have taken an interest in the Fortas affair.

The President began by mentioning the disturbing headline in the *Times*. "It is most desirable," he said pointedly, "not to involve this matter in partisanship." Whatever action Congress took should involve both parties; moreover, Nixon hoped that his legislative lieutenants would not offer "aid and comfort to anyone doing something rash."

If that remark was directed, as it seemed to be, at the talk of impeachment, Gerald Ford missed the point. Like an earnest schoolboy who had diligently done his homework, Ford plunged into an enthusiastic discussion of impeachment lore. "I'm amazed," he said, "how easy it is to start impeachment proceedings and how broad the grounds are." It was even possible, Ford mentioned, for the President himself to initiate the process by sending a special message to Congress.

That was all Richard Nixon wanted to hear about that. It would be, he said firmly, an "improper" intrusion for the President to get involved in an impeachment. Besides, he reminded Ford, impeachment was bound to drag on and on, thus interfering with his new Administration's legislative program, and it was likely to lead to a partisan fight, which, the President once again declared, was precisely what he sought to avoid. He had a feeling, Nixon said, that it might be best for all concerned if the Supreme Court worked out its own problems.

By this time his guests were beginning to grasp what the President was driving at. He wanted Fortas's resignation.

Now the group launched into a discussion of how this might be achieved. Everett Dirksen was quick to point to a serious obstacle. For Fortas to quit, said Dirksen, would be tantamount to admitting wrongdoing, an admission which the Justice so far had steered away from. Inevitably, Dirksen was reminded of an anecdote, which concluded with an epigram Daniel Webster had supposedly delivered to a nineteenth-century jury: "Confession is suicide and suicide is confession."

At this apparent impasse, it at last occurred to the legislators that the President must have had some purpose in bringing his attorney general into their company. John Mitchell, who had so far been a silent participant in the proceedings, was asked an obvious and vital question: Had the Justice Department learned more about the Fortas affair than the *Life* article revealed?

"Yes," said the attorney general. That was all the answer he volunteered. Since extracting information from Mitchell is rather like removing an impacted molar, no one pressed him further. After issuing yet another warning against partisanship and hasty action, the President turned the discussion to more routine matters, leaving his visitors to digest the ominous scrap of news Mitchell had provided.

Since Richard Nixon's motives for staging this exercise are subject to interpretations varying from his own, his intentions can perhaps best be judged by considering what he had accomplished. He had forestalled, at least for the time being, the messy business of impeachment. He had encouraged his guests to conclude that he wanted Fortas off the bench, and he had furnished them, through his attorney general, with a tantalizing bit of information that could be used to expedite the Justice's departure.

Congressmen talk. Richard Nixon had been around Washington long enough to know that. The lawmakers who had shared his confidence that Tuesday morning could be counted on to spread the word to their staffs, to other congressmen, then to their staffs and ultimately to the press, where it would do the most good—or harm, depending upon one's point of view.

A hint of what was in the wind came immediately after the White House meeting from the venerable weathervane, Everett Dirksen. The day before, he had remarked that he saw no grounds for impeachment in Fortas's conduct. But, following the session with Nixon and Mitchell, Dirksen told reporters: "There's going to be heavy pressure for some kind of action, I can tell you that."

Such remarks served, of course, as self-fulfilling prophecies, heating the furor in Congress and inciting the curiosity of the press. On Wednesday morning, the day after the White House meeting, Robert Griffin held a press conference at which a reporter asked what he knew about rumors "that there is more yet to come" on the Fortas case. Griffin deftly kept the rumors blazing. "There is more information, I think, that might come out," he said, "and I am not at liberty at this time to say what it is."

There certainly was, as Griffin well knew by this time, more information, and it was in the hands of the Justice Department, which was working night and day on the case.

If the department needed impetus for its efforts, it had been provided by Fortas's statement on Sunday. When the attorney general and his aides first learned of Fortas's relations with Wolfson, some thought, as Jack Landau later recalled, "that Fortas was too intelligent to have done anything this foolish. We had been waiting for his reply. But when he came up with that rather elliptical statement, it did nothing to help him." Even Will Wilson, who took the darkest view of the matter from the start, conceded that "if Fortas had simply kept his mouth shut, I don't know what would have come out of it. The problem of establishing what the $20,000 was for and what he was doing might have gotten fuzzed up."*

As it was, Wilson roared ahead full throttle. When he arrived at his office on Monday after Fortas had issued his statement, William Bittman, Wolfson's attorney, was already waiting to keep the appointment he had made the week before. Wilson talked to Bittman, then brought him in to see the attorney general. Bittman was advised that the IRS was already in the process of obtaining a subpoena to examine the records of the Wolfson Foundation's office in Jacksonville. He was also told that the Justice Department wanted to question

---

* Wilson would later have further reason to ponder the ethical standards demanded of public servants. In 1971, after his name was brought into a major scandal involving a Texas financier and former client, Wilson quit the Justice Department.

Wolfson. Bittman said he would discuss that with Wolfson and left. How much, if anything, Bittman volunteered at that point about Fortas's relations with Wolfson is not known. At any rate, by the next morning, Mitchell knew enough, either from Bittman or from the first reports from the IRS in Jacksonville, to tell the congressional leaders there was more to come on the case.

The search of the foundation's files yielded correspondence between Wolfson and Fortas having to do with Fortas's services to the foundation. A much more dramatic and significant discovery was Fortas's contract with the foundation providing him with $20,000 a year for as long as he and his wife should live.

By Tuesday afternoon the Justice Department in Washington knew the terms of the contract and was awaiting a copy, which was to be flown up from Jacksonville. That evening Mitchell had a speaking engagement in New York at a private dinner tendered by the Lawyers' Committee on Civil Rights Under Law. Civil rights was not the subject uppermost in the attorney general's mind at the moment, but the New York lawyers could not easily be rebuffed. Mitchell kept the date, taking Landau with him. The dinner, at Manhattan's University Club, ran on quite late. The attorney general and his press officer took the last plane out of New York to Washington, which brought them into Dulles Airport after one o'clock on Wednesday morning. At the airport to welcome them were Will Wilson and Henry Petersen, a veteran of the criminal division whom Wilson had made his deputy. Wilson had a copy of Fortas's foundation contract with him.

The four men piled into the back of Mitchell's limousine and pulled up the glass separating them from the chauffeur. As the car headed back into town on the long road through the Virginia countryside, Wilson turned the contract over to Mitchell. "It was one thing just to know the contract existed," said one member of the party. "But it was something else to see everything spelled out in black and white." Mitchell looked the document over and "sucked in his breath."

[246]

Landau went home to bed. The other three passengers went to Mitchell's residence at the Watergate apartments, the luxurious condominium whose popularity with Nixon's appointees had made it into a symbol of the new Administration. Amidst the Mitchells' French antiques they sat down with a round of drinks to map strategy.

The importance of the contract could hardly be overestimated. Out of the welter of hearsay and surmise the Justice Department had been dealing with, here at last was a tangible piece of evidence. This was no innuendo; it was a legal document that made a mockery of Fortas's efforts to obscure his relationship with the foundation. The question remained how it could best be used. After some deliberation Mitchell decided that he should bring it to the attention of the Chief Justice of the United States.

Mitchell later explained that the decision reflected his "basic training" as a lawyer. "When a lawyer has a problem involving the courts, the first thing he does is to go and talk to the judge about it," he said. "When you find that a witness is being bribed, or the prosecutor is crooked, or the clerk is stupid or whatever, you go to talk to the judge. It's just as simple as that."

It was not, of course, anywhere near that simple. If it had been, then Mitchell could have talked to Fortas himself, as Ramsey Clark had done some months before. Mitchell said he considered this, but decided against it, because "the last thing the department normally does is to have the attorney general discuss with the individual under investigation any of the aspects of it." Otherwise, Mitchell explained, if the case were to go to trial, the attorney general might be forced to go through the embarrassment of testifying.

Other considerations carried greater weight than this legalism which, had roles been reversed, Fortas himself might have devised as a rationale. For one thing, to Mitchell the prospect of a personal confrontation with Fortas seemed distinctly unpleasant. For another, Mitchell felt that Fortas had shown bad faith by the statement he had already made in the case.

Beyond that, a visit to Warren seemed more likely to help achieve the Administration's major objective in the case, which was Fortas's removal.

"This was the Court's problem," Mitchell said later. But the attoney general and the President had also made it their problem and they had decided on a solution. The Administration had already helped to build up the pressure on Fortas in the Congress and in the press. Now Mitchell had the opportunity to create additional pressure from within the Court itself.

On Wednesday morning following the Watergate conference Mitchell got in touch with the President and, as he put it, "informed" him of what he intended to do. "There was no intervention or even discussion of an approach by the President or anybody in the White House," he said later. "The decision was made entirely by myself." Officials at the White House, who were desirous of keeping the President in the background of the Fortas affair, later greatly stressed that it was Mitchell's idea, not Nixon's, to call on Warren. The distinction is thin. Whoever thought of it first, the President certainly could have cancelled the plan when he heard about it. But if Nixon had any comment on his proposal, Mitchell said he could not recall it.

The attorney general was given an appointment with the Chief Justice at 11:30 Wednesday morning. Mitchell took what precautions he could to avoid discovery. His chauffeur drove around to the back entrance of the Court and pulled into the basement garage, where Mitchell was met by a marshal who escorted him to Warren's chambers.

Warren himself has never discussed this meeting, beyond confirming later that it took place, and Mitchell has said only a little more. By his account, the attorney general showed the Chief Justice "certain documents," which could have only been the foundation contract and related correspondence unearthed by the IRS in Jacksonville. Their meeting lasted less than thirty minutes, and, Mitchell recalled, "I did most of the talking." Mitchell had been "apprehensive" about the Chief's reactions "under this unprecedented circumstance." But these misgivings turned out to be "entirely unfounded." Indeed, according to Mitchell, Warren was "appreciative" of the visit. "He accepted it entirely in the spirit with which I approached him." If Warren was shocked or dismayed at the information Mitchell conveyed to him, he gave no sign. Later Mitchell said drily: "I wouldn't believe that Earl Warren at this stage of life would be shocked about anything." The Chief "did not express any opinions or make any statements" at all. He simply said "he would take the matter under consideration. He indicated no course of action."

Mitchell had no way of knowing exactly what Warren would do, or could do. It was possible that he might keep the matter to himself, but his "appreciative" response indicated otherwise. "We certainly assumed that he would tell Fortas," one Justice official said. "And we thought that he might also tell the rest of the Justices and they might have some procedure for dealing with this."

Warren was deeply disturbed. He later described the Fortas affair as "a matter of intense controversy and emotion," and has refused to say anything further that might "reopen wounds that have now healed." According to sources close to the Court, Warren, as the Justice Department fully expected, did discuss Mitchell's visit with Fortas and also informed the other Justices. The Chief had very clear standards of right and wrong. In this case, he is said to have taken "a very strong position" that Fortas's arrangement with Wolfson "should not have happened." His feelings were intensified by the untimeliness of the disclosure—only a month preceding his retirement from the Court after sixteen years of service. He could not help but look upon the incident "as a blot on the image of the Warren Court." His views were shared by most of his brethren. While some were sympathetic, they felt that the plight Fortas had gotten himself into left him little choice but to resign.

Whatever their attitude, the Justices could do little about it directly. Though the Chief Justice is chief administrator of the Court's affairs, he has no authority to discipline any of the other Justices. Nor are the Justices as a group empowered, either by the Constitution, statute, or the Court's own rules, to act in such a situation. Indeed some Justices, jealous of their own independence, would almost certainly oppose anything that resembled interference in the affairs of one of their brothers.

In 1966, following the disclosures of Justice Douglas's retainer from the Parvin Foundation, Hugo Black was asked by the *Los Angeles Times* if he thought the Court should attempt to govern the outside activities of its members. Black's answer was a flat no. Black himself was not much of an activist off the bench. His main outside interest seemed to be tennis, a sport which he credited with helping preserve his vigor in his eighties, but that was by his own choice, and he felt strongly that no one should tell Justices what not to do. "The Constitution provides for an independent judiciary," he said, "one which is not controlled by special ruling of the judges. I do not consider it to be a part of my responsibility or duty to sit in judgment upon the outside activities of my brethren on this Court."

Though the Fortas affair presented unique problems, the Court had in the past been troubled by aging members whose all too evident infirmities were a burden and an embarrassment. Informal efforts to deal with such problems had left a bad taste with all concerned. In 1870, when Justice Robert Grier became enfeebled by age, a committee of Justices that included Stephen Field called upon him and tactfully suggested that he retire. Years later, Field himself reached such a state of "decrepitude" that he often forgot how he had voted on decisions and lapsed into periods of "dull stupor." One of Field's colleagues was then delegated to call on him to remind him of that earlier encounter. But when Field was approached and asked if he remembered his visit to Grier, the old man's eyes blazed. "Yes," he said. "And a dirtier day's work I never did in my life."

Thus, it seemed difficult for Warren and the others to take

any action that might not damage the Court as much internally as it was now threatened from outside. What solution, if any, the Justices might have worked out among themselves will never be known, because the attorney general's secret visit to Earl Warren suddenly became a matter of public knowledge.

The far-reaching controversy over Fortas's relations with Wolfson had been touched off by a story in *Life.* Now it was pushed toward a climax by *Newsweek,* which learned of Mitchell's extraordinary trip to the Court and duly reported it. The public disclosure embarrassed the Administration, but its impact was more damaging to Fortas.

As the Fortas affair and subsequent events demonstrated, the press is a potent instrument for advancing the interests of whatever side in a public controversy is best equipped to use it. Restrained only by the limits of libel, and hopefully by a concern with accuracy and fairness, journalists usually publish whatever they consider interesting and significant. The results may be seriously damaging to one side or the other, but if the press allows such considerations to influence its decisions on what to print, it risks its freedom and defaults on its obligations.

Long afterward, John Mitchell professed still to be puzzled over how his meeting with Earl Warren came to light. "It has disturbed me ever since," he said, "because the information that the department had was very closely held."

It was and it wasn't. Within the Justice Department itself, the handful of officials who knew kept the matter to themselves. The Administration, however, for reasons best known to itself, passed the word to a few key figures in the Congress, men who were important in the legislative hierarchy or who had particularly interested themselves in the Fortas affair. In one instance, the President himself made a point of personally delivering the news by phone. The motives for these disclosures are open to conjecture. The President, who earlier in the week had argued against rash action, may have wanted to reassure the legislators that the Administration had the situation well in hand. Or he may have wanted the information to leak out. Or he may simply have wanted to flatter a loyal supporter by letting him in on a state secret.

At any rate, soon after the secret was known on Capitol Hill, *Newsweek's* Samuel Shaffer, a veteran of that citadel of gossip, learned about it. Spurred by his first tip, Shaffer gathered enough information from several sources not only to confirm the attorney general's visit with the Chief Justice, but also to reconstruct in part the President's earlier strategy session with the Republican legislators. *Newsweek* made Shaffer's exclusive story the centerpiece of its next issue.

Abe Fortas's picture, in judicial robes, graced the magazine's cover under the headline: "Justice on the Spot." A lengthy chronicle of the Fortas controversy opened with the news that Attorney General Mitchell had paid "a backstairs call on Chief Justice Warren. The message: There was still more damaging material in the Fortas file and it was sure to surface unless Fortas withdrew." The magazine offered no inkling of what this damaging material might be. The terms of Fortas's foundation contract still remained secret, but the story created a sensation comparable to the reaction to Lambert's initial article.

Washington first heard of it on news broadcasts on Sunday evening, May 11, after a week of public debate about Fortas's relations with Wolfson. The initial response from the White House was a denial. Then it developed that all the White House was denying was *Newsweek's* assertion that the President had directed Mitchell to call on Warren. The President, it was insisted, had merely been told by Mitchell what he was going to do.

Semantics mattered little at the moment. The news was out, and Mitchell decided to make the most of it. It was arranged with Warren that both he and Mitchell should acknowledge that they had met. That was all Warren said. Mitchell went further. "As a courtesy to the Chief Justice," he announced on Monday morning, "I felt it incumbent upon me to inform him of certain information known by me which might be of aid to him." Once again the attorney general had said more than he needed to. He had confirmed not only the meeting but also the report that the Justice Department knew more about Fortas and Wolfson than the public did.

In fact, Mitchell had since collected even more information on the case than he had passed on to Warren. The new evidence had been furnished by Louis Wolfson himself. From the very first, Will Wilson had wanted to interview Wolfson, but he did not want to bargain with him for his testimony. Wolfson for his part was leery of incriminating himself. Solving these problems required negotiation and legal rigmarole. After Wolfson declined to testify voluntarily, Wilson told Wolfson's lawyer, William Bittman, that the Justice Department was prepared to bring him before a grand jury under subpoena and, if necessary, to grant him immunity from prosecution to compel him to speak. Wolfson thus was left with little choice in the matter. To spare himself the trouble and possible notoriety of appearing before a grand jury, he agreed to answer questions in his prison cell, where he was formally served with a subpoena.*

Wolfson was questioned by FBI agents on Thursday, May 9, the day after Mitchell talked to Warren. Eager to be in the thick of things, Will Wilson flew to Florida for the occasion. He came back to Washington with the signed statement from Wolfson about his relations with Fortas and copies of more letters that Wolfson had written to the Justice.

Wolfson's statement has never been made public, but whatever he might have said damaging about Fortas was still only his word, which would take time to confirm. Of more immediate use were the letters. While their details are also still secret, it is known that the correspondence between Wolfson and Fortas, like the conversation between Mitchell and War-

---

* When it later became publicly known that Wolfson had been questioned, the Justice Department took pains to announce that it had compelled him to testify and to deny reports that he had been offered concessions as an incentive. This assertion gained credence a few months later when Wolfson was denied parole. He ultimately served out nine months of his one-year sentence, with time off for good behavior.

ren, was one-sided. Wolfson did most of the writing. He was in fact a great letter writer at the time of his troubles. As Fortas himself later pointed out, Wolfson wrote about his problems to a number of people, including several friendly congressmen. In general, he described his difficulties with the SEC, complained of unfair treatment and asked for help or advice of one sort or another. Officials who saw the Wolfson-Fortas correspondence found no evidence that Fortas had actually given Wolfson any help, but if the letters were not proof of criminal conduct, taken together with the foundation contract, they were suggestive of impropriety. Before locking them in his safe, Mitchell had copies made and sent them on to Earl Warren at the Supreme Court, where they could be expected to add to the pressures on Fortas.

So far, however, Fortas had seemed impervious to all pressure. Never easily bluffed or cowed, he had decided to try riding out the storm. "He's resigned to the criticism he's going to get," said Fred Rodell, a former colleague at Yale who talked to Fortas early in the crisis. "But he's not resigned to the idea of resigning." Fortas was playing for time. Any day, some new sensation might arise to distract the public and the press. Besides, he wanted the chance to confer with Justice Douglas, who was still away in Brazil.

He came to his chambers regularly and carried on his judicial business as usual. "We worked on petitions for the next conference," one of his clerks recalled. "We took papers in to him, which he read and commented on as he always did. It was another example of how he could compartmentalize his life." With the Court not meeting, Fortas was spared the need for any public appearance there, but months before he had agreed to give a series of speeches while the Court was in recess. If he reneged now he would seem to be hiding from sight. He decided to stick to his schedule.

It was a difficult course to follow, and it became more difficult as the controversy mounted. Speaking at Northeastern University in Boston on Thursday, May 8, Fortas glanced around the crowded auditorium and said slyly that he was "very impressed by all the cameramen here just for an ordinary speech." He added that the pleasant afternoon he had spent on the campus had made him feel "a little more kindly about *Life*," putting enough emphasis on the final word to draw a laugh from his audience.

In his address, which dealt with "the generation gap," Fortas made no attempt to answer the questions that had been publicly raised about his conduct, but his words could be taken as a comment on the nation's quickening sense of moral discontent, to which his behavior had already contributed. Many of his critics, of course, had political and personal axes to grind, but others were resentful on broader grounds. They feared Fortas had further undermined the old liberal orthodoxies in which they themselves were finding it increasingly difficult to believe.

Writing in the *Washington Post,* Edward P. Morgan described the Fortas affair as "a stunning blow" to liberalism. "It explodes," he pointed out, "just as the attacks on the Establishment for eroding their ideals with hypocrisy and squeezing institutions to serve special interests rather than the public good are mounting from the student left and black militants." James Reston wrote that the Fortas case had aggravated "the crisis of belief." "The most idealistic of our young people," he said, were watching the developments "and wondering and condemning. Where are sincerity and integrity? Where are honesty and plain speaking?"

Where indeed? They were not evident in Fortas's speech at Northeastern, which answered the youthful challenge to his generation with a defense resembling the lawyer's ploy of confession and avoidance. He understood, Fortas said, the younger generation's discontent with the problems of war, race and poverty, but he contended that these problems had always been there. His generation, which was now called "the Establishment," had launched "a great social revolution" to solve them. "Now this is the work that is unfinished," he said. "It is work that is like building a new house—in the early stages everything is a mess, torn up and disordered." The time had come, Fortas declared, for the younger generation to join the old in putting the house in order and "to take part in the great and heroic ventures that we have started." But it detracted something from the inspiration of his message that when the Establishment's spokesman was finished, he had to be hustled from the auditorium into a waiting car, shouting over his shoulder to reporters: "No, no, no."

The shadow of the Wolfson Foundation fee followed him the next night to Richmond, Virginia, where as he began another speech on the differences between the generations, a heckler shouted: "Honest Abe!" Fortas plunged ahead, warning the audience that lawless protest against injustice would only invite repression. His office took the occasion to announce that he had donated his $2,500 fee to a scholarship fund at the law school and added primly that for "some time" Fortas had not accepted any payment larger than his expenses.

It was late in the game for him to worry about such niceties. On Monday night, May 12, when Mitchell's visit to Warren was already public knowledge, Fortas returned to his hometown to speak at Memphis State College on "Justice and Equality." Circumstances seemed to mock his words. When he declared: "He who seeks respect for the law must give respect in equal measure," a student in the audience snickered. The newsmen were still snapping at his heels. When his plane landed in Washington that night, one reporter asked whether it was fair to assume that he was standing on the one public statement he had made. "Whether it is fair or unfair," Fortas snapped, "I am saying nothing."

Then he drove home to Georgetown, where Bill Douglas, finally returned from abroad, awaited him. Douglas had been under attack for one thing or another most of his public life. To the best of anyone's memory, he had never given ground. Now, as an old friend, and as a colleague who had his own foundation to answer for, he urged Fortas to stand firm.

As each day passed, Fortas's enemies and his former friends pressed him harder. H. R. Gross was said to be on the verge of instituting impeachment proceedings. On May 10, Senator

Walter Mondale, a liberal Democrat from Minnesota, publicly suggested that Fortas resign. Three days later Maryland Senator Joseph Tydings, another liberal Democrat and a member of the Judiciary Committee, called a press conference to make that suggestion a demand. Tydings disclosed that he had written Fortas asking for an explanation of the foundation fee and had received none. The situation, Tydings said, "has deteriorated beyond recall. Mr. Justice Fortas must resign. He must resign immediately."*

In the midst of the furor, one senator spoke out for "thoughtful consideration and a strict adherence to the Constitution." Sam Ervin, who had plagued Fortas so persistently before the Judiciary Committee, rose in the Senate to call the current controversy "a crisis for the Supreme Court of a seriousness rarely matched in our history." Reminding his colleagues that they would sit as judge and jury in the event of impeachment, Ervin warned them against prejudging the issue. Even more than the senators, the President, too, should be restrained in his conduct, Ervin said. "Care should be taken not to establish any precedent suggesting that the President has any power or influence to discharge a member of the judiciary from office." On the Court itself, Ervin pointed out: "Each judge is an independent officer. Judges are not dependent for their positions on the good will or tolerance of their brethren on the courts. It would be most unfortunate," he said, "if the independence of the judiciary were weakened by making judges subject to the opinions of other members of the judiciary."

But the congressional mood was not receptive to lectures on the independence of the judiciary. The open denunciations continued on the House and Senate floors. In the cloakrooms the whisper spread that as bad as the Fortas case looked on

---

* A year later Tydings himself was the target of another story by William Lambert in which the senator was accused of behaving unethically by using his official influence to foster his financial interests. Though Tydings denied the charges, the allegations were generally considered to have contributed to Tydings's defeat in the 1970 election.

the surface, even worse information was still hidden in the Justice Department's files. There was no letup in the press either. "Justice Fortas's tragic lack of discernment has irreparably harmed his usefulness on the High Court," said the *Los Angeles Times*. And even the *Memphis Press-Scimitar,* which in the past had proudly recorded how its local boy had made good, now called upon him to explain or resign.

Fortas now had almost no room in which to maneuver. He had foreclosed his options at the very start of the controversy. Then he had two obvious choices: to give a full and frank account of his relations with Wolfson or to ignore the matter entirely, hoping that it would blow over. Both courses were alien to his nature. The statement he had issued from his chambers was not an explanation, but rather a motion for dismissal. It said not nearly enough, yet far too much. Not only was it unpersuasive, its clumsiness would undermine the credibility of anything further he attempted to say.

He could no longer ignore the clamor in the press and the Congress. Plainly, the controversy was not going to fade away. Knowing that the Justice Department had uncovered his lifetime contract with the foundation, Fortas must have assumed that the department was hot in pursuit of more information. He could also assume that his foes would not limit their probings to his relations with Louis Wolfson. Senator Griffin, for one, was prepared to delve into the past for any indications of questionable behavior, a prospect that threatened to discomfit not only Fortas himself, but also his close associates, Lyndon Johnson among them.

Then there was the Court to consider. On Friday, May 15, the Justices would return from recess to meet together in formal conference. Votes would be taken, opinions assigned and cases scheduled for next term's docket. If Fortas was going to resign it would be better to leave before he involved himself further in the business of the Court. And Fortas was enough of a realist to realize that little choice remained to him but to resign.

His decision was signaled on Tuesday afternoon, May 13,

when he was scheduled to appear at a New Hampshire resort town to address the judges of the First Circuit. At the last minute he sent his law clerk to announce that he could not attend. It was the first break in his schedule. That night he met with Douglas and with Paul Porter for several hours in his home. Douglas was still in a combative mood. Porter had prepared himself by reading the biography of John Marshall, with particular emphasis on the section dealing with the impeachment of Justice Chase 165 years before. But there would be no combat and no impeachment. Fortas talked to his two friends, then sent for his secretary to begin work on a statement that would make him the first Justice in the history of the Court to quit under fire.

By midafternoon of the next day he had advised his colleagues of his decision and had given to the Chief Justice a four-page letter of resignation and explanation.* In far more detail than he had previously provided, the letter traced Fortas's relationship with Wolfson and the foundation. At last he set forth the lifetime terms of his contract with the foundation, his decision to resign as consultant in June of 1966, his return of the $20,000 six months later. Since he had joined the Court, Fortas acknowledged, Wolfson had written and talked to him about his legal troubles. But, he said, he had never interceded for Wolfson.

"There has been no wrongdoing on my part," Fortas said. "There has been no default in the performance of my judicial duties." He was leaving, he said, only because of his concern for "the welfare and maximum effectiveness of the Court." He hoped that his departure, "by terminating the public controversy, will permit the Court to proceed with its work without the harassment of debate concerning one of its members." And he also hoped that in private life he would be able "to continue to serve the nation and the cause of justice which this Court so ably represents."

Fortas's last act before he left was to call his office staff to-

---

* See Appendix B for full text of letter.

gether to tell them he was resigning. He seemed to them to be greatly relieved. After recounting his letter to Warren, Fortas changed the subject and began to reminisce about the early days of his career and old New Deal friends. He even recalled the article he had written for the *Yale Law Journal* in 1933 on wage assignments. "He sounded regretful, but not bitter," said one of his clerks. "He was sort of sentimental."

While Fortas was saying farewell to his staff, his letter to Warren, along with a two-sentence letter of resignation to the President, was on the way to the White House. It arrived there at 5:30 P.M. in plenty of time to make the Thursday morning papers. But the war in Vietnam which had burdened Fortas while Lyndon Johnson was President intruded on him even now. Richard Nixon planned a major address to the nation that night on the war and wanted nothing to distract attention from his speech. Nixon set Fortas's letter aside.

John Mitchell was promptly informed, however. That evening as the attorney general was preparing for a speech of his own on "Fair Trials and the Administration of Justice," one of his aides mentioned the Fortas case. "Don't worry," Mitchell told him. "It will all be over tomorrow."

Even at the last, information on the case continued to leak out. While Fortas's letter sat on the President's desk, the *Los Angeles Times* went to press with a story that disclosed the terms of Fortas's contract with the Wolfson Foundation. The *Times* also reported that other documents bearing on the case were in the government's possession, along with a statement Wolfson had made to the FBI. This information, the paper said, was being interpreted by Justice Department officials "to mean that Fortas appeared to be willing to assist Wolfson in a Securities and Exchange Commission investigation of the financier."

By Thursday morning, with that news in the public domain and still no word from the White House, Fortas called Banning Whittington, the Court press officer, and told him to announce his resignation. Several hours later the White House finally released Fortas's letter and Nixon's curt response: "I have received your letter of resignation and I accept it, effective as of its date."

From his chambers at the Court, Earl Warren issued a brief epitaph on his departed colleague. He praised Fortas as "a learned and compassionate Justice" and expressed hope that "throughout the years which lie ahead he will enjoy both success and happiness in the pursuit of his profession."

Fortas spent the day at home, playing Mozart and Haydn on his Guidantus and taking phone calls from newsmen. He was relaxed enough to joke about the offer of a job by one of his musician friends, as second fiddle, he said. If he did well, he speculated, he might get to be first violin. He had no serious plans for the future, which, he said, he was "trying not to think about." His decision to resign he had come to regard as inevitable. Unless he left the Court, he said, "there would be this great constitutional confrontation that would go on for months. Hell, I feel there wasn't any choice for a man of conscience."

The events of the past ten days had not made him bitter. "I made no criticism. I harbor no animosity. I make no judgment on anyone." He saw neither plot nor purpose in what had happened. "I'm not the kind who looks for that kind of thing," he said. "It's just as if an automobile hit me as I stepped off the curb."

CHAPTER NINE

CODA

AMIDST the funereal atmosphere that prevailed at Arnold & Porter following Fortas's fall from grace, Thurman Arnold offered a visitor his own anguished postscript to his friend's judicial career. "Thank God," Arnold said, "that he didn't get to be Chief Justice."

The thought was small consolation to most of Fortas's long-time liberal allies and admirers to whom his forced resignation from the Court was a staggering blow. "It is a famous defeat for all of us," wrote columnist Joseph Kraft. Emanuel Celler, chairman of the House Judiciary Committee, declared: "The Fortas affair is a tragedy—almost Greek in nature." Grecian or not, the affair did have tragic results: A brilliant public career wrecked and the reputation of the Supreme Court damaged. But the reasons have been obscured by the tangle of politics, morality and law which surrounded the episode from the beginning.

David Broder contended in the *Washington Post* that the Fortas case "was in many ways the culmination of New Deal liberalism." But that seems too sweeping an indictment. Many New Dealers have preserved their honor, and some of their idealism is still bearing fruit. It is true that the "great social revolution" which Fortas helped set in motion did open important personal opportunities for him, as it did for others. It is also true that he was part of most of the great events of his time. His own values reflected his own characteristics, however, and the climax of his career was largely shaped by the happenstance of his friendship with Lyndon Johnson.

Fortas was unusually bright and ambitious, and strikingly insensitive to what others thought of his behavior. He fought for principle when it suited him, but he usually kept his eye on the main chance and the big money. His corporate clients who made him wealthy, and Lyndon Johnson who made him powerful, cared mainly for the results he delivered. Men presumed to be more meticulous about principles accepted his success as the stamp of greatness. They classified Fortas's expediencies as realism, the altar on which ideals are regularly sacrificed. Then it was discovered that in his supposed realism Fortas had struck a very foolish bargain with Louis Wolfson. This disclosure was all the more embarrassing because it came in the midst of a period of national soul searching and touched on the Supreme Court, the institution the nation could least afford to have compromised.

The error of Fortas's ways is hard to classify. He did not commit a crime; we have the Justice Department's word for that. "We reviewed that for quite a long time after the event," said John Mitchell. "And the determination of the people in the criminal division was that there was no actual breach of the criminal statute." Following Fortas's resignation, Will Wilson had the FBI interview several SEC officials close to the Wolfson case and ordered a check of telephone logs at the SEC for records of calls from Fortas. One of Wilson's own men went to New York to interview Alex Rittmaster. Wilson was looking for evidence that Fortas had tried to interfere in the investigation of Wolfson, perhaps by inveigling the transfer of the case from Robert Morgenthau's office. When all was done, Wilson was left with some suspicions, but without enough evidence to warrant further investigation. In midsummer he reluctantly gave up and closed the case.

While the absence of incriminating evidence does not necessarily prove innocence, common sense strengthens that conclusion. If Fortas did attempt to intervene, it must surely have been one of the least successful attempts in legal history: Wolfson's two convictions testify to that. Moreover, any attempt to meddle in the case would have been so risky as to be foolhardy for both Wolfson and Fortas. The government's investigation of Wolfson had aroused the intense interest of officials in the SEC and in Morgenthau's office; they would have been alert to any retreat and quick to complain. Rescuing Louis Wolfson from Robert Morgenthau would have approached, to borrow Lee Loevinger's phrase, "robbing Tiffany's at high noon."

Considering the available evidence, Fortas's conviction in impeachment proceedings would have been difficult to achieve. At any rate it would have been unprecedented. True, Congress was in an uproar at the time, and the standards of impeachments have been the subject of long debate. After Fortas resigned and Justice Douglas had become the prime target for congressional anger, Gerald Ford asserted "that an impeachable offense is whatever a majority of the House of Representatives considers it to be at a given moment in history." But the Congress has yet to accept that dubious criterion. As Representative Paul McCloskey has pointed out, judicial misbehavior that is not criminal has never resulted in a successful impeachment unless the judge was misusing his judicial power.

Fortas's connection with Wolfson had no bearing on his duties at the Court, where Fortas had always been careful to stay out of cases involving clients of his former law firm. If it was influence that Wolfson was interested in, it was Fortas's influence at the White House, not at the Supreme Court. For an impeachment to succeed, Fortas's accusers probably would have had to demonstrate that the Justice had tried to use his friendship with Lyndon Johnson to Wolfson's advantage. This was the sort of evidence the Justice Department looked for but failed to find.

What is left, then, is a case of noncriminal, nonjudicial

misbehavior. This does not make it trivial, but does make it difficult to deal with appropriately. The only formal judgment on Fortas's relations with Wolfson was delivered by the ethics committee of the American Bar Association. The committee found that his conduct was "clearly contrary" to the canons of judicial ethics. The gist of the eight canons cited as bearing on the case was that judges should avoid any activity, on or off the bench, that might cause even the suspicion of impropriety. But these canons have been described, in one observer's elegant phrase, as "but poles at which judges may look for guidance of length and direction of shadow when light hits upon them." More succinctly, Justice Tom Clark called them "most ambiguous and unenforceable."* Reason therefore suggests that in judging adherence to these guideposts an allowance should be made for forgivable error.

Whether Fortas's particular transgression should have been forgiven is difficult to determine, partly because he himself has never asked forgiveness. He declared he had done no wrong, likened what happened to him to a traffic accident, and began the reconstruction of his life along the lines it had followed before he joined the Court.

Some of his former colleagues at Arnold & Porter wanted him to return there, but the sentiment was by no means unanimous. Some lawyers worried that taking him back might tarnish the firm's prestige. Others were disturbed because they still had unpleasant memories of their existence under Fortas's rigorous domination. At any rate, Fortas made other plans, though Carol Agger stayed on with the firm.

By the spring of 1970 Fortas had found a partner, a Chicago lawyer named Howard Koven, and established a "small, small" firm in a newly fashionable section of Georgetown. Soon he was back at the SEC and his other old haunts. When the Supreme Court convened in the fall, Fortas filed a peti-

---

* A few months after Fortas resigned, the American Bar Association appointed a panel of lawyers and judges to create a "clear and unequivocal" code of conduct for the judiciary.

tion for a review in a patent case, appealing a decision written by, of all people, Judge Homer Thornberry. Until the Court summarily rejected the appeal, the ex-Justice considered arguing the case himself before his former colleagues. After all, he reminded a reporter, Charles Evans Hughes had argued before the Court after *he* had resigned as a Justice.

Fortas kept up his music and other outside interests. For months after his resignation he worked on another book, dealing, he said with "the current crisis in individual liberty," and tentatively titled *Freedom in Crisis*. Later Fortas decided that its theme of "converting the social revolution into national assets" was too optimistic. The Nixon Administration's policies at home and abroad made him less hopeful for the nation's future, he said, and he recalled the manuscript from his publisher.

He was still making a good many speeches, mostly at college campuses, an experience which he described as enlightening and inspiring. With "our institutions in danger of cracking and crumbling," he told a group of young Washington lawyers, the best hope for the future rested with the younger generation, who had added "a new dimension" to national life. "There is a formidable body of young people who are no longer satisfied with materialistic goals," Fortas declared. "American destiny, American goals will no longer be limited by the dollar sign."

If Fortas saw any connection between the folly of materialism and his own experience he did not choose to mention it. Nor for that matter has he ever adequately explained his association with Wolfson. So some important questions still beg an answer. What specific services was Fortas going to perform for the foundation? Why did he delay so long before returning the money? How did he respond to Wolfson's appeals for advice?

Fortas later said that his "only regret" was that he failed to treat Louis Wolfson more graciously at the time of their parting. "I didn't see him man to man," he told an interviewer, "and explain my admiration for the work he was doing and express my feeling of propriety which forced me to terminate the nature of the arrangement."

Whatever obligation Fortas felt to Wolfson, he owed the country and the Court a complete explanation of what he had done, along with an acknowledgment that he had made, to put the most favorable face on it, an error in judgment. If he had spoken out in time, with sufficient candor and sense of the proprieties involved, he might have saved his seat. At the least he would have cleared the air of some of the darker innuendoes and helped to restore public confidence in the Court.

It remains to be seen whether the Fortas case, and ensuing controversies over judicial conduct, will teach judges to be above criticism in their off-bench activities. Experience suggests that until clearer guidelines are established, some judges are bound to stray into difficulty. The most effective answer is probably the simplest. The late Dean Acheson argued convincingly for broad prohibitions against judges accepting outside income, serving outside organizations and counseling political figures, with no exceptions allowed even for Presidents of the United States. Whether the regulations should be promulgated by Congress or by the Judicial Conference is a question of mechanics. Certainly no such code would have much meaning unless it covered the Justices of the Supreme Court, whose powers, Acheson asserted, "are tolerable only when performed by men believed to be disciplined by a strict sense of duty under the Constitution and the law."

Acheson's proposals would allow no deviation from abstinence except for lectures on legal subjects delivered to legal audiences. Charities, civic commissions and Presidents would thus have to survive without the benefit of judicial energies and insights. But these contributions can be more readily sacrificed than respect for the courts, which is far too important to allow judges, or Justices, to endanger it.

That respect is already seriously threatened from other quarters. The protection of the Supreme Court's reputation was proclaimed by the Nixon Administration to be its dominant concern in the Fortas case. John Mitchell, who was the

President's chief agent in the affair, said afterwards: "Every lawyer, and certainly everybody in government who has anything to do with the Court, wants to help maintain and improve the public posture of the Court so that the judiciary is held in the highest possible esteem by the people of this country." But whatever damage Fortas may have done to the Court's public esteem, the Administration added to it. In responding to *Life's* disclosures about Fortas's financial connection with Wolfson's foundation, the Administration did far too much, and talked far too much about what it did.

The Justice Department has no authority to police the ethical behavior of the Supreme Court. By law and tradition this is a matter left to the consciences of the individual Justices. The results may not always seem satisfactory, but the problem awaits a more appropriate remedy than the heavy hand of the attorney general.

The attorney general does have authority to investigate the possibility of criminal conduct. Whether circumstances justify an investigation is a question of judgment. Ramsey Clark answered that question one way; months later John Mitchell reached a different conclusion. The merits of each decision could be debated. The point is that the sensitive ramifications of the case should have obliged the Justice Department to conduct any investigation in the strictest confidence. Instead, Attorney General Mitchell indulged himself in gratuitous comments to the press and, together with the President, in indiscreet confidences to the Congress which influenced the outcome of the episode.

Later, Mitchell declared himself pleased with the end result. "I think it's much better that the circumstances developed the way they did," he said, "rather than to have some proceeding in the Congress." But as Sam Ervin sought to remind everyone at the time, it was up to Congress itself to decide what procedures should be followed. Impeachment is a cumbersome process. It was designed that way to discourage precipitous use. By forcing a solution more convenient to itself, the Administration tampered with the independence of the judiciary guaranteed by the Constitution.

Fortas's resignation left a legacy of animosity and marked an end to the Nixon Administration's brief venture in consensus politics. Most liberals nursed their wounds in silence, for the time being. But Senator Gore declared that if the attorney general had engaged in "intimidating use of information . . . then this is as plainly in contradiction of ethics as the action of which Fortas is accused." Among Republicans, Senator Javits confessed that he too had doubts about the attorney general's behavior. The attacks on Fortas, Javits suggested, might have been partly inspired by hostility toward the Warren Court.

For its part the Administration, particularly the Justice Department, veered sharply and stridently to the right. In short order after Fortas quit, the attorney general sought to delay school desegregation in the South, to establish preventive detention in the District of Columbia and to expand his authority for electronic surveillance of suspected domestic subversives everywhere in the country. These actions might have been taken in any event. But it is hard to doubt that Nixon and Mitchell were emboldened and encouraged by the disarray in liberal ranks and the anticipated shift in the balance of power at the Court.

The controversy that drove Fortas from his seat was the second stage in the struggle for control of that institution which began with Lyndon Johnson's attempt to make Fortas Chief Justice. As it turned out, the battle continued long after Fortas left, at considerable cost both to the Court and to the Administration. The President and the attorney general contributed to their own difficulties. They failed to gauge the depth of liberal resentment and failed to understand that the issues raised in the Fortas case could be turned against the Administration.

Probably the Administration was reassured by the Senate's swift approval of Warren Burger, whom Nixon nominated as

Chief Justice within a week after Fortas's resignation. In making the announcement, the President pointedly called attention to Burger's "unquestioned integrity." It turned out that Burger, like Fortas, had a connection with a foundation. For eleven years he had been a trustee of the Mayo Foundation which in recent years had paid him $2,000 annually. Liberals were still too stunned by the Fortas debacle to make serious objection and Burger was confirmed by a seventy-four-to-three vote. The liberals needed time to recover and a more vulnerable target. The President obligingly provided them with both.

In August of 1969, Nixon nominated Clement Haynsworth, chief judge of the Fourth Circuit Court of Appeals, to fill Fortas's seat. Since Haynsworth hailed from Strom Thurmond's South Carolina his nomination was considered another in a series of gestures designed to foster Republican strength in the South. This in itself was enough to arouse the suspicions of the liberals. Civil rights groups and organized labor soon found more specific reasons in Haynsworth's judicial record to oppose his nomination. The press, with fine impartiality, probed into his background. In 1963 Haynsworth had joined in a controversial decision favorable to a big textile company. William Eaton of the *Chicago Daily News* learned that the judge had a large financial interest in a vending-machine concern that did substantial business with the textile firm.

The cry of unethical conduct was heard again in the land. The liberals on the Senate Judiciary Committee, led by Birch Bayh of Indiana, pried deeper into Haynsworth's affairs, which the Administration had not bothered to examine. They learned that he had an extensive stock portfolio and had occasionally neglected to disqualify himself from cases involving companies in which he was an investor. Stephen Schlossberg, general counsel of the United Auto Workers, told the Judiciary Committee that some legal authorities believe "that Haynsworth's conduct makes Fortas look like an altar boy." His nomination had created "a crisis of confidence in this country," Schlossberg contended. "People want to know, is the test the same? Will the standards be the same? Will the same senators and commentators who demanded the purity of one judge demand it also of another?"

The answer inevitably had to be yes. Nixon and Mitchell stubbornly pressed the fight and the Justice Department sought to justify Haynsworth's actions. But too many senators who had joined the attacks against Fortas could not afford to ignore the ethical charges against Haynsworth. The nomination was defeated in October by fifty-five votes to forty-five, after which the President issued a statement praising Haynsworth's "unimpeachable integrity" and condemning his critics as politically motivated.

The Senate was now in a conciliatory mood. No one there wanted another battle with the President and another controversy over the Court. The belief prevailed that Nixon could win approval of any nominee who had managed to steer clear of the stock market and foundations. "Anyone who hasn't been convicted of murder—recently," joked Senator George Aiken. Nixon and Mitchell looked to the South again and picked Judge George Harrold Carswell of the Fifth Circuit Court of Appeals.

Carswell's financial activities presented no problem, but his record on civil-rights cases made Haynsworth by comparison appear to be an agent of the NAACP. The liberals, who had consumed their choicest expletives against Haynsworth, were frustrated at first, but the press and the Administration's own ineptitude again furnished them with ammunition. Ed Roeder, a TV reporter, unearthed a twenty-year-old political speech, overlooked by the Justice Department, in which Carswell had pledged his undying belief in racial segregation and white supremacy.

Carswell immediately disowned those sentiments, and his supporters claimed the remarks were merely the result of youthful intemperateness. Then evidence came to light that suggested that Carswell's views had not really changed much at all. While he was serving as a U.S. attorney, he had helped to organize a private golf club whose main reason for existence was to get around a recent Supreme Court decision banning segregated public recreational facilities. Carswell told the Judiciary Committee that he was unfamiliar with the incorporation papers for the golf club. But it was subsequently disclosed that the judge had been shown the papers in question on the eve of his testimony, and thus evidently had attempted to deceive the committee and the Senate.

Not only was Carswell a bigot, his critics contended, he was an incompetent one at that. After examining his judicial record, Dean Louis H. Pollak of Yale Law School concluded "that the nominee presents more slender credentials than any nominee for the Supreme Court put forth in this century." The *New York Times* charged that the President's selection of a man so lacking in excellence "almost suggests an intention to reduce the significance of the Court by lowering the caliber of its membership." Perhaps the most devastating blow to Carswell's chances was struck by one of his strongest supporters, Senator Hruska. Bristling at charges that Carswell was at best a mediocre judge, Hruska declared: "Even if he were mediocre, there are a lot of mediocre judges and people and lawyers. They are entitled to a little representation, aren't they, and a little chance?"

When the roll was finally called in the Senate in April, the count was fifty-one to forty-five against mediocrity and Carswell. Nixon thus became the first President since Grover Cleveland to have two successive Supreme Court nominees rejected by the Senate, a setback he suffered with little grace. While John Mitchell, who had personally approved both defeated nominees, looked on, the President delivered a bitter post-mortem to the press. He characterized Carswell's defeat as "an act of regional discrimination" and promised the "millions of Americans who live in the South" that "the day will come when judges like Carswell and Haynsworth can and will sit on the High Court."

Having extracted what political benefit he could from the two disasters, the President made his third choice for Fortas's seat, Judge Harry Blackmun of the Eighth Circuit Court of Appeals. By contrast with Carswell, Blackmun seemed possessed of sterling qualifications. Nor could anyone find objections to his personal life, although some thought it a peculiar coincidence that of all the judges in the land the President should settle on one who had been a friend since childhood of Warren Burger. Nevertheless, the battle-weary Senate rushed to confirm Blackmun. In June of 1970, after the Court had gone without a ninth justice for more than a year, the longest period it had been below full strength since the Civil War, the vacancy Fortas left was filled at last.

Soon after Blackmun took his seat, it became apparent that the Administration had at last succeeded in halting the Court's activist thrust. With Blackmun and Burger combining on nearly every vote, the liberals were beaten back on a number of important cases, particularly in the criminal law, where Nixon had concentrated his campaign rhetoric.

But even as Mr. Justice Blackmun began his first term, another attack on the Court was under way. Following Carswell's defeat the conservatives decided it was their turn for revenge. Led by Gerald Ford, a group of congressmen launched a formal effort to impeach Justice Douglas, the first serious attempt aimed at a member of the Supreme Court since 1804. The main charges were aimed at Douglas's connection with the Parvin Foundation and at his outside writings, some of which were alleged to be pornographic and others seditious. As Professor Philip Kurland of the University of Chicago Law School has pointed out, the pattern for the attack on Douglas was established by the Fortas case. Like Fortas, Douglas had a liberal judicial record and a penchant for controversial outside activity. The distinction was that Douglas, with three decades of service behind him and without Fortas's controversial connection to Lyndon Johnson, made clear from the first that he would not resign. The President, who had discouraged talk of impeaching Fortas, so far as is known made no attempt to restrain the assault on Douglas.

[273]

Unfortunately for Douglas's accusers, the case was taken over by a special subcommittee headed by Congressman Celler, a long-time liberal stalwart in the House. Celler saw to it that the issue did not come to a head during the 1970 congressional campaign, when political pressures might have produced a vote against Douglas in the House. Instead, Celler's subcommittee spent months gathering evidence, then, in January of 1971, issued a report clearing Douglas of all the charges against him.

Though Douglas remained on the Court, the death of Justice Black and the retirement of Justice Harlan in September 1971 gave President Nixon an enviable opportunity to strengthen the conservative position. His first attempts to do so, however, caused him considerable difficulty. Reports that Congressman Richard Poff of Virginia would be named to replace Black caused so much criticism from civil-rights groups that Poff withdrew himself from consideration. Nixon then sought to nominate Judge Mildred Lillie of California and Herschel Friday, a lawyer from Little Rock, Arkansas, but both failed to win the endorsement of the hitherto complaisant American Bar Association. Finally, Nixon settled on Lewis Powell of Virginia, a former ABA president, and Assistant Attorney General William Rehnquist. Both were confirmed, though twenty-six liberal senators cast their votes against Rehnquist's views on civil rights and civil liberties.

The battle over Rehnquist prolonged one of the most jarring chapters in the Court's history. In less than three years one Justice was forced to quit and two designated replacements were rejected by the Senate. Another Justice was threatened with impeachment. The President was forced to discard three potential nominees. Rehnquist's nomination provoked the largest vote against a successful Supreme Court candidate since Charles Evans Hughes was confirmed as Chief Justice in 1930.

This chain of events has resulted in large part from Richard Nixon's determination to reshape the philosophy of the Court, a concern more intense than any other Chief Executive's since

Franklin Roosevelt. Nixon's attitude was reflected in his Administration's handling of the Fortas case, and also in his choice of nominees for the Court, which is a more normal part of our political process. Presidents cannot be blamed for trying to influence the outlook of the Court by their appointments, but a prudent President will realize that his power to do so is severely limited when he faces strong opposition in the Senate. If the President is genuinely interested, as he has said, in establishing a balanced Court, he might be better served to choose Justices whose own views are balanced, not loaded on one side. Heavy-handed attempts to play politics with the Court inevitably arouse resistance that is just as heavy handed.

It is a dangerous game for Presidents to play. The Court is a uniquely American instrument of government; it makes the difference, Alexis De Tocqueville believed, between anarchy and union. Though its authority and responsibility are awesome, it is extremely vulnerable. The Justices "are the all powerful guardians of a people which respects law," De Tocqueville wrote, "but they would be impotent against popular neglect or popular contempt." The partisanship and hypocrisy that have so far marked the struggle over the Court threaten to undermine respect for the law and to diminish the Court as an institution. If that happens, no matter who wins control of the Court, the Republic will suffer a shattering loss.

APPENDIX A

STATEMENT BY ABE FORTAS:

SINCE I became a member of the Court (October 1965):

1. I have not accepted any fee or emolument from Mr. Wolfson or the Wolfson Family Foundation or any related person or group.

In 1965, before I became a member of the Court, my law firm was retained in connection with civil litigation by one of Mr. Wolfson's companies. In this connection I met Mr. Wolfson and discussed with him the significant and commendable work of Mr. Wolfson and his family foundation in the field of harmonious racial and religious relations. This is an area in which I have and have had a continuing interest apart from my official judicial or legal functions.

In 1966, in the hope that I would find time and could undertake, consistently with my Court obligations, research functions, studies and writings connected with the work of the foundation, the Wolfson Family Foundation tendered a fee to me. Concluding that I could not undertake the assignment, I returned the fee with my thanks. At no time did I have any reason to believe, nor do I now believe that the tender of the fee was motivated by or involved any hope or expectation

[277]

that it would induce me to intervene or make representations on Mr. Wolfson's behalf.

2. At no time have I spoken or communicated with any official about Mr. Wolfson, whether with respect to a pardon or his criminal cases or his SEC matters.

3. At no time have I given Mr. Wolfson or any of his family, associates, foundations, or interests any legal advice or services, since becoming a member of the Court. I have not participated, as a Justice or otherwise, in any legal or judicial matter affecting any of them. In accordance with general judicial practice, I disqualify myself in cases which come to my attention concerning former clients or associates.

May 4, 1969

Supreme Court of the United States
Washington, D.C. 20543

Chambers of
JUSTICE ABE FORTAS

May 14, 1969

The Honorable Earl Warren
Chief Justice
Supreme Court of the United States
Washington, D. C. 20543

My dear Chief Justice:

I am filing with you this memorandum with respect to my association with the Wolfson Family Foundation, and a statement of the reasons which in my judgment indicate that I should resign in order that the Court may not continue to be subjected to extraneous stress which may adversely affect the performance of its important functions.

As you know, I have delayed issuing a detailed report or announcing my decision until it could first be communicated to the members of the Court. In my judgment, this was the only proper

[279]

course open to me as an Associate Justice of this Court, because of the Court's position as a separate and independent branch of the government under the Constitution. Because of the Court's recess, this report was not possible until yesterday.

In the spring or summer of 1965, before I was nominated as Associate Justice of the Supreme Court, my law firm represented New York Shipbuilding Corporation, a company controlled by Mr. Louis E. Wolfson, with respect to various civil claims. Later in the summer of 1965, and also before my nomination, my firm was retained in connection with some securities problems of Merritt-Chapman and Scott Corporation, of which Mr. Wolfson was Chairman of the Board.

I became acquainted with Mr. Wolfson and he told me about the Wolfson Family Foundation and his hopes and plans for it. He knew that its program—the improvement of community relations and the promotion of racial and religious cooperation—concerned matters to which I had devoted much time and attention.

Mr. Wolfson stated that he intended to increase the Foundation's resources, and he hoped that the Foundation might expand its work so as to make unique and basic contributions in its field. As we proceeded in our discussions, Mr. Wolfson suggested that he would like me to participate in and help shape the Foundation's program and activities. I told him I was interested in these objectives and that I hoped we would continue our discussions.

I became a member of the Court in October 1965. Shortly thereafter, Mr. Wolfson was in Washington and again conferred with me about the Foundation's work and my possible association with it. I again indicated my interest in the Foundation's program and in expanding its scope, and we discussed the possibility of my participating in the project on a long-term basis. Because of the nature of the work, there was no conflict between it and my judicial duties. It was then my opinion that the work of the Court would leave me adequate time for the Foundation assignments.

The Board of the Foundation met in December 1965, and approved, by resolution, an agreement under which I was to perform services for the Foundation. It was understood between us that the program in question was a long-range one and that my association would be meaningful only if it were on a long-term basis. The agreement, therefore, contemplated that I would perform continuing services, and, instead of fixing variable compensation from time to time for work done, it provided that I would receive Twenty Thousand Dollars per year for my life with arrangements for payments to Mrs. Fortas in the event of my death.

In January 1966, I received a check for Twenty Thousand Dollars under the agreement, and began my association with the Foundation. In June of that year I attended and participated in a meeting of the Trustees of the Foundation at Jacksonville, Florida. It is my recollection that Mr. Wolfson did not attend the meeting. I went from Jacksonville to his farm at Ocala where I had an overnight visit, as I recall, with him and his family.

Later, in June 1966, I reached the decision that the continuing role in the Foundation's work which our agreement contemplated should be terminated. There were two reasons for this decision: My work for the Court was much heavier than I had anticipated and my idea of the amount of time I would have free for non-judicial work had been a substantial overestimate. I had also learned shortly before informing the Foundation of my decision to terminate the arrangement, that the SEC had referred Mr. Wolfson's file to the Department of Justice for consideration as to criminal prosecution.

I therefore wrote a letter to the Foundation, addressed to its General Counsel, dated June 21, 1966, cancelling the agreement we had entered into, subject to completing the projects for the year. I recited as my reason only the burden of Court work.

In September and October of 1966, Mr. Louis E. Wolfson was indicted on separate charges stemming from stock transactions, and in December 1966, I returned to the Foundation, in its entirety, the sum of Twenty Thousand Dollars previously paid to me. I concluded that, because of the developments which had taken place, the services which I had performed should be treated as a contribution to the Foundation.

Since becoming a member of the Court, I have not, at any time, directly or indirectly, received any compensation from Mr. Wolfson or members of his family or any of his associates for advice, assistance or any reason whatever, except the Foundation fee which was returned.

Since I became a member of the Court, Mr. Wolfson on occasion would send me material relating to his problems, just as I think he did to many other people, and on several occasions he mentioned them to me, but I have not interceded or taken part in any legal, administrative or judicial matter affecting Mr. Wolfson or anyone associated with him.

It is my opinion, however, that the public controversy relating to my association with the Foundation is likely to continue and adversely affect the work and position of the Court, absent my resignation. In these circumstances, it seems clear to me that it is not my duty to remain on the Court, but rather to resign in the hope that this will enable the Court to proceed with its vital work free from extraneous stress.

There has been no wrongdoing on my part. There has been no default in the performance of my judicial duties in accordance with the high standards of the office I hold. So far as I am concerned, the welfare and maximum effectiveness of the Court to perform its critical role in our system of government are factors that are paramount to all others. It is this consideration that prompts my resignation which, I hope, by terminating the public controversy, will permit the Court to proceed with its work without the harassment of debate concerning one of its members.

I have written a letter asking President Nixon to accept my resignation, effective as of this date.

I leave the Court with the greatest respect and affection for you and my colleagues, and my thanks to all of you and to the staff of the Court for your unfailing helpfulness and friendship. I hope that as I return to private life, I shall find opportunities to continue to serve the Nation and the cause of justice which this Court so ably represents.

Sincerely,
(signed) ABE FORTAS

BIBLIOGRAPHY

OFFICIAL SOURCES

NATIONAL ARCHIVES:

Papers of the Agricultural Adjustment Administration. Record Group 145. Abe Fortas correspondence file. (Referred to in notes as AAA papers.)

Records of the Department of the Interior. Record Group 48. File of Undersecretary Abe Fortas. This file contains twelve boxes of general correspondence and memoranda related to various Interior Department agencies. (Referred to in notes as Undersecretary's File.)

HOUSE OF REPRESENTATIVES:

Judiciary Committee. *Associate Justice William O. Douglas.* First and Final Reports of special subcommittee on impeachment resolution, 91st Congress, 2nd session, 1970.

SENATE:

Judiciary Committee. *George Harrold Carswell.* Hearings on nomination to be Associate Justice of the Supreme Court, 91st Congress, 2nd session, 1970.

Judiciary Committee. *Clement F. Haynsworth, Jr.* Hearings on nomination to be Associate Justice of the Supreme Court, 91st Congress, 1st session, 1969.

Judiciary Committee. *Judicial Reform Act.* Hearings of the subcommittee on improvements in judicial machinery, 91st Congress, 1st and 2nd sessions, 1969–70.

[283]

Judiciary Committee. *Measures Relating to Organized Crime.* Hearings of the subcommittee on criminal laws, 91st Congress, 1st session, 1969.

Judiciary Committee. *Nomination of Abe Fortas.* Hearings on nomination to be Associate Justice of the Supreme Court, 89th Congress, 1st session, 1965.

Judiciary Committee. *Nominations of Abe Fortas and Homer Thornberry.* Hearings on nominations to be Chief Justice and Associate Justice of the Supreme Court, 90th Congress, 2nd session, 1968.

Judiciary Committee. *Nonjudicial Activities of Supreme Court Justices and Other Federal Judges.* Hearings of the subcommittee on separation of powers, 91st Congress, 1st session, 1969.

BOOKS AND PERIODICALS

Arnold, Thurman. *Fair Fights and Foul.* New York: Harcourt, Brace & World, 1965.

Baker, Leonard. *Back to Back: The Duel Between FDR and the Supreme Court.* New York: Macmillan, 1967.

Biddle, Francis. *In Brief Authority.* Garden City, N.Y.: Doubleday, 1962.

Bird, Caroline. *The Invisible Scar.* New York: David McKay, 1965.

Black, Hugo L. *A Constitutional Faith.* New York: Knopf, 1968.

"Chief Confidant to Chief Justice," *Time,* July 5, 1968.

Clapper, Raymond, "Felix Frankfurter's Young Men," *Review of Reviews,* January 1936.

Corry, John. "Strom's Dirty Movies," *Harper's,* December 1968.

De Tocqueville, Alexis. *Democracy in America.* New York: Oxford University Press, 1947.

Evans, Rowland and Novak, Robert. *Lyndon B. Johnson: The Exercise of Power.* New York: New American Library, 1966.

Fairfield, Roy P., ed. *The Federalist Papers.* Garden City, N.Y.: Anchor Books, 2nd edition, 1966.

Fortas, Abe. *Concerning Dissent and Civil Disobedience.* New York: Signet Books, 1968.

———. "Mr. Justice Douglas," *Yale Law Journal,* May 1964.

———. "Thurman Arnold and the Theater of the Law," *Yale Law Journal,* May 1970.

———. "Wage Assignments in Chicago," *Yale Law Journal,* February 1933.

Frank, John P. "William O. Douglas," *The Justices of the United States Supreme Court 1789–1969,* Vol. IV, Leon Friedman and Fred L. Israel, ed. New York: Chelsea House, 1969.

Frankel, Jack. "Removal of Judges," *Journal of the American Judicature Society,* Vol. 48, No. 9.

Freedman, Max, ed. *Roosevelt and Frankfurter*. Boston: Little, Brown, 1967.

Goldman, Eric. *The Tragedy of Lyndon Johnson*. New York: Alfred A. Knopf, 1969.

Goulden, Joseph C. *The Money Givers*. New York: Random House, 1971.

Graham, Fred. "Abe Fortas," *The Justices of the United States Supreme Court, 1789–1969*, Vol. IV.

————. "The Many Sided Justice Fortas," *New York Times Magazine*, June 4, 1967.

Hammer, Richard. "Why Things Went Sour for Louis Wolfson," *Fortune*, September 1961.

Harris, Richard. *Decision*. New York: E. P. Dutton, 1971.

Hoopes, Townsend. *The Limits of Intervention*. New York: David McKay, 1969.

Ickes, Harold. *The Lowering Clouds*, Vol. III of *The Secret Diary of Harold Ickes*. New York: Simon and Schuster, 1964.

Johnson, Lady Bird. *A White House Diary*. New York: Holt, Rinehart and Winston, 1970.

Kramer, Victor. *Selections from the Letters and Legal Papers of Thurman Arnold*. Washington: Merkle Press, 1961.

Lambert, William. "Fortas of the Supreme Court," *Life*, May 9, 1969.

————. "How LBJ's Family Amassed Its Fortune," *Life*, August 21, 1964.

Lewis, Anthony. "A Tough Lawyer Goes to the Court," *New York Times Magazine*, August 8, 1965.

————. *Gideon's Trumpet*. New York, Vintage Books, 1964.

Lilienthal, David. *The TVA Years*, Vol. I of *The Journals of David Lilienthal*. New York: Harper & Row, 1964.

Loevinger, Lee. "A Washington Lawyer Tells What It's Like," *George Washington Law Review*, May 1970.

MacDonald, Dwight. *Henry Wallace: The Man and the Myth*. New York: Vanguard Press, 1948.

Manchester, William. *The Death of a President*. New York: Harper & Row, 1967.

Moley, Raymond. *The First New Deal*. New York: Harcourt, Brace & World, 1966.

Navasky, Victor. "A Famous Prosecutor Talks About Crime," *New York Times Magazine*, February 15, 1970.

————. "In Washington, You Just Don't Not Return a Call From Abe Fortas," *New York Times Magazine*, August 1, 1971.

Nixon, Richard M. *Nixon on the Issues*. Nixon-Agnew Campaign Committee, 1968.

————. *Six Crises*. Garden City, N.Y.: Doubleday, 1962.

[285]

Oberdorfer, Don. "Ex-Democrat, Ex-Dixiecrat, Today's Nixiecrat," *New York Times Magazine,* October 6, 1968.

Payne, Melvin M., ed. *Equal Justice Under Law: The Supreme Court in American Life.* Washington: The Foundation of the Federal Bar Association, 1965.

Peek, George N. "In and Out, the Experiences of the First AAA Administrator," *Saturday Evening Post,* May 16, 1936.

Phillips, Cabell. *The Truman Presidency.* New York: Macmillan, 1966.

Reeves, Richard. "This Is the Battle of the Titans?" *New York Times Magazine,* November 1, 1970.

Rodell, Fred. "The Complexities of Mr. Justice Fortas," *New York Times Magazine,* July 28, 1968.

Rostow, Eugene V. "Professor Fortas—A Student's Reminiscence," *Yale Law Report,* Fall 1965.

Schlesinger, Arthur M., Jr. *A Thousand Days.* Boston: Houghton Mifflin, 1965.

———. *The Coming of the New Deal.* Boston: Houghton Mifflin, 1959.

———. *The Politics of Upheaval.* Boston: Houghton Mifflin, 1960.

Seib, Charles B. and Otten, Allen L. "Abe, Help!—LBJ," *Esquire,* June 1965.

Shannon, David A. *The Great Depression.* New York: Prentice-Hall, 1960.

Sidey, Hugh. *A Very Personal Presidency.* New York: Atheneum, 1968.

Steinberg, Alfred. *Sam Johnson's Boy.* New York: Macmillan, 1968.

Swindler, William F. *Court and Constitution: The New Legality, 1932–1968.* Indianapolis and New York: Bobbs-Merrill, 1970.

Walworth, Arthur. *Woodrow Wilson.* Boston: Houghton Mifflin, 2nd edition, 1965.

Weaver, John D. *Warren: The Man The Court The Era.* Boston: Little, Brown, 1967.

Whelan, Richard. *The Founding Father.* New York: New American Library, 1964.

White, Theodore. *The Making of the President.* New York: Atheneum, 1964.

Wilson, Edmund. *The American Earthquake.* Garden City, N.Y.: Doubleday, 1958.

MISCELLANEOUS SOURCES

Wolfson, Louis E., Press Conference, Tuesday, March 3, 1970, Jacksonville, Florida. This is a 121-page booklet distributed by Wolfson containing his prepared statement to the press conference and other related material and correspondence. (Referred to in notes as Wolfson

Press Conference.) Wolfson also furnished the author with a transcript of the questions and answers at the press conference. (Referred to in notes as Wolfson Transcript.)

Yale Law School Association. Transcript of remarks at a dinner on the occasion of the presentation of a portrait of Justice Fortas to Yale University, November 15, 1968. Provided by the Office of Alumni Relations, Yale Law School, New Haven, Connecticut. (Referred to in notes as Presentation Transcript.)

REFERENCE NOTES

CHAPTER ONE

PAGE

1 *The marshal's errand:* Author's interviews with William Lambert and Jack Landau.

1 *The President's stroll: Washington Post,* May 3, 1969.

2 *Nixon's One Hundred Days: Newsweek,* May 12, 1969, pp. 33–34; *New York Times* (hereafter referred to as NYT), April 15, 1969, and Washington *Star,* March 30, 1969.

3 *Lambert's story: Life,* May 9, 1969.

4 *Wolfson's plea: Washington Post,* May 7, 1969.

5 *Warren dinner: Ibid.,* April 24, 1969.

7 *On rare occasions:* During the 1880s, Justice Stephen Field embarrassed his colleagues by his close association with railroad officials when regulation of the railroads was a major issue before the Court. See *Everyman's Constitution* by Howard Jay Graham (State Historical Society of Wisconsin, 1968), pp. 101–109, 569–571. In 1923 attacks by the Hearst papers prompted Chief Justice William Howard Taft to give up a $10,000 annuity from the Carnegie Corporation. See *William Howard Taft: Chief Justice* by Alpheus T. Mason (Simon & Schuster, 1965), Ch. XI. In 1966 press criticism was directed at Justice Douglas's connection with the Parvin Foundation. See p. 250.

7 *"The Cases that come to us":* Text of address to Judicial Conference of the District of Columbia, June 2, 1969.

8 *FDR avoided the Court issue:* Baker, *Back to Back,* pp. 43–46.

8 *Murder and rape:* Text of campaign speech delivered in Cincinnati,

October 21, 1968. *"Weakening the peace forces"*: Text of television speech, Atlanta, October 3, 1968.

9   *The Southern caucus:* Chester, Hodgson and Page, *American Melodrama,* pp. 461–463.

9   *Nixon's vision:* From speech in Michigan, July 7, 1968, quoted in *Nixon on the Issues,* p. 80.

9   *Quiet encouragement:* Author's interview with a confidential source.

12   *Nixon's leadership formula:* Nixon, *Six Crises,* pp. xv, 19, 74.

12   *The Derby trip: Washington Post,* May 4, 1969.

14   *Nixon's dinner remarks: Ibid.,* April 9, 1970.

16   *"He had it made"*: This and other comments about the attorney general in this chapter are from author's interviews.

18   *"Not overjoyed"*: This and other quotations from the attorney general in this chapter not otherwise attributed are from author's interviews with him, August 13, 1969, and February 16, 1971.

20   *Mitchell complained:* NYT, March 19, 1969, also Organized Crime Hearings, pp. 146–147.

23   *"A profound thinker": Ibid.,* July 29, 1965.

23   *"Insufficiently holy"*: Lewis, "A Tough Lawyer Goes to the Court."

23   *"Reputation as a fixer"*: Author's interview with Griffin, January 26, 1970.

24   *Views on Washington lawyers: Business Week,* April 23, 1969; *True,* September 1969, and *The Washingtonian,* August 1967.

24   *"I don't like the s.o.b."*: Lewis, *Gideon's Trumpet,* p. 52.

25   *Moynihan's warning:* NYT, March 11, 1970.

27   *"We ought to quit"*: Fortas hearings, p. 46.

CHAPTER TWO

28   *"Standing on its head"*: Arnold, *Fair Fights and Foul,* p. 54.

28   *Thirteen million unemployed and farm discontent:* Schlesinger, *The Coming of the New Deal,* p. 3. *Russian jobs:* Shannon, *The Great Depression,* p. 12. *Miners' and steel workers' plight and starvation deaths:* Bird, *The Invisible Scar,* pp. 26–35.

29   *"A little terrifying"*: Schlesinger, *The Coming of the New Deal,* pp. 42–43.

29   *"A possible dictatorship"*: Wilson, *The American Earthquake,* p. 479.

30   *Frankfurter's role:* Clapper, "Felix Frankfurter's Young Men."

30   *Fortas's early years:* Based on files of *Memphis Commercial Appeal* and personal interviews by Angus McEachran, Jr. See also *Memphis Down in Dixie,* by Shields McIlwaine (New York: Dutton, 1948).

PAGE

31 *"Nineteen and ten-twelfths"*: Recalled by Professor Fleming James, Presentation Transcript, pp. 12–14.

32 *Intellectual ferment at Yale*: Arnold, pp. 54–70.

33 *Douglas on Arnold*: Kramer, *Letters of Thurman Arnold*, pp. viii–ix.

33 *"He could see life"*: Fortas, "Thurman Arnold and the Theater of the Law."

33 *Arnold's point system*: Frank, "William O. Douglas."

33 *Emerson recalled*: quoted by James, Presentation Transcript, p. 10.

33 *"The brightest mind"*: author's interview.

34 *Fortas's article*: Yale Law Journal, Vol. XLII, No. 4, February 1933.

34 *"A classical Yale investigation"*: Rostow, "A Student's Reminiscence."

35 *Sturges sent word*: By telegram, June 26, 1933, AAA papers.

35 *"A perfect bedlam"*: Arnold, p. 131. For other descriptions of AAA's early days see Moley, *The First New Deal*, pp. 258–263; Schlesinger, *The Coming of the New Deal*, pp. 46–60, and MacDonald, *Henry Wallace*, pp. 45–57.

36 *"A plague of lawyers"*: Peek, "In and Out."

36 *Phone call to Memphis*: Memo to Jerome Frank from James E. Jones, August 12, 1933, AAA papers.

36 *Salary dispute*: Fortas memo to Chester Davis, August 26, 1933; and Jerome Frank memo to Davis, October 17, 1933, AAA papers.

37 *Esta Fortas's report*: Memphis Commercial Appeal, November 27, 1933.

37 *Fortas's activities* at AAA: AAA papers.

38 *Peek's denunciation*: Peek, "In and Out."

39 *Fortas's personal life*: Author's interviews with Thomas Emerson and Leon Keyserling.

41 *Carol Agger in class*: Author's interview with Norman Diamond, a fellow student.

41 *Fortas's stature at Yale*: Rostow, "A Student's Reminiscence."

41 *Fortas's relations with his colleagues, his athletic feats and the Hunt Club*: Presentation Transcript.

43 *"The men down the line"*: Schlesinger, *The Politics of Upheaval*, p. 227.

44 *Kennedy's call to Douglas*: Whelan, *The Founding Father*, p. 382.

44 *SEC investigation*: Business Week, June 25, 1938, pp. 36–38.

44 *SEC vs. holding companies*: Schlesinger, *The Politics of Upheaval*, pp. 324, 448, 501; Newsweek, August 1, 1938, pp. 36–37.

45 *Ickes background*: Current Biography (New York: H. W. Wilson, 1941), pp. 426–428; Ickes, *The Lowering Clouds*.

45 *Fortas's work at coal division: Newsweek,* July 5, 1943, p. 52, and author's interview with Norman Diamond, April 20, 1970.

46 *Ickes's differences with Lilienthal:* Minutes of Ickes's staff meeting, April 18, 1941, Undersecretary's File. Also, Lilienthal, *The TVA Years,* pp. 313, 375–377.

47 *Clash with Morse: Washington Post,* August 31, 1965.

47 *Cold sarcasm:* Fortas letter to W. L. Batt, November 3, 1942, Undersecretary's File.

48 *Bureaucratic humor:* Fortas to James Rowe, December 11, 1942, Undersecretary's File.

48 *Exchange with Ickes:* November 9 and 10, 1943, Undersecretary's File. *Ickes's attitude toward Fortas:* Ickes, *The Lowering Clouds,* pp. 379, 479, 524.

48 *FDR passed a note:* Biddle, *In Brief Authority,* p. 176.

49 *Fortas and the draft: Washington Post,* May 12, 1943; September 5, 1943; November 17, 1943; December 14, 1943; *Washington Times Herald,* November 5, 1943; *Time,* September 20, 1943, p. 21.

50 *Warren's views on Japanese expulsion:* Weaver, *Warren,* pp. 105–114.

51 *"A terrific mistake":* Fortas to Eugene Rostow, June 28, 1945, Undersecretary's File.

52 *"A dangerous situation":* LaGuardia to Ickes, April 21, 1944, Undersecretary's File.

53 *The Court upheld the government: Korematsu vs. U.S.,* 323 U.S. 214 (1944).

53 *Fortas's bargaining tactics:* Author's interview with Adrian Fisher, July 21, 1970.

54 *"Not an enthusiast":* Holly Camp's interview with Arthur Goldschmidt, July 29, 1970.

55 *"The luckiest thing":* Arnold, p. 190.

CHAPTER THREE

56 *The firm's purpose:* Fortas, "Thurman Arnold and the Theater of the Law."

56 *"A cynical friend":* Arnold, *Fair Fights and Foul,* p. 191.

57 *Truman never believed:* Phillips, *The Truman Presidency,* p. 357.

57 *The Friedman case: Friedman v. Schwellenbach,* cert. denied, 330 U.S. 838 (1947); Arnold, p. 205; Fortas, "Thurman Arnold."

58 *The loyalty program:* Phillips, p. 361.

58 *Many turned to Arnold, Fortas & Porter:* Author's interviews with Milton Freeman and G. Duane Vieth; Arnold, pp. 204–227; Fortas,

"Thurman Arnold." See also *Bailey v. Richardson*, 341 U.S. 918 (1951), and *Peters v. Hobby*, 349 U.S. 331 (1954).

61 *Arnold's letter:* Kramer, p. 73.

62 *"Will he fight?":* Lattimore, *Ordeal by Slander*, p. 38.

62 *Fortas letter: Ibid.*, pp. 20–21.

65 *Arnold's letter to ACLU:* Kramer, pp. 82–83.

65 *Porter's anecdote:* Fortas, "Thurman Arnold."

67 *Starting from scratch: Ibid.*

68 *Counsel to Puerto Rico:* Marquis Childs's column is reprinted in Fortas-Thornberry Hearings, pp. 1111–1115; Fortas's comments are on pp. 177–180, *ibid.*

69 *"Banana by banana":* Rodell, "The Complexities of Mr. Justice Fortas."

69 *Argument for Otis: Kaiser-Frazer Corp. v. Otis & Co.*, 195 F. 2nd 838.

71 *Wry jokes:* Louis Cassells, "Arnold, Fortas & Prosperity," *Harper's*, November 1951.

72 *Carol Agger's life style: Washington Post*, March 22, 1964, and July 30, 1965; NYT, July 25, 1968.

73 *A martini for the cello:* Seib and Otten, "Abe, Help!—LBJ."

73 *Fortas on Minuteman Hill:* "Chief Confidante to Chief Justice."

73 *Albert Schweitzer Award: Washington Post*, November 22, 1965.

73 *Interest in psychiatry:* Seib and Otten.

74 *Fortas's role in the Gideon case:* Lewis, *Gideon's Trumpet*.

77 *"This is my life":* Confidential source.

78 *Rauh's comment:* Author's interview with Joseph Rauh, June 1, 1970.

78 *"Nothing dishonorable":* Fortas, "Thurman Arnold."

78 *"A new estate": Hard Times*, No. 36, June 16–23, 1969.

78 *"Like robbing Tiffany's":* Loevinger, "A Washington Lawyer Tells What It's Like."

CHAPTER FOUR

80 *"He deliberately cultivated":* Steinberg, *Sam Johnson's Boy*, p. 124.

80 *Lower Colorado River project: Ibid.*, pp. 130–131.

81 *Sunday suppers: Washington Post*, January 16, 1968.

81 *"No vacancy":* Fortas to Johnson, February 27, 1943, Undersecretary's File.

82 *"I appreciate it":* Fortas to Johnson, October 23, 1943, *ibid.*

82 *Johnson's Senate campaigns:* Steinberg, pp. 154–182, 235–272.

84 *"Lyndon's in trouble":* Seib and Otten.

85 *In Black's chambers: Washington Daily News*, August 3, 1965.

PAGE

86 *Reversing Parr's conviction:* Lewis, "A Tough Lawyer Goes to the Court."

88 *Fortas's role in civil-rights bills:* Evans and Novak, *Lyndon B. Johnson,* p. 134; Seib and Otten.

89 *"I knew the man":* Seib and Otten.

90 *"Check it with Abe": Ibid.*

91 *Bobby Baker affair:* Evans and Novak, pp. 332–333; Steinberg, pp. 595–599.

91 *"A spectral presence":* Schlesinger, *A Thousand Days,* p. 1018.

93 *"More than he did":* Manchester, p. 639; Evans and Novak, pp. 340–343.

93 *Fortas on the phone:* Steinberg, p. 611.

94 *Editing the speech: Ibid.,* p. 627; Manchester, p. 606n; Evans and Novak, p. 348.

95 *Setting up Warren Commission:* Manchester, pp. 458–459; Evans and Novak, p. 337.

95 *The Baker case:* Evans and Novak, pp. 413–415; *Washington Post,* December 4, 1963; *Newsweek,* November 16, 1964.

96 *Fortas's ties to White House:* Washington *Star,* July 29, 1965; author's interviews.

96 *"Extraordinary ability":* Author's interview with G. Duane Vieth.

97 *Cigarets and health:* Seib and Otten; *Washington Post,* March 20, 1964.

97 *Negotiations with Lipchitz:* Goldman, *The Tragedy of Lyndon Johnson,* pp. 145–148.

98 *The greatest influence: Ibid.,* p. 38.

98 *The 1964 campaign:* White, *The Making of the President,* pp. 275, 367.

99 *The Johnson fortune:* Seib and Otten; Sidey, *A Very Personal Presidency,* pp. 183–184; Lambert, "How LBJ's Family Amassed Its Fortune."

100 *"A damn vice squad":* Seib and Otten.

101 *The Jenkins case: Ibid.;* Fortas-Thornberry Hearings, pp. 48–49; Evans and Novak, pp. 479–481.

CHAPTER FIVE

104 *Offer of the attorney generalship: Washington Post,* February 3, 1965; Seib and Otten.

105 *The Dominican affair:* NYT, May 6, 1965; "Chief Confidant to Chief Justice."

107 *Johnson urged Warren:* Manchester, p. 630.

107 *"That or doom":* NYT, July 21, 1965.

REFERENCE NOTES

108   *"So do I"*: Reeves, "This Is the Battle of the Titans?"

109   *"His only regret"*: Freedman, *Roosevelt and Frankfurter,* p. 482.

110   *"Abe was moved"*: Johnson, *A White House Diary,* p. 299.

110   *A $250,000 home: Newsweek,* May 19, 1969.

110   *"A heart full of gratitude"*: Henry Hubbard of *Newsweek,* who was shown a copy of the letter to Johnson.

110   *"With a wry smile"*: Johnson, p. 304.

110   *Moyers on Fortas: Washington Post,* July 28, 1965.

111   *"Abe says no"*: Author's interview with confidential source.

111   *With mock solemnity:* Author's interview with confidential source.

112   *Johnson's statement:* NYT, July 29, 1965.

113   *"She refused to believe it"*: Confidential source; see also *Washington Post,* July 30, 1965.

113   *"A quiet participant"*: NYT, July 30, 1965.

114   *Editorials and questioning of Miss Shearon and Fortas:* Fortas Hearings, pp. 3–4, 8–16, 38–57.

118   *"Bombastically pretentious"*: Harlan Fisk Stone, quoted in Payne, *Equal Justice Under Law,* p. 114.

119   *Harlan's rating:* This statement and all others in this chapter dealing with Fortas's work at the Court not otherwise attributed are based on author's interviews with Fortas's law clerks. The clerks interviewed were Daniel Levitt, John Griffiths, David Rosenbloom and Walter Slocombe, whose combined service spanned Fortas's four years on the Court.

120   *"Powerless to change"*: Powell v. Texas, 392 U.S. 518 (1968).

120   *"Few things more rewarding"*: NYT, May 16, 1969.

120   *"A general alarm"*: Shuttlesworth v. Birmingham, 382 U.S. 87 (1965).

120   *"Strange classification"*: U.S. v. Grinnell Corp. 384 U.S. 563 (1966).

121   *Georgia election case: Fortson v. Morris,* 385 U.S. 231 (1966).

121   *The startled attorney: Graham,* "Abe Fortas."

121   *Fortas's remarks: Washington Post,* March 2, 1966.

122   *Escobedo case: Escobedo v. Illinois,* 378 U.S. 478 (1964).

123   *"If God be Fortas"*: Graham, "The Many-Sided Justice Fortas."

123   *The Miranda ruling: Miranda v. Arizona,* 384 U.S. 436 (1966).

124   *"Worst of both worlds": Kent v. U.S.* 383 U.S. 541 (1966).

124   *Gault arguments: Washington Post,* December 7, 1966; *In re Gault,* 387 U.S. 1 (1967).

125   *Carol Agger explained:* Unpublished interview with Richard Stout of *Newsweek,* June 1968.

125   *The quintessential statement: Baltimore & Ohio R.R. vs. United States,* 386 U.S. 372 (1967).

125   *New York Times v. Sullivan:* 376 U.S. 254 (1964).

PAGE

127 *Nixon slipped: Washington Post*, April 28, 1966; *Time Inc. v. Hill*, 385 U.S. 374 (1967).

128 *Obscenity not protected: Roth v. U.S.*, 354 U.S. 476 (1957).

129 *Ginzburg v. U.S.*: 383 U.S. 463 (1966).

130 *Contrasts self with Warren:* Rodell, "The Complexities of Mr. Justice Fortas."

131 *Tribute to Douglas:* Fortas, "Mr. Justice Douglas."

132 *Jackson's letter:* Swindler, *Court and Constitution: The New Legality*, pp. 159–160.

132 *"My legal bible":* Black, *A Constitutional Faith*, p. 66.

133 *A claim against SBA: United States v. Yazell*, 382 U.S. 341 (1966).

133 *"Limitless areas": Adamson v. California*, 332 U.S. 46 (1947).

133 *Louisiana sit-in: Brown v. Louisiana*, 383 U.S. 131 (1966); *Washington Post*, February 24, 1966.

135 *Califano's comments:* Author's interview, April 28, 1970.

135 *"An opinion from Fortas": Newsweek*, July 8, 1968. *"Any figure too low":* "Chief Confidante to Chief Justice."

135 *Fortas tended to minimize:* Fortas-Thornberry Hearings, p. 104.

136 *Fortas's union card:* Johnson, p. 627.

137 *Fortas's advice to First Lady: Ibid.*, pp. 518–519.

137 *Analytical help:* Fortas-Thornberry Hearings, pp. 104, 170.

137 *Goldberg's anger:* Hoopes, *The Limits of Intervention*, p. 185.

138 *Fortas's curious role: Ibid.*, pp. 216–217.

138 *Legal ground rules:* Fortas, *Concerning Dissent and Civil Disobedience*, pp. 91, 103–104.

139 *Urged more bombing:* Hoopes, p. 215.

139 *Israeli go-between:* Confidential source.

140 *Recommended friends:* Graham, "The Many-Sided Justice Fortas."

141 *Wilson consulted Brandeis:* Walworth, *Woodrow Wilson*, Book II, pp. 158, 172n, 210; *FDR called him Isaiah:* Schlesinger, *Politics of Upheaval*, pp. 220–222, 234–236.

141 *Frankfurter and FDR:* Freedman, pp. 500, 523, 526, 545, 596, 608, 671.

141 *"Like a piker":* Author's interview with Rauh.

CHAPTER SIX

143 *The Senate football team:* Evans and Novak, pp. 104–105.

146 *"I left politics": Washington Post*, July 6, 1968.

147 *The White House pool:* Johnson, p. 594.

147 *LBJ's visit:* Weaver, p. 336.

147 *Warren-Johnson letters:* NYT, June 27, 1968.

PAGE

148 *Johnson's views:* Interview with Henry Hubbard of *Newsweek*, June 28, 1968. Also see *Newsweek*, July 8, 1968, p. 17.

148 *The President's decision:* Author's interview with Califano.

149 *Thornberry's ties to Johnson:* "Chief Confidant to Chief Justice."

150 *Russell's reaction:* Confidential source who was told the story by Johnson. Also, Joe Califano later told the author: "We thought we had commitments from Russell and Eastland before the nominations went up. I heard that many times and that was the way LBJ operated."

151 *Winning Dirksen's support: Newsweek*, July 15, 1968, p. 27; *Washington Post*, September 24, 1968.

151 *Past nominations by lame ducks:* Fortas-Thornberry Hearings, pp. 400–401.

153 *Warren press conference: Washington Post*, July 6, 1968.

153 *Griffin's background:* NYT, September 28, 1968.

154 *Griffin's reaction:* Author's interview with Griffin, January 26, 1970.

155 *White House pressure: Newsweek*, July 15, 1968, p. 27.

156 *The anti-Semitism issue: The Jewish News* of Detroit, July 5, 1968; *New York Law Journal*, September 19, 1968. *Javits's statement:* NYT, September 14, 1968. *Griffin's counter-charge: Washington Post*, September 21, 1968.

158 *Nixon's reaction:* "Chief Confidant to Chief Justice," Baltimore *Sun*, June 28, 1968; *Nixon on the Issues*, p. 80.

158 *Griffin's phone call:* Sam Shaffer interview with Griffin.

160 *"Majestic generalities":* Quoted by Fortas, Fortas-Thornberry Hearings, p. 105.

162 *Clark's testimony: Ibid.*, pp. 8–39.

162 *"Calculated vagueness":* NYT, June 30, 1968; *New Republic*, July 20, 1968.

163 *Griffin's testimony:* Fortas-Thornberry Hearings, pp. 41–65.

163 *Dirksen's reply: Ibid.*, pp. 51–54.

165 *Fortas's opening points: Ibid.*, pp. 105–107.

166 *Full disclosure: Ibid.*, p. 106.

166 *Lazarus letter: Ibid.*, pp. 167–168, 225–229.

166 *Fortas dug into history: Ibid.*, pp. 164–166. *"That opportunity will be concluded": Ibid.*, p. 124. *"In a class with Jack Benny": Ibid.*, p. 168.

167 *Outlined by Gore: Ibid.*, pp. 100–101.

168 *Cited Ervin ruling: Ibid.*, p. 110. *"Mr. Chief Justice": Ibid.*, p. 234. *"Zero, absolutely zero": Ibid.*, p. 106.

168 *Fortas cites dissent: Ibid.*, p. 111. *"I shall not comment": Ibid.*, p. 128.

169 *Fortas cites Scottsboro case: Ibid.*, p. 173.

PAGE
169 *Thurmond background:* Oberdorfer, "Ex-Democrat, Ex-Dixiecrat."
170 *"I have never":* Fortas-Thornberry Hearings, pp. 182–183. *Mallory: Ibid.,* pp. 191–192, *Washington Post,* July 19, 1968.
171 *Frankfurter's position:* Quoted by Senator Hart, Fortas-Thornberry Hearings, p. 123. *"Nobody likes to be disagreeable": Ibid.,* p. 273. *"The smut industry": Ibid.,* p. 295. *"How much longer?": Ibid.,* p. 359.
173 *"A scandalization":* Corry, "Strom's Dirty Movies." *Fortas's position:* Fortas-Thornberry Hearings, pp. 1312–1316.
174 *Porter's efforts:* Confidential source.
174 *Judicial restraint memo:* Fortas-Thornberry Hearings, pp. 1110–1113. *Judicial performance memo: Ibid.,* pp. 1115–1123.
175 *Ervin denounced: Ibid.,* p. 312.
176 *"The phrase that should ring":* NYT, August 4, 1968.
177 *Eastland announced:* NYT, September 5, 1968. *Mansfield's report:* NYT, September 6, 1968. *Johnson's attack:* NYT, September 7, 1968.
178 *Phone call to Griffin:* Author's interview with John Hushen, former press aide to Griffin. *Porter confided:* Author's interview with Califano. *Tennery explanation:* Fortas-Thornberry Hearings, pp. 1286–1304.
180 *Further charges: Washington Post,* September 15, 1968; NYT, September 17, 1968. *Fortas's statement:* Fortas-Thornberry Hearings, p. 285.
181 *Griffin's statement:* NYT, September 15, 1968.
181 *Mansfield's distress: Washington Post,* September 26, 1968. *Dirksen's position: Washington Post,* September 28, 1968.
181 *Fortas-Johnson letters:* NYT, October 3, 1968. *Warren to stay:* NYT, October 11, 1968.
182 *Thurmond's suggestion:* NYT, October 3, 1968.
183 *"I shall persevere":* NYT, October 4, 1968.
183 *"The most denounced":* NYT, November 5, 1968.

CHAPTER SEVEN

185 *"He told us nothing":* Author's interview with Jerry Kabel, press aide to Senator Hart, May 9, 1969.
186 *Wolfson background:* Hammer, "Why Things Went Sour for Louis Wolfson." *Wall Street Journal,* April 22, 1969; *Washington Post,* May 16, 1969; NYT, June 1, 1969.
189 *Wolfson to Leahy:* Wolfson Press Conference, p. 100.
189 *"Only by imagination":* Goulden, *The Money Givers,* p. 25.
189 *"A genuine interest":* Wolfson Press Conference, p. 10.

PAGE

190   *Correspondence with Goldberg: Ibid.,* pp. 111–112.

190   *"A million dollars":* Wolfson Transcript.

190   *Contributions to Fuller Warren: Ibid. "Someone has to tell me":* *Ibid.*

191   *Offers to Wilkinson, Ribicoff, Roosevelt and Collins:* Wolfson Press Conference, pp. 101–118.

191   *"Truth of the matter": Ibid.,* p. 13.

191   *"Wolfson urged Fortas": Ibid.,* p. 12.

192   *"I did not seek":* Fortas-Thornberry Hearings, p. 124.

192   *"I might go to seed":* Navasky, "A Call from Abe Fortas."

193   *Justice's outside activities:* "Overview of Extrajudicial Activities," Final Douglas Report, pp. 431–450.

195   *Invitation to Wolfson:* Wolfson Press Conference, p. 11.

195   *"Technical violations": Ibid.,* p. 12.

195   *"A long-range program":* Fortas letter to Warren, May 14, 1969 (see Appendix B).

195   *Foundation's disbursements:* Figures are from the foundation's returns filed with the Internal Revenue Service for fiscal years ending September 30, 1965 and 1966.

196   *"This man's knowledge":* Wolfson Transcript.

197   *"Political vendetta":* Wolfson letter to U.S. Parole Board, Wolfson Press Conference, p. 55. *Dreyfus Case: Ibid..* p. 65.

197   *Origins of SEC probe:* Author's interview with Stuart Allen. See also government brief in U.S. Court of Appeals, *U.S. v. Wolfson, Gerbert, Kosow and Staub,* Docket No. 33326, pp. 28–36.

199   *Freeman's first move:* Author's interview with Milton Freeman, April 20, 1970.

199   *Fortas later acknowledged:* In letter to Warren, May 14, 1969.

200   *"I was comforted":* Wolfson letter to author, April 21, 1970.

200   *"Each case different":* Author's interview with Manuel Cohen.

200   *Continental case:* The background on this case and the Merritt-Chapman case is based on author's interviews with staff members of the SEC and the U.S. Attorney's office, plus appeals briefs filed by the government and the defense.

204   *The SEC announcement:* NYT, June 23, 1966.

204   *Wolfson letter to Cohen:* Affidavit of Michael Armstrong, U.S. District Court, 66, Cr. 832, *U.S. v. Wolfson, Gerbert, Kosow, Rittmaster and Staub.*

205   *Morgenthau's reputation:* Navasky, "A Famous Prosecutor Talks About Crime."

205   *"Enforce all the laws":* Author's interview with Robert Morgenthau, December 8, 1969.

PAGE

206   *Wolfson grumbled:* Hammer.

207   *Rittmaster's story:* Armstrong's notes on this interview are on file as government exhibit 3503-A in the Merritt-Chapman case.

208   *Armstrong braced him:* Appellants' Supplemental Appendix, Second Circuit Court of Appeals, *U.S. v. Wolfson and Gerbert,* Docket No. 31993, p. A223.

210   *Concern among Fortas's staff:* Confidential source.

212   *Douglas's fee: Los Angeles Times,* October 16, 1966.

212   *"Because of developments":* Fortas to Warren, May 14, 1969.

212   *Fortas and Wolfson met:* Wolfson Press Conference, p. 12.

213   *"Not exactly":* Government appendix, Second Circuit Court of Appeals, *U.S. v. Wolfson and Gerbert,* Docket No. 31993, p. 118 A. *"Not a detail man": Wall Street Journal,* September 27, 1967.

213   *In bitter terms:* Wolfson Press Conference, p. 62–63.

CHAPTER EIGHT

215   *Morgenthau called Clark:* Interview with Ramsey Clark, March 16, 1970.

216   *Due in February 1967:* Foundation tax returns are due on the fifteenth day of the fifth month following the close of the foundation's fiscal year, which in this case was September 30, 1966.

216   *Reached Lambert's ear:* The ensuing account of Lambert's inquiries is based on a series of interviews with him in 1970.

217   *Morgenthau made it his business:* This information, from a confidential source, was confirmed by Morgenthau in an interview with the author. Vinson told the author he had only a "hazy recollection" of Morgenthau's call.

218   *Clark's visit to Fortas:* This information, originally from another source, was confirmed by Clark in an interview with the author, April 27, 1971.

219   *Glowing tribute:* Presentation Transcript, pp. 3–5.

224   *Fortas's answer:* Lambert, "Fortas of the Supreme Court."

226   *"Covered up with work":* Author's interview with Will Wilson, February 23, 1970.

227   *Wilson swung into action:* Information on Wilson's activities comes from Wilson himself and confidential sources in the Department of Justice.

228   *Wolfson's interview: Wall Street Journal,* April 22, 1969.

229   *"Natural feebleness":* Fairfield, *The Federalist Papers,* No, 78, pp. 228–230.

229   *Impeachment precedents:* Final Douglas Report, p. 33.

PAGE

230 *A sitting judge:* Three Federal judges had previously been indicted —after they had resigned or retired. See Borkin, *The Corrupt Judge,* pp. 27, 116, 181.

233 *Rehnquist memorandum:* Author's interview with William Rehnquist; Borkin, pp. 25–28, 41–46, 79–82, 141–186, 221–222; Judicial Reform Act Hearings, Rehnquist's and Borkin's Testimony.

233 *"We were quite sure":* This and other quotations from Landau are from author's interviews with him.

239 *"Extremely important":* NYT, May 6, 1969.

240 *"Most serious":* Statement issued May 5, 1969, by Griffin's office.

240 *Congressional indignation:* See *Congressional Record,* Vol. 115, May 5, 1969. House, p. 11209; Senate, pp. 11259–11267, 11419.

241 *Ford's reaction and the White House meeting: Newsweek,* May 19, 1969.

246 *The Watergate meeting:* Confidential source.

247 *"Basic training":* These and other quotations from Mitchell in this chapter are from author's interviews with him on February 16 and March 31, 1971.

249 *"A matter of controversy":* Letter from Warren to author, March 24, 1971.

250 *A flat no:* Letter from Black to Robert J. Donovan of *Los Angeles Times,* November 21, 1966, reprinted in Nonjudicial Activities Hearings, pp. 222–223.

250 *Field and Greer:* This anecdote is from *The Supreme Court of the United States* by Charles Evans Hughes, quoted by Frankel.

252 *"Justice on the Spot": Newsweek,* May 19, 1969.

252 *Mitchell went further: Washington Post,* May 13, 1969.

254 *Found no evidence:* From confidential sources; see also Goulden, pp. 302–303.

255 *"Very impressed": Washington Post,* May 9, 1969. Other details from press release provided by Northeastern University, May 8, 1969.

255 *"A stunning blow": Washington Post,* May 10, 1969. "Crisis of belief":* NYT, May 14, 1969.

256 *"Honest Abe": Washington Post,* May 11, 1969.

256 *Return to Memphis: Los Angeles Times,* May 13, 1969. "Fair or unfair": Washington *Star,* May 13, 1969.

256 *Gross on the verge: Washington Star,* May 12, 1969. *Mondale suggests: Washington Post,* May 11, 1969.

257 *Tydings demands: Congressional Record,* Vol. 115, Senate, May 13, 1969, P. 12329. *Ervin's statement: Ibid.,* p. 12208.

261 *Fortas's comments: Newsweek,* May 26, 1969, p. 33.

CHAPTER NINE

262   *Arnold's postscript:* Confidential source.

262   *"A famous defeat":* Washington Post, May 19, 1969. *"Greek trag-edy":* Newsweek, May 26, 1969, p. 33. *New Deal liberalism:* Washington Post, May 20, 1969.

263   *"We reviewed that":* Author's interview with Mitchell.

264   *Ford's assertion:* First Douglas Report, p. 31. *McCloskey's argument:* Final Douglas Report, pp. 369–370.

265   *ABA's findings:* Washington Post, May 21, 1969.

265   *"Poles for guidance":* Edward L. Wright, quoted in Nonjudicial Activities Hearings, p. 519. *"Most ambiguous":* Ibid., p. 175.

266   *A patent case:* Beckman v. Chemtronics, cert. denied, Docket No. 711, 1970 term.

266   *Hughes had argued:* National Observer, November 2, 1970.

266   *"In danger of cracking":* From author's notes of Fortas speech to Young Lawyers' Section, District of Columbia Bar Association, November 13, 1970.

267   *His only regret:* Navasky, "A Call from Abe Fortas."

267   *Acheson's proposals:* Nonjudicial Activities Hearings, pp. 112–125.

267   *Mitchell's comment:* Author's interview.

269   *Gore's and Javits's reaction:* Washington Post, May 16, 1969.

270   *Burger's foundation connection:* NYT, June 9, 1969.

270   *"People want to know":* Haynsworth Hearings, p. 354.

271   *"Unimpeachable integrity":* Newsweek, December 1, 1969, p. 21.

271   *Carswell's civil-rights record:* Carswell Hearings, pp. 21–24, 31–37, 139–196. *Attempted to deceive:* Harris, Decision, pp. 133–135.

272   *"More slender credentials":* Ibid., p. 242.

272   *"Lowering the caliber":* NYT, January 23, 1970.

272   *"Even if he were mediocre":* Harris, Decision, p. 110.

272   *Nixon's post-mortem:* Newsweek, April 20, 1970, p. 35.

273   *Most serious attempt:* A resolution calling for Douglas's impeachment had been introduced in the House once before, in June 1953, after he had granted a stay of execution in the Rosenberg espionage case. But the move failed for lack of support. See NYT, June 18. In 1868 a resolution was referred to the House Judiciary Committee proposing the investigation and possible impeachment of an unnamed Supreme Court Justice who reportedly had asserted to friends that recently passed reconstruction legislation was unconstitutional. The resolution died in committee. See *Hind's Precedents of the House of Representatives, Vol. 3, Section 2503.*

275   *"All powerful guardians":* De Tocqueville, *Democracy in America,* pp. 86–87.

INDEX

Abt, John, 114
Acheson, Dean, 88, 89, 267
Agger, Carol; *see* Fortas, Carol Agger
Agricultural Adjustment Administration (AAA), 29, 35–7, 114–5
Aiken, George, 271
Allen, Stuart, 197–8, 200, 206–7, 210
American Bar Association, 174, 193, 265
American Civil Liberties Union, 65
American College of Trial Lawyers, 176
American Motors, 187, 197, 206
American Nazi Party, 157
American University seminars: fee to Abe Fortas, 178–9, 181, 182, 184, 185, 223, 239, 240
Animal Welfare Institute, 73
Archbald, Robert, 229, 232
Armstrong, Michael F., 205–10, 213
Arnold, Fortas & Porter, 96, 137, 221; loyalty cases, 23, 55–67; formation of firm, 54, 55; practice flourishes, 67–72, 77–9, 96; criticism of firm's clients and tactics, 77–9; Fortas leaves firm, 105, 110, 113

Arnold, Thurman, 28, 69, 78, 192, 262; law firm loyalty cases, 23, 58, 60, 61, 63–6; at Yale, 32–3, 42; at AAA, 35, 37; law practice flourishes, 67–71; *see also* Arnold, Fortas & Porter; Arnold & Porter
Arnold & Porter: memo on Fortas as Chief Justice candidate, 174–5; settlement with Fortas, 192; Wolfson case, 199, 200; Fortas decides not to return, 265
Avery, Sewell, 186

Bailey, Dorothy, 59–60
Baker, Bobby, 90–1, 95–6, 100, 113
Bankruptcy Act (1938), 44
Bayh, Birch, 270
Beck, Dave, 221
Benítez, Jaime, 105
Betts vs. Brady, 75–6
Biddle, Francis, 49
Bidwell, Truman, 205
Bittman, William, 225, 228, 245–6, 253
Bituminous Coal Division, 45–7
Black, Hugo: Supreme Court Justice, 58, 85–6, 108, 119, 122, 125, 129, 144, 250; *Gideon* case, 76–7; rivalry with Fortas, 132–4

[303]

Hawaii, 47
Haynsworth, Clement, 270–1
Hearst press, 51
Herald Tribune, 114
Hill, James, 126, 128
Hiss, Alger, 11, 35, 114–5
Holland, Spessard, 4–5
Holmes, Oliver Wendell, 118, 144, 162
Hoopes, Townsend, 138
Hoover, Herbert, 28, 160
Hoover, J. Edgar, 227
Hruska, Roman, 115, 116, 272
Huffnagel, Charles, 210
Hughes, Charles Evans, 266
Humphrey, Hubert, 12, 145
"Hunt Club," 42
Hutchins, Robert M., 32

Ickes, Harold, 23, 45–9, 51, 81
Impeachment: threats against Fortas, 4, 10, 230–3, 241, 243, 244, 256, 264; historical precedents, 7, 229, 232; threats against Warren, 8; cumbersome process, 229–33, 268; threats against Douglas, 273–4
Inflation, 140
Internal Revenue Service: investigation of Wolfson Family Foundation, 216, 245–6; investigation of Fortas, 216–9, 222
International Juridical Association, 115
Israel, 139

Jackson, Robert, 132, 231
Japanese-Americans resettlement, 50–4
Javits, Jacob, 156, 269
Jay, John, 166
Jenkins, Walter, 95, 101–3, 113, 116, 126
Jewish factors, 109, 130, 151, 155–7
Jewish News, 156
John Birch Society, 157
Johnson, Albert W., 232
Johnson, Lady Bird, 99, 110, 134, 136–7, 222

Johnson, Lyndon B., 183, 228, 274; Abe Fortas as friend and adviser, 3, 10, 23, 24, 79–82, 84–98, 105, 116–7, 119, 134–42, 165–7, 170, 184, 211, 219, 221–2, 227, 263, 264; elected to Senate (1948), 82–6; presidential candidate, 88–9; Vice President, 89–91; and Bobby Baker, 90–1, 95–6, 100; assumed presidency after Kennedy assassination, 93–5; election campaign (1964), 98–103; personal wealth, 99–100, 221–2; Walter Jenkins incident, 101–3; wanted Fortas to be attorney general, 104–6; and Dominican Republic civil war, 105; Goldberg to United Nations, 106–8; and Vietnam War, 106, 111–2, 137–9, 145; "Great Society," 106, 143; Supreme Court seat for Fortas, 108–14, 116–7, 192, 193; decides not to seek reelection, 137, 145; nomination of Fortas as Chief Justice, 143–4, 147–59, 269; skill with Congress, 143, 155; and Chief Justice Warren, 147; and Everett Dirksen, 150–2; Senate considers Fortas nomination as Chief Justice, 160–4, 177–8; and opposition to Fortas, 153–9, 163–4; withdrawal of Fortas nomination, 181–2; and Attorney General Ramsey Clark, 219; and Will R. Wilson, 226
Judiciary: constitutional protection, 229–30, 250, 257; investigation of accountability, 229–33; Acheson's proposed rules of behavior, 267
Justice Department: investigations of Abe Fortas, 1, 4, 12, 226–8, 230–2, 236–7, 239, 244–5, 253, 258, 263, 268; John Mitchell's views on functions, 20; Owen Lattimore prosecution, 64–5; investigation of Bobby Baker, 95; memo on Abe Fortas, 174–5;